BUILDING REGULATIONS

BUILDING REGULATIONS

A Self-Help Guide for the Owner-Builder

Edmund Vitale

CHARLES SCRIBNER'S SONS / NEW YORK

Copyright © 1979, 1976 Edmund Vitale

Library of Congress Cataloging in Publication Data
Vitale, Edmund.
   Building regulations.
   Includes index.
   1. Building laws—United States—Popular works.
I. Title.
KF5701.Z9V57   343'.73'078   78-26682
ISBN 0-684-16068-4

५५710

This book published simultaneously in the
United States of America and in Canada—
Copyright under the Berne Convention

1 3 5 7 9 11 13 15 17 19   v/c   20 18 16 14 12 10 8 6 4 2

Printed in the United States of America

Excerpts from the following books are reprinted by permission of the publishers:
The Basic Building Code/1975, copyright © 1975 by the Building Officials and Code
Administrators International, Inc., 1313 E. 60th St., Chicago, Ill. 60637
Standard Building Code, copyright © 1976 by Southern Building Code Congress In-
ternational, Inc., 3617 Eighth Ave. South, Birmingham, Ala. 35222
Uniform Building Code, copyright © 1973, together with *1975 Accumulative
Supplement,* copyright © 1975, by International Conference of Building Officials, 5360
S. Workman Mill Rd., Whittier, Calif. 90601
One- and Two-Family Dwelling Code, 1975 Edition, published and copyrighted by all
of the model code groups listed above, together with the Council of American Building
Officials, 560 Georgetown Building, 2233 Wisconsin Ave. N.W., Washington, D.C.
20007
Dwelling, by River, copyright © 1974 by Freestone Publishing Co., Box 357, Albion,
Calif. 95410
Finding and Buying Your Place in the Country, by Les Scher, copyright © 1974 by
Les Scher, published by Collier Books, a Division of Macmillan Publishing Co., Inc.,
866 Third Ave., New York, N.Y. 10022
Low-Cost, Energy-Efficient Shelter for the Owner-Builder, edited by Eugene Eccli,
copyright © 1976 by Eugene Eccli, published by Rodale Press, Inc., Emmaus, Pa.
18094
Your Engineered House, by Rex Roberts, copyright © 1964 by Rex Roberts, published
by M. Evans and Company, Inc., 216 E. 49th St., New York, N.Y. 10017
"Local Regulation of Building: Agencies, Codes, and Politics," by Charles G. Field and
Frank T. Ventre, in the *1971 Municipal Yearbook,* copyright © 1971 by the International City Management Association, 1140 Connecticut Ave. N.W., Washington, D.C.
20036
The Building Code Burden, by Charles G. Field and Steven R. Rivkin, copyright ©
1975 by D. C. Heath and Company, Lexington Books, Lexington, Mass. 02173
The Owner-Builder and the Code, by Ken Kern, Ted Kogon, and Rob Thallon,
copyright © 1976 by the authors, published by Owner-Builder Publications, P.O. Box
550, Oakhurst, Calif. 93664

To Judie, Lisa, and Tara

ACKNOWLEDGMENTS

I wish to extend my thanks and appreciation to the following people: Robert M. Eisenhard of the National Bureau of Standards, U.S. Department of Commerce, for his help and guidance with the material in Appendix C; Walter Melvin, for the architect's drawings in Appendix B; Hariett Verret-Prentice, who had to read my writing and type the manuscript; my family, who had to put up with my weird working habits; and finally Terry Krautwurst, who, while a fellow editor at *Mother Earth News*, encouraged me at the time when the idea for this book was conceived and who, after we both left *Mother*, read the final draft and made critical comments, suggestions, and editorial changes that were invaluable to me . . . with Terry always taking the role of the owner-builder for whom the book was written.

CONTENTS

BUILDING
REGULATIONS

Introduction

When the idea that eventually led to this guide first dawned on me, I didn't intend to write a book. No. All I wanted to do was try to show owner-builders how to obtain a building permit. I thought that the quick, almost off-the-cuff statements in most of the do-it-yourself home-construction books—"check to see if you're governed by a building code, and if you are, get a building permit"—left unexplained a vast area of controversy, confusion, and possible disappointment for the owner-builder.

But when I attempted to sit down and set forth how owner-builders can go about getting a building permit, I then knew why most construction books only skirt the issue: The problem is so complex! Which building code out of the very many construction ordinances should I use to write about? . . . How detailed do I get? . . . Should I explain about fire districts, standards, and types of contruction? . . . How do I handle all the other variables? And even though my legal schooling and experience had prepared me to understand the legal niceties, I really wasn't sure I could *explain* these engineering/legal/construction requirements in nonlegal language so that every owner-builder could understand and benefit.

Then Ken Kern, Ted Kogon, Rob Thallon (in their book *The Owner-Builder and the Code: The Politics of Building Your Home*) and River (in her book *Dwelling*) placed the building-code issue for me on a philosophically fundamental plane: the right of an individual to provide his or her own shelter without unreasonable governmental regulation or interference.

Out of all these crosscurrents, viewpoints, and problems grew the book: an attempt to guide the owner-builder through the complexities of a building code on—as it turns out—about five different levels.

First and foremost, this is a guide through all the provisions of the building codes of which the owner-builder must be aware if he desires to see his project through to completion. Whatever other criticism might be made of this book, it can't be said that it does not specifically give innumerable and concrete examples of all different kinds of code provisions (and even different versions of the same regula-

tion!) that you might face, as well as an Index in which all the material
from *each particular code* (no matter where it appears in the book) is
collected for your easy reference.

Second, for those readers who have a particularly tough building
inspector to contend with, or who have a project that will take a lot of
creative reasoning to realize, I've interspersed throughout the
chapters "Code-Reading Techniques" that will not only give you a
deeper understanding of the legal regulations known as a building
code, but will also provide a better insight into *any* governmental
regulation you may face (and to which we are each becoming increas-
ingly subjected in all walks of life).

On the third level, I also wanted specifically to document the
case for code reform from the point of view of the owner-builder—to
continue and reinforce the fight Ken Kern and his co-authors, River,
and others had started. This tack led to much editorial comment and
criticism of codes throughout the book, which culminates in a last
chapter devoted entirely to "How to Change Your Building Code."

This criticism of the codes (and the last chapter in particular) is
intended to give owner-builder groups the hard facts with which to
make the fight against overregulation and for meaningful and responsible code changes. But this criticism has resulted in some people's
writing me (when the first three chapters appeared as articles, in
slightly altered form, in *The Mother Earth News*) and accusing me of
being a little crazy to advocate the abolishment of all construction
regulations.

I do not favor the repeal of all construction regulations. I do,
however, strenuously object (1) to building codes that were originally
designed for the cities being imposed on rural areas, and (2) to building codes that don't take into account the very special problems of the
owner-builder. I just want to go on record here, so you don't think
I'm crazy, too!

The fourth level was unintentional. I decided that the only way
to explain building codes to owner-builders everywhere in the United
States was to use examples from the four model building codes that
are published in this country. This led me to put similar provisions
from the different codes side-by-side—and the results were interesting: there were some inconsistencies and some significant differences
among similar model-code provisions, which, as you will see, sometimes lead to different results.

This comparison could stimulate reform by the model-code
groups themselves. In fact, William J. Tangye, Director of Engineering Services of the Southern Building Code Congress (the body that
adopts and publishes the Standard Building Code), wrote me and
commented on the first three articles in *Mother*: "I believe that ar-

ticles such as yours would be beneficial to the owner-builder as well as the code-writing bodies. The latter in providing some constructive criticism and input to help us get our act together and remove conflicting and ambiguous criteria."

And finally—and this may be the most important level of all—I think the book shows how overregulated we've become in a particular aspect of our lives. We have absolutely no conception of how to build and provide for our own shelter and, further, have allowed that basic function to become so regulated that few of us could even follow the rules if we *had to* build our own house.

I hope this work will act as a rallying cry for all of us to take back some control over our own lives. And, if we all don't go out and build our own shelters tomorrow, let's at least get the rules and regulations changed so that when we're ready to build, we'll be allowed to do so.

1. Problem and Background

Building regulations (those amorphous, contradictory, dictatorial, and highly technical governmental edicts) and the building inspector (the physical embodiment of the construction establishment) are part of the harsh realities that the "new pioneer" of American society—the homesteader, back-to-the-lander, and owner-builder—must face.

The individual self-builder generally feels that he or she should have the right to do what he or she wants with his or her land . . . to build the shelter he or she desires . . . to use different and unusual materials in the fabrication of a house that doesn't look like the neighbors'. But building regulations—in solidifying the status quo of construction technology and housing aesthetics—often do not permit this basic freedom!

The right to build your own dwelling according to your own desires, then, is the major area in which alternative, ecological, and simpler life-styles run head-on into the energy-consuming, resource-wasting, creature-comforted majority of our society and, further, hit construction contractors, labor unions, and building material producers right in the breadbasket.

(Yes, there are sections of the country that don't have building or health codes yet, but as the movement of the people from the large metropolitan areas to the rural countryside increases, can even more building regulations be far behind?)

How harsh a reality are these construction regulations? Ask the people who've innocently started (or completed) a self-built dwelling—only to have the building inspector "red tag" the structure for demolition because it does not conform to the local code. Ask the good people of United Stand, a group of owner-builders in Mendocino County, California, about their long and continuing fight against the Golden State's building regulations—regulations that often unreasonably impose construction restrictions throughout that state without regard to the special circumstances of the rural owner-builder.

Or look at the contradictions of a building code that in one locality seems to allow Karen and Jim's yurt while denying Ken and Katie the right to build a log cabin; or the municipality in Virginia where

Tom's 50-foot windtower (built to help meet his energy needs) violates the code, whereas Jeff and Joanne erected the same tower in a town in Nebraska with the building inspector's approval; or the county that allows Jan and George to build a house from scrounged materials while Terry and Laurel's barn-converted-into-a-home in a neighboring county is posted as being uninhabitable.

The fact of the matter is that there are currently some two thousand different building codes in effect throughout the U.S. And they vary from state to state, county to county, and sometimes even from town to town.

Worse yet, none of the regulations is geared to the needs of the energy-saving, resource-recycling, low-income self-builder.

On the other hand, it is this author's contention—after a careful study of the problem—that anyone who has the vigor, temperament, creativity, and willingness to build his or her home (and that's everyone who puts his or her mind to it) can also apply those traits to deal favorably with building codes and inspectors. Why? Because (1) building officials are not nearly as knowledgeable in code-reading (though very well informed about construction techniques) as one is led to believe, and (2) a person with a good, sound understanding of a building code frequently can talk himself into exemptions to, and variances from, the code that the building inspector would not have thought of.

So instead of just saying that building regulations are confusing, complicated, and must be dealt with, this book will lead you through the regulatory maze—clarifying (as well as possible under the circumstances) an admittedly hazy, fuzzy, and maddening area of the law. I won't provide specific answers, but I *will* give every one of you who's been bitten by the do-it-yourself building bug—no matter where you live in this country—a knowledge of the complications you'll face, an insight into the reading and understanding of the codes you're most likely to confront, and an approach to finding practical, legal, administrative, and maybe even political solutions to your problems.

Let's start with a few definitions, a little history, and some comments.

The laws that govern the planning and construction of your shelter are many and varied. There are housing codes . . . which are different from building codes . . . which are different from health codes . . . etc. It's easy to get confused and the owner-builder should be aware of these differences, and the possibility of conflict among the various codes.

Let's begin, then, by defining the different codes. The explanations are presented here in the form of a narrative checklist (including some background and editorializing to put the terms in their proper perspective) of the points an owner-builder should consider as she or he prepares to buy a piece of property on which to construct her or his own shelter. A few of these laws have less impact on the rural self-builder than others, but an understanding of all the various regulations—and the differences between them—can put you just one step farther along toward the successful completion of your own building.

At the same time I'm defining the different codes, I'll also try to give you the reasons why each particular regulation came into being. Because—as you'll see—these rules are not bad in and of themselves. They were enacted to meet real problems and are entirely appropriate to certain situations and locales. The difficulty arises (1) when these codes are applied to new and different circumstances where they shouldn't be applied (at least not without significant changes to accommodate the new situation), (2) when they are used to accomplish an objective that they weren't designed to do, or (3) when the original rules were not amended to meet changed circumstances. (I think you'll see what I mean by all this after you've read through this checklist.)

ZONING ORDINANCES

The first consideration that an owner-builder must contemplate when he or she buys a piece of land is whether the local zoning ordinance (if any) allows the property to be used for the construction and occupancy of a single-family dwelling.

A zoning code is a local ordinance that places all the property in a city, town, or county into different land-use classifications. That is, a certain section of town may have a business classification (where the permitted uses are, for example, business offices and stores), another section of the hamlet may be designated single-family residential, while still another portion of the community might contain only manufacturing companies. Having a town divided into such different use classifications means that only those uses that meet the definitions of each zoning classification are allowed to be built in that section of town.

The homesteader, farmer, or rural owner-builder will not be confronted with zoning ordinances to a large degree since such land-use laws are generally found only in metropolitan and suburban areas and not—at least not yet!—in places where there has been no significant population growth. But please *don't make the assumption* that there is no zoning ordinance in effect. Go to town hall and make certain.

If you find out there is a zoning ordinance in the town where you are thinking about buying land, your next step is to locate that piece of property on the zoning map (which you will also find at town hall). The zoning map should tell you what use classification is designated for that area in which your property is located. If the permitted use is anything other than single-family residential, you should forget about buying the land. A single-family dwelling can't be built in a business or manufacturing zone without going through an expensive, time-consuming, and not always successful variance procedure.

As for you suburban owner-builders, not only will you probably be faced with a zoning ordinance, but your search of the local code may be a bit more complicated than just ensuring the lot you want to buy is in a single-family zone. You see, many suburban communities don't have just one residential zone. They sometimes divide the residential classification into three or four *different kinds* of single-family use . . . and may even throw in garden and high-rise apartment zones for some diversity. What generally differentiates one single-family zone from the other is the size of the lot upon which you can build your house.

You owner-builders in suburban areas, therefore, must not only determine that the property you want to buy is in a residential zone, but also that you have the right size lot upon which to build for the zone in which it's located. If you're in a residential zone but the lot is too small, you have to get a variance to build upon it. (I wouldn't recommend that procedure for owner-builders; you might have enough difficulties attempting to get your house built without having to fight the zoning board of adjustment for a variance too.)

If you already own a lot (or just *have* to buy a particular piece of property) that is subject to a zoning ordinance, and plan to build your own home thereon, I would strongly advise you to study very carefully the regulations contained in the zoning code. (You can purchase your own copy if you wish—at a cost of between $1 and $5—from the municipal clerk at your town hall.) Being familiar with and understanding the zoning ordinance is a good start on learning to read, and understand, the building code that is probably also in effect.

Zoning laws may seem to be a rather severe intrusion on the individual's right to develop his property as he sees fit, and in some instances they are! These ordinances, however, did grow out of many municipalities' legitimate desire to have an orderly growth pattern for their community. The regulations attempt to create stability of land use and property values in specified areas. If you construct your house in a single-family residential zone, you can be sure that a factory belching black smoke will not at some later date be built right next door and therefore depreciate your property's value (both monetarily and emotionally).

This method of governmental regulation of private property—zoning—was constitutionally sanctioned by the Supreme Court of the United States back in the mid-twenties. Thus, the government's right to dictate to a limited degree the ways you and I use our land has been firmly established in our nation's jurisprudence.

How zoning laws come into effect is that the state (the federal government does not get into the zoning act), through its constitution or by virtue of a statute adopted pursuant to its police powers, authorizes—but does not compel—a municipality or county to enact a zoning ordinance. Then the local or county government that wants to pass such an ordinance studies all the land within its boundaries and classifies it into various proposed land uses.

Once the study has been completed, the town or county can officially adopt its zoning ordinance—if, that is, the use classifications assigned to each portion of town in the zoning ordinance are "reasonable." If they're not, the ordinance is unconstitutional. What "reasonable" means in this situation is that the classified use must bear some relationship to the uses that already exist in the district. In other words, if an area is predominately single-family residential, it may be unreasonable—and therefore unconstitutional—for that area to be placed in a heavy manufacturing zone by the town fathers.

In addition to regulating land use, zoning ordinances also contain other regulations—and this is where these laws often become burdensome. For instance, such an ordinance can dictate the minimum size of the building lot for each different use classification, and/or how far a building must be located from the front, rear, and side property lines, and/or the height of the structure. (These provisions are sometimes known as "bulk requirements.") Some ordinances even try to legislate aesthetics—how a building should look!

If you propose a structure that is the correct use for the zoning classification but violates one or more of these bulk requirements, then—as we've already seen in the case of the undersized residential lots—you'll have to go to the zoning board of adjustment for a time-consuming and expensive application for a variance . . . and that variance may or may not be granted.

So I think you can see by now how zoning has veered from its original goal (the orderly development of a municipality) to a weapon (the bulk requirements) that help perpetuate construction conformity and stifles creative approaches to home-building. In fact, some of these ordinances—such as those that don't permit apartments or that do require very large lots for a single-family dwelling or that use zoning to try to maintain a high-class residential community—are under court attack as being discriminatory to the low-income segment of our population.

SUBDIVISION ORDINANCES

Another factor that you as an owner-builder must consider before you purchase land is whether or not you will be buying all the land the seller has, or whether that owner is keeping a portion of the land for him- or herself. If the seller is conveying only a portion of one larger piece of property to you, you'll have to find out for your own good whether there is a subdivision ordinance that controls the situation.

You see, a subdivision ordinance regulates the division of land—like carving out 250 individual lots from one 100-acre farm, or even dividing that 100-acre farm in half. These ordinances require that before a portion of property can be legally conveyed a subdivision approval must be obtained.

A good idea, therefore, if you intend to buy a part of someone's land, is to provide in the contract of purchase (1) a statement that the conveyance is conditioned upon official subdivision approval being obtained and (2) a specific designation of exactly who will make application for the approval. (It's generally the seller's responsibility; if the buyer seeks approval, there should be an appropriate reduction in the purchase price.)

In any case, here's the procedure for subdivision approval: Application is made to the planning board or subdivision committee (or whatever name the ordinance uses to designate the governmental body empowered to pass on subdivisions) on a form the board provides. The application, in most cases, will have to be accompanied by an accurate, scaled sketch (possibly even a professionally engineered survey) that shows (1) the entire property in question, (2) the portion (or portions) being subdivided, and (3) the existing improvements (such as buildings, access, etc.) and contemplated improvements on the entire land. Sometimes, if you're dividing land in a suburban area, the planning board may also require the sketch plat to show all property and improvements within 200 feet of the land in question.

The planning board then reviews the sketch to determine that it contains all the information called for by the subdivision ordinance, that all parts of the property have proper access, and that the property division and development won't cause problems such as flooding, erosion, etc. If all these requirements are satisfied, the planning board will approve the subdivision. Once the subdivision has been approved and recorded (you'll have to check your individual ordinance as to how, when, and where to record), the specified portion or portions of property can be sold.

If a subdivision ordinance has not been adopted by a county, municipality, or other governmental body, any division of land within the jurisdiction in question can take place without governmental approval. And even if there is a subdivision ordinance in effect, when you purchase *all* the property in a particular tract the subdivision ordinance is of no consequence because there is no division of land.

Sometimes there is a tricky problem, however, concerning what constitutes one complete parcel of land—and you owner-builders who are looking for land in rural areas governed by a subdivision code are more likely to confront this situation than your suburban counterparts. So for your benefit, I'll explain.

Now, it's clear that a seller who owns two parcels of land that are separated by property owned by others does not need a subdivision to sell one of those parcels: he's not dividing a single piece of land. It's also clear that if a seller has two pieces of property separated by a state-, county-, or municipality-owned and -maintained road, he does not need a subdivision to convey one of those parcels.

The situation is unclear, however, when a seller has accumulated his one large tract of land by purchasing many smaller tracts and he wants to sell you one of those smaller parcels described exactly as shown on the deed when he bought it. Don't sign the contract to buy! In most cases this would be considered a subdivision . . . but not always. It's a matter of the definitions in the particular subdivision ordinance in effect. So if you're in this situation, go to town hall and get an opinion—in writing—from the municipal or planning board clerk that a subdivision is not required. If you can't get such an opinion, require the seller to get a subdivision.

Caution: Don't think you've avoided the subdivision problem by signing an agreement with a rural landowner that allows you to erect your dwelling on a portion of his land (on which there are three or four other owner-builders doing the same thing) without actually purchasing the property. There are usually prohibitions—tucked away in the fine print of either a subdivision or zoning ordinance—against more than one primary use of a piece of property under a single ownership.

Actually, there are very good reasons for the existence of subdivision regulations. The uncontrolled division of land can easily result in unnecessarily intensified use of that very precious and nonrenewable resource. Increased use creates increased traffic, water runoff, and sanitation problems. And these are some of the bad effects that subdivision ordinances attempt to keep to a minimum by requiring proof that a proposed division of land will be a constructive (rather than destructive) process.

As with zoning, each municipality or county within a state that authorizes subdivision ordinances has the option of whether or not to adopt such a code—and not all of them do. Again, the areas ex-

periencing the most population growth are the ones most likely to
adopt such ordinances in order to prevent (or at least slow down) hap-
hazard and destructive development.

BUILDING CODES

These are the regulations that specify how—and of what materials—a building must be constructed. As we shall see, they assign
specific legal responsibilities to builders. They require that you (1)
obtain a building permit before you start construction, (2) submit, at
times, plans and specifications for review, (3) subject the structure
you're building to three or four inspections, and (4) subject yourself to
criminal penalties if you do not comply.

Unfortunately, some owner-builders don't bother finding out
about the existence of these regulations until *after* they've purchased
a piece of property. If you have very definite plans in mind for your
shelter, make sure—*before you buy that land*—that the building code
(if any) in the municipality or county where you contemplate the
purchase of land permits the construction of your house. Otherwise,
you may have to change your building plans to conform to the code
that governs the property you've bought.

Lest this seem horribly arbitrary and unfair, perhaps a quick
review of how building codes have developed over the years will put
the present situation into a more honest perspective.

Cities on the North American continent began to adopt building
codes even before the revolution that gave birth to this country. The
regulations grew out of a real need to protect city dwellers from fire,
wind, snow, floods, earthquakes, overcrowding—and sheer unsafe
construction. Some codes outlawed thatch roofs and a few even
prohibited wooden construction (in municipalities where fire was
especially feared).

Building codes started to proliferate to the then-rural areas of
this country about the turn of the century, when a group of insurance
companies—in   the   best   tradition   of   American   enterprise—
promulgated a model building code in an attempt to stop its losses
from fires. Thus, the National Building Code—still with us today—
came into being. (The present address of the American Insurance Association is 85 John St., New York, N.Y. 10038.)

At about the same time, building officials were banding together
in different parts of the country and drafting their own model codes,
and all of them (in amended form, of course) are still with us today.
The International Conference of Building Officials (5360 S. Workman
Mill Rd., Whittier, Calif. 90601) issued the Uniform Building Code,
which predominates in the West. The Building Officials and Code

Administrators International (1313 E. 60th St., Chicago, Ill. 60637) wrote the Basic Building Code, prevalent in the Midwest and East. The Southern Building Code Conference (3617 Eighth Ave. South, Birmingham, Ala. 35222), unhappy with the way the other groups addressed themselves to the unique problems of that section of the nation, drafted still another model: the Standard Building Code.

These organizations have, over the years, broken down the whole construction process into a number of individual components—plumbing, mechanical (heat and air conditioning), etc.—and have codified each part in a separate set of regulations. Thus the existence of a plumbing code, mechanical code, etc. The main building code itself in each case, however, is still the basic construction document that guides a contractor in the erection of everything from a single-family dwelling to high-rise building to huge shopping centers.

And that's the problem: the attempt of each major code to cover so many different kinds of construction (not only the high-rises and shopping centers mentioned above, but also farm buildings and factories) in a single document. This has resulted in a general building code (*not* including the separate plumbing, mechanical, and other codes) that is hundreds of pages long and so tightly crammed with charts, graphs, formulas, equations, and appendices that only an engineer can decipher it. This, of course, puts the owner-builder who wants to construct his own simple dwelling at a decided disadvantage.

There has been, however, an attempt to solve this particular dilemma of the builder of residential dwellings. All four model-code organizations have collaborated to produce the *One- and Two-Family Dwelling Code.* Its title is self-explanatory; and besides buiding code regulations, it also contains those provisions of the plumbing and mechanical codes that are applicable to single-family residential construction. (The main building codes themselves do not contain plumbing and mechanical specifications. As indicated above, such regulations have been relegated to separate volumes.)

The chapters of the *One- and Two-Family Dwelling Code* are presented in a logical construction sequence and this manual is therefore much easier to follow than any of its four bigger brothers (the Basic, National, Standard, and Uniform Building Codes). This code, in addition, is compatible with the other four and is an excellent reference and instruction book if you're considering the construction of your own shelter in a code-dominated municipality. The manual costs $8 and is available from any of the four model-code groups at the addresses listed above for each, or from the Council of American Building Officials, 560 Georgetown Building, 2233 Wisconsin Ave. N.W., Washington, D.C. 20007.

Bear in mind that all of the codes discussed above remain nothing more than mere models, without force and effect, unless and until they've been adopted by either a state, county, or municipal government (which—with the possible addition of the federal government—are the only entities that have the legal power to regulate building construction). Furthermore, the municipality (or county or state) may (1) adopt an entire model code as written, (2) pass part of a model code and substitute its own requirements for certain specific sections, (3) draft its own construction (or plumbing or mechanical) code, or (4) not adopt any code at all.

I hope that you can now understand how and why construction codes differ from town to town, county to county, and state to state. And although I don't ask you to understand it, I also hope you can see how the one really positive accomplishment made by the code organizations—the promulgation of the *One- and Two-Family Dwelling Code*—is completely negated by the fact that each group has failed to remove from its voluminous buiding codes those specific provisions relating to single-family residential construction. Thus, many jurisdictions which adopt one of the model building codes and do not adopt the model Dwelling Code still force the owner-builder to do battle with the bigger and more complicated code.

Enough said at this point. The remaining chapters in this book are devoted to each and every aspect of the model building codes that relates to the owner-builder of his or her own single-family dwelling.

FIRE PREVENTION CODES

Fire prevention codes have closely paralleled building codes in their origin and development. These codes are supposed to be different in that fire prevention codes are concerned exclusively with potential fire hazards in buildings (such as high-rises, where fighting a fire is difficult) or the fire hazards created by certain kinds of occupancies (such as grain elevators, chemical factories, etc.) and how to prevent, eliminate, or contain those hazards.

But the line of demarcation between a building code and a fire prevention code is fuzzy at best. Building regulations, as we've just seen, incorporate fire prevention standards and requirements. The National Fire Prevention Association attempted to explain the difference in the fourteenth edition of the *Fire Prevention Handbook:*

> To decide which items go into a fire prevention code and what should be included in the building code is a difficult task. In general, all construction requirements should be part of the building code and administered by the building department. The equipment and machinery incidental to a process or hazard in a building should be part of

the fire code and regulated by the fire department. Original requirements for exits and fire extinguishing equipment are usually found in building code provisions, but the maintenance of such items is covered in a fire prevention code.

Even with that explanation, I'm still confused. But we have learned that the fire prevention codes are enforced not by the building inspector's office but by the fire department.

I would like to be able to tell you owner-builders not to worry about fire prevention codes, but I can't. Because there are isolated instances, like the state of Alaska, where there are no state building regulations but there is a state fire protection code that incorporates a building code. In such a situation, it just depends on whether the state or local fire marshall will enforce the building provisions that are part of the fire prevention code.

So my advice is: If you're governed by a building code, don't worry about a fire prevention ordinance; most of the fire regulations will probably be incorporated into the building code. If, however, you're *not* governed by a building code, check at the town hall or county seat to see if there's a fire prevention code in effect and if the governmental authorities use that code to enforce building regulations. This would be rare, but it sometimes happens!

HOUSING CODES

These ordinances are basically maintenance codes; they're designed to regulate the living conditions of multifamily residential units. They set the requirements for the water, heating, and sanitary facilities that a landlord is supposed to supply to his or her tenants.

At least that's what the housing codes were *originally* designed to do! These codes, you see, were first enacted in this country in response to the deplorable living conditions which the flood of European immigrants in the 1800s produced in U.S. cities. Many urban dwellers at the time were lodged in overcrowded, unhealthy death traps—and housing regulations were adopted to provide a minimum of protection for the helpless tenant. Fire escapes, toilets for every twenty occupants, tap water on each floor, and banisters for the stairways were some of the early standards required of multifamily dwelling owners.

Even though you may not think that a housing code should concern an owner-builder, it—unfortunately—can. And that's because the original target of these codes—rental property and multifamily living quarters—has been expanded in some cases to embrace all residential uses *including* single-family dwellings. The change came about, in part, when many cities included housing regulations within their building codes. When people began moving to the suburbs en masse, these very same building codes moved with them, and thus the regulation of residential environment and living conditions was imposed as part of the overall building code itself and not just a separate chapter dealing specifically with multifamily housing. (I entitled Chapter Five of this book " 'Nonconstruction' Construction Requirements" because of this very trend.)

To make matters worse, even though some of these "environmental living conditions" provisions have been incorporated into the building codes, there still can be a separate housing code. And furthermore, just to compound the complexity, these separate housing codes might also still regulate single-family dwellings. So you end up contending with a maddening multiplicity of code requirements from several different sources!

Therefore, before you buy land or build, it's important (especially for suburban owner-builders) to find out from the county and/or municipal clerk (1) if there is a housing code in the jurisdiction where you intend to build, and, if there is, (2) whether that code governs single-family dwellings. If it does, then you'll have to read it and determine which of its provisions are applicable and make sure your proposed dwelling complies with them.

SANITARY (OR HEALTH) CODES

These are the regulations that govern the disposal of human waste and "gray water" (the colloquial name given to water in which clothes, dishes, and humans have been washed).

Owner-builders often don't consider the implications of these health regulations until after they've bought a piece of property on which they plan to construct their house. *Don't make the same mistake*—especially if you are in an area where there are no municipal sewers to tie into (generally a rural section). Always look into the requirements of the local health code *before* you buy land, particularly if it is unsewered.

Why? Because: (1) rural owner-builders are more likely to be subjected to a health ordinance than they are a building code, since more jurisdictions have adopted a health regulation than have enacted a building code. And, (2), these sanitary codes will more than likely require that you install a septic tank/leach field disposal system—an expensive proposition that may not even be possible if the soil on your land doesn't pass certain specified tests.

I won't go into all the details of this subject here. Chapter Six of this book is entirely devoted to the topic (and, incidentally, includes directions on how to conduct those soil tests I just mentioned). For now, just remember that a review of the requirements of your local health code is as important *before* purchasing property as it is when you actually start construction. Maybe more so; because once you buy that land and later find out you aren't allowed to build on it, you'll have a difficult time selling it.

The same concerns for safety, health, and disease prevention that gave rise to building and housing codes also produced our sanitation laws. And the purpose of these laws is entirely justified. Obviously, for instance, there must be some regulation of the disposal of human excrement because of the disease and death that can result from open sewers and contaminated water supplies.

Unfortunately the regulations take a somewhat one-dimensional, and severely restrictive, approach to the problem. For instance, the health codes have decreed that a flush toilet—one connected either to a municipally operated sanitary sewer system or to a septic tank—is the *only* way to treat human waste. There are, however, other alternatives—such as the composting toilet or the old pit privy (outhouse)—that also safely treat human waste and are completely viable and inexpensive. But they're forbidden under nearly every health regulation in the nation.

Furthermore, the same unfortunate process that injected housing code requirements into building codes has occurred with sanitation regulations. Most of the model *building* codes require flush toilets and private sanitary disposal systems (a septic tank by its official name) for residential dwelling as part of the requirements for a building permit. So even if a given sanitary ordinance doesn't require septics, its "brother" building code might.

As I said, you'll have to wait for Chapter Six for the full poop (so to speak) on this subject, but I did want to warn you early on just how important the local health laws can be—both before and after you buy that piece of land.

ELECTRICAL CODES

Believe it or not, here is a code that isn't as confining as the others we've reviewed. The provisions of this regulation govern the installation of electrical fixtures and equipment but do *not* mandate that you *must* have electricity. So owner-builders who don't want commercial or homemade current can go right ahead without legal hassle and build and use their homes as "kosher" residential dwellings.

Once you do decide to have electricity, however—even if it's from your own wind or hydro system—you must (if you're governed by an electrical code) conform to the installation and safety precautions prescribed by this code. In fact, even if you're not required by a local ordinance to install your electricity in a code-approved manner, I would strongly urge you—for safety's sake—to follow the provisions of the National Electrical Code.

It's also important to remember that although the National Electrical Code is the only electrical code used extensively throughout this country, there can be slight variations in the actual code a town or county adopts. Municipal authorities have the power to amend the National Electrical Code to serve the needs, tastes, and whims of their local jurisdiction, and they often have exercised that power.

One of the resulting variables that an owner-builder should look for in the local code (because this particular subject is not covered by the National Electrical Code) is whether that ordinance permits an owner-builder to do his or her own wiring. Some municipalities allow self-builders and homeowners to do their own electrical work, while others permit do-it-yourselfers to perform such work only after the payment of a considerable fee for the privilege. And still others prohibit anyone but licensed electricians from doing the job. Like everything else we've discussed so far, you should thoroughly investigate this subject and how it's handled in the municipality where you intend to build—*before* you purchase the piece of property on which you hope to put up your owner-built house.

ENERGY REGULATIONS

If all the above codes, ordinances, rules, and regulations aren't enough, a new field of building regulations has grown out of the fuel shortages of the seventies. Now that all of us in this country have finally begun to realize that our fossil fuel energy supply is not an infinite and cheap commodity, we've started to look for ways to save that finite and precious product. Some people have realized that buildings could be built in such ways as to use less fuel to heat and/or cool them.

Thus energy-conservation building regulations were born. These energy codes can generally be divided into two classes: (1) those that regulate the insulation of your new house (an example is the "Energy Conservation in New Building Design" adopted by the American Society of Heating, Refrigerating, and Air-Conditioning Engineers, which regulation is known as ASHRAE 90-75). Or, (2), those that take into account not only insulation, but also window placement in south-facing walls, the use of shutters, and other passive solar-energy techniques (an example is the local ordinance adopted by the City of Davis in California).

The difficulty here for owner-builders is that these energy regulations might be incorporated into a local or state building code or might be found in its very own code—usually a statewide, mandatory energy-conservation regulation.

This kind of code would never have been necessary if we had always designed our dwellings and buildings to conserve rather than waste energy. Since energy codes are here, you should be concerned with them if they are applicable in your jurisdiction.

I have attached an Appendix—C—to this book which gives you the current status of statewide building, plumbing, mechanical, electrical, and fire prevention codes. Use it as a start or reference (not the final answer, which only your local authorities can give you) in your (1) selection of property on which to build your house, or (2) design choices for the home you can build on the property you already own.

2. The Building Permit

Now that we have a few definitions under our belt, let's set the stage for an in-depth review of the building code—the regulation that dictates minimum construction standards for a building.

Let's assume that you—the owner-builder—have a piece of vacant property on which you want to build a house, or that you've bought an old farmhouse you want to fix up. Let's also assume that the municipality in which the property is located has (1) a building code that you must abide by, (2) a subdivision ordinance that you've not violated (because there was no division of the land you purchased), (3) a zoning ordinance—the provisions of which are satisfied because your property is in a single-family district and meets all the requirements of the ordinance—and (4) a health or sanitary code that allows you to use an old-fashioned privy. (This last assumption is, unfortunately, contrary to reality in most areas today. I'll deal with that subject in a later chapter. For now, let's just set up an ideal situation so that we can focus specifically on building codes alone.)

If you followed the advice I gave you in Chapter One, you will have at least looked at, if not purchased, a copy of the building code ordinance in effect in your municipality before you bought your property. (If you don't have a copy of the code yet, I strongly advise that you get one from the municipal clerk's office.)

Read the handbook's table of contents, or the division headings if there isn't such a table. (There also may be an index to your code. But at this preliminary stage, when we're reviewing the broad outlines of the codes, you don't need it. I will discuss the use of a code's index—if you're lucky enough to have one in your building code—in Chapter Five of this book when we start to get down to specific provisions.) Building code manuals are usually divided into chapters (or articles or parts) and you will quickly note that many of the chapters—such as those on sprinklers and standpipes, steel construction, elevators and dumbwaiters, signs, etc.—simply don't apply to your project, and therefore can be disregarded.

You should, however, immediately review with care the chapter on administration (usually the first one in the code). This is the part of the ordinance that deals with the first two obstacles you'll face: the building permit and the building inspector.

Before examining what you need to do to overcome those obstacles, please let me qualify my coming remarks in two ways:

One: I don't know exactly how your building code is written—each code is organized differently—but I do know that all such regulations should be similar to one of the four model codes. So no matter how your particular code is set up, this book's discussion of the Basic Building Code (BBC, also sometimes referred to as the BOCA code), the National Building Code (NBC), the Standard Building Code (SBC), and the Uniform Building Code (UBC)—plus the *One- and Two-Family Dwelling Code* (Dwelling Code)—will give you a pretty good idea of what to look for in, and how to interpret, your own area's construction regulations.

In other words, at this point our discussion and review of the different model-code provisions important to the owner-builder is valuable to you mainly as a checklist against which you can compare your own local ordinance, so that *you* will know what has been left out, revised, or added to the code which governs your situation.

Two: I'll use the section numbers of the various code provisions as they appear in each of the respective model-code volumes. But remember that the numbering system contained in each of the four model building codes will probably be different from that used in your code—even if your regulation is patterned after one of the models. This situation comes about because each municipality or county has its own numbering system for its own ordinances.

All right. With those qualifications out of the way, we're ready to proceed.

A cursory examination of the chapter on administration in your code makes it apparent that you can hardly do any construction without a building permit; in other words, without the authorization and approval of some kind of governmental body. The BBC's language pretty much exemplifies this condition: "The permit shall be a license to proceed with the work and shall not be construed as authority to violate, cancel, or set aside any provisions of this code . . ." (§115.2).

The implications of that quote are enormous. Imagine that our government requires us to get a *license* to construct our own shelters! Strange . . . I always thought that you and I had the right to build our own homes subject only to reasonable regulations for the protection of others. Individual rights and governmental authority seem to have been turned around in the construction field—to the detriment of you and me!

Also, just reading the all-encompassing situations in which a building permit is required will give you an idea of the widespread reach of the building codes themselves:

> Permits Required. No person, firm, or corporation shall erect, construct, enlarge, alter, repair, move, improve, remove, convert, or demolish any building or structure in the city, or cause the same to be done, without first obtaining a separate building permit for each such building or structure from the Building Official. [UBC §301(a)]

You can't even tear down a structure without a building permit, as incongruous as that sounds! And all the other model codes have similar all-inclusive language (BBC §113.1, NBC §102.1, SBC §105.1).

So before showing you how to go about getting a building permit to construct a new home on a vacant lot, let's first take a look at the situations in which you need to get a building permit just to make repairs on an existing dwelling under the different codes. This should be instructive because (1) you'll see how the various model codes often treat the same problem differently, and (2) it will be a relatively simple and easy way to learn the code-reading techniques that you should develop. Furthermore, you may be able to use some of the theories (arguments) presented here to persuade your building inspector that you don't need a permit to fix up that old farmhouse you just bought (for instance), or that you don't have to alter that old building to conform to the requirements of a newer code (another for-instance).

REPAIRS

Okay. Now let's set the stage for this discussion on repairs with a hypothetical situation. Suppose you have a leaky roof to repair, and suppose that you also intend to replace a section of an interior wall that was damaged by water coming in through that leaky roof. Do you think you'll need a building permit just to replace a few roof shingles and take out damaged Sheetrock in order to install new material?

Most of us wouldn't even think of obtaining a building permit in such a situation. We'd just go ahead and make the needed repairs. But what do the building codes say on this topic? Read on, and see how many of us would have been in violation of an all-encompassing governmental licensing authority.

The BBC states in §113.1 that you must get a building permit to construct or alter a building "except that ordinary repairs, as defined in Section 102.0, which do not involve any violation of this code shall be exempt from this provision." When you turn to §102.1, you find the following: "Ordinary repairs to structures may be made without application or notice to the building official; but such repairs shall not include the cutting away of any wall, partition or portion thereof . . ." It continues, to state other definitions of what "ordinary repairs" are *not!* Though it's nice to know that you can make ordinary repairs without application or notice to the building inspector, you can't really tell for sure, from the language of this section, just what ordinary repairs *are.*

CODE-READING TECHNIQUE: In almost every code there's a chapter (or article or part) containing definitions. You should always refer to that chapter for every word that you find ambiguous, for whenever you try to make a noun or verb or adjective that you *think* you know fit a particular situation, you will find that the word's meaning becomes fuzzy. So look up that term you're sure you can define anyway: you may not always find the word defined in your code, but more often than not you will (and sometimes that definition will be very different from what you thought the meaning was). Remember: How any given word in your code is defined can make all the difference in the world to your situation!

Now let's continue to pursue our search through the BBC for a clear description of ordinary repairs. When you look in Article 2 of the BBC (entitled "Definitions and Classifications") you'll find that the *O*'s don't include any definition of ordinary repairs (although the meaning of "ordinary materials" *is* given). When you look under the *R*'s in Article 2, however, you'll find "repair" defined as: "The reconstruction or renewal of any part of an existing building for the purpose of its maintenance." There's no meaning given for "repairs, ordinary" so you still don't know if repairs and ordinary repairs are two slightly different concepts. But you *are* sure—if you're subject to a building code similar to the BBC—that you can reconstruct, renew, and repair *for the purpose of maintenance* without first obtaining a building permit.

CODE-READING TECHNIQUE: As you can see, there may be two or three different places in a code to look up the meaning of a word, and, as I stated before, many words in the codes are not defined at all. Some codes do provide that undefined words "shall have their ordinary accepted meanings or such as the context may imply" (BBC §201.3, NBC §200.c), but in any case it's these undefined words and unclear provisions that allow you to argue knowledgeably with the building inspector that what you want to do is not really prohibited by the code.

I think that we can conclude (in our hypothetical leaky-roof situation) that under the BBC you *can* replace shingles on the roof without a building permit. But to replace the damaged Sheetrock may be a different story—after all, the BBC says that ordinary repairs "shall not include the cutting away of any wall, partition or portion thereof" (§102.1). But wait . . . you won't have to cut into the wood studs of the wall. You need only to take portions of the water-damaged Sheetrock out. So you can argue that this is an ordinary repair and not one that requires a building permit.

The NBC has provisions similar to those found in the BBC. Section 102.8 of the NBC states that "repairs may be made without filing an application or obtaining a permit." Repairs are defined in §200 the same way as in the BBC; thus all the comments made in the discussion of the BBC are applicable to codes derived from the NBC.

The SBC is a different story, however. This code defines repairs—in §201.2—as does the BBC, but that's the last of the similarities. Why? Because §105.1(c) of the SBC requires that "ordinary minor repairs may be made *with the approval of the Building Official* without a permit; provided that such repairs shall not violate any of the provisions of this code." (The italics are mine.) In other words, under the SBC you may not need a permit to make repairs, but you certainly need the building inspector's approval! (By the way, there are no definitions for "ordinary," "minor," or "ordinary minor" repairs in the SBC.) I don't know how it's possible to enforce the mandate of §105.1(c). Imagine summoning a do-it-yourselfer to court for failure to get the approval of the building inspector just to replace a window broken by a child's baseball! Or, for that matter, imagine summoning you to court because you didn't get the approval of the building inspector to replace a few shingles and a few square feet of Sheetrock in your house!

The UBC is even worse. There seem to be absolutely no exceptions to its requirements for obtaining a building permit to make repairs. You simply must—pursuant to §301(a), quoted on page 22 of this book—get one! Whether or not you are cited and convicted of violations of this building code when you replace those shingles or patch the wall that needs fixing without first obtaining a building permit simply depends on whether the building inspector wants to go by the book.

I think you can now start to see that these codes sometimes reach the point of absurdity in their attempt to be all-pervasive. This is a perfect example of how more and more laws create less and less respect for the law (you just can't legislate everything)! And this over-regulation to the point of absurdity is also the key to understanding the concept—which will be developed later in this book—that it's sometimes the *building inspector*, rather than the written words of the ordinance, that is the code.

Before I leave this discussion on repairs, there's one important problem that the owner-builder who is making extensive renovations on an old house must be aware of, and that is the problem of determining the point at which the building inspector is likely to deem your renovations major enough to require that the *entire* old structure be made to conform to current code standards.

I'm sure you'll not be surprised if I tell you that this situation is also covered in these omnipotent codes (with the sole exception of the NBC, which has no such provisions). If additions, alterations, or repairs (cumulative within a twelve-month period) exceed 50 percent "of the value of an existing building," then the whole building has to conform to code standards—BBC §106.2, SBC §101.4(a), UBC §104(b). If the alterations exceed 25 percent of value (but not more than 50 percent within the twelve-month period), the BBC and the SBC—§106.4 and §101.4(c), respectively—state that it's up to the building inspector to determine how much of the repaired portion of the building shall be made to conform, while the UBC §104(c) provides that all parts of the building being repaired need be brought up to code standards. If the alterations are under 25 percent during a twelve-month period, all three codes—BBC §106.5, SBC §101.4(f), and for nonstructural repairs in UBC §104(e)—allow that the repairs can be made of the same materials as those in the original construction.

So your course of action if you're in this kind of situation is clear: Don't make repairs totaling more than 25 percent of building value during a single twelve-month period!

CODE-READING TECHNIQUE: Watch for these time-period stipulations in the codes and learn to use them to your advantage. For example, check your local code to see if it tells you when to start counting the twelve-month repair cycle (the model codes don't). If your code is silent on this point, then it seems to me that for repairs totaling 40 percent of value done over a span of two months, you might argue that one twelve-month period ended after the first month in which you made repairs and a new twelve-month cycle started at the beginning of the second month! It's at least worth a try.

THE APPLICATION

So. Now that we know that you have to get a building permit to build a house (and in most cases to make major renovations and improvements to an existing dwelling), let's examine exactly how you actually get this license. The first thing you do—after you've taken my advice and reviewed a copy of the building code in effect in your jurisdiction—is to go to town hall (or the county seat) and pick up an application form for your building permit.

Each of the model codes requires that you make application for a building permit—but they don't spell out the actual application form itself. The codes do list, however, the minimum requirements that the application must include, and then leave it to the local building inspector to draft the actual document.

The list in UBC §301(b) is typical of the information required on an application for a building permit:

> (b) Application. To obtain a permit the applicant shall first file an application therefor in writing on a form furnished for that purpose. Every such application shall:
>   1. Identify and describe the work to be covered by the permit for which application is made;
>   2. Describe the land on which the proposed work is to be done, by lot, block, tract, and house and street address, or similar description that will readily identify and definitely locate the proposed building or work;
>   3. Indicate the use or occupancy for which the proposed work is intended;
>   4. Be accompanied by plans and specifications . . . ;
>   5. State the valuation of the proposed work;
>   6. Be signed by the permittee, or his authorized agent, who may be required to submit evidence to indicate such authority;
>   7. Give such other information as reasonably may be required by the Building Official.

(See also BBC §113, NBC §102.3, and SBC §105.2 for similar requirements.)

This list might seem uncomplicated to you, and actually it is. But some of the application forms that have been devised pursuant to this provision have been long and overwhelming, with up to four pages of questions! Why? Because most municipalities use just one standard application form for every and any kind of building project. Chances are, a person in your area who's building a shopping center will probably have to fill out the same application form that you will to erect your single-family dwelling.

It's obvious from this that not every question on the application form will apply to you or require an answer from you. If you have any difficulty in completing the form, ask the building inspector to help you; he or she should be able to explain any confusing points.

Just so you'll know what to expect, I've reproduced a sample building-permit application form in Appendix A, and it is one that's filled in for the house plans reproduced in Appendix B. But since each state or county or municipality can make up its own application form, your particular building-permit application will in all likelihood be different from this one. You should, however, be prepared to provide information similar to that contained in §301(b) of the UBC quoted above and contained in the form I've reproduced in Appendix A.

Two of the more important requirements for the owner-builder in §301(b) are the valuation of the proposed work, and the plans and specifications that are sometimes required to accompany the application . . . so let's move on now and discuss those subjects.

THE FEE

When a building inspector tells you to state the valuation of the proposed work on a building-permit application form, he's asking you to help him determine the fee you'll have to pay for that permit. (Yes, you must pay the government a fee just to build your own house!) Under the UBC, these fees are charged on a sliding-scale formula based on the valuation of the contemplated construction:

Table No. 3-A
BUILDING PERMIT FEES

TOTAL VALUATION	FEE
$1.00 to $500.00	$5.00
$501.00 to $2,000.00	$5.00 for the first $500.00 plus $1.00 for each additional $100.00 or fraction thereof, to and including $2,000.00.
$2,001.00 to $25,000.00	$20.00 for the first $2,000.00 plus $4.00 for each additional $1,000.00 or fraction thereof, to and including $25,000.00.
$25,001.00 to $50,000.00	$112.00 for the first $25,000.00 plus $3.00 for each additional $1,000.00 or fraction thereof, to and including $50,000.00.
$50,001.00 to $100,000.00	$187.00 for the first $50,000.00 plus $2.00 for each additional $1,000.00 or fraction thereof, to and including $100,000.00.
$100,001.00 to $500,000.00	$287.00 for the first $100,000.00 plus $1.50 for each additional $1,000.00 or fraction thereof, to and including $500,000.00.

The justification for collecting fees for a building permit is that such fees reimburse the local government for the "services" it performs—for instance, for the four inspections the building inspector makes during actual construction to determine whether or not your house is being built "according to code."

Some building codes also require you to pay another fee called a plan-checking fee. This payment, supposedly, is to cover the costs the local government incurs for the manpower and time it takes to review your plans and specifications to determine if they conform to the code.

The UBC—whose fee schedule is reproduced above—has such a plan-checking fee (§303[b]); it's fixed at one-half of the cost of the building permit. And if you start construction without first getting a permit, the UBC, in §303(a), requires double fees!

As we've seen from Table 3-A, quoted above, the building-permit fee is based on the total valuation of what you're constructing. But *how* is total valuation determined, and *who* fixes that figure? Each of the codes answers those questions in a slightly different way.

Under the UBC, it's the building inspector who has the power to determine the value (defined in §423 as "the estimated cost to replace the building in kind, based on current replacement costs") of the proposed construction. So even though you consider your dwelling priceless (and it will be with all the hard work you put into it!), try to make it appear to be worth less in the eyes of the building inspector.

The BBC, in §118.3, requires that the building-permit fee be based on "the volume of the structure, or as otherwise prescribed in the local ordinances. . . ." (How to compute volume is set forth in §119.) This code also leaves it to the building inspector to establish a schedule of unit rates to be charged. (There is no plan-checking fee or doubling of fees if you start construction without a permit under this code, though local jurisdictions that adopt the BBC may collect a plan-checking fee.)

CODE-READING TECHNIQUE: Not all definitions of words or explanations of concepts are found in the chapter on definitions. Many times you'll find words or concepts explained in other sections of the code (as §119 is used to clarify §118.3 in the example above). Generally, if the explanatory material is not immediately preceding or following the section where the ambiguous phrase appears, that section itself should direct you to the explanatory provision.

The NBC doesn't even mention building-permit fees in the main part of its text, but has relegated that requirement to §10 of the ordinance (set forth in its Appendix Q), which it recommends that local jurisdictions use when adopting the NBC. The standard by which the building inspector sets the fee under this code is based on the "estimated cost" (defined in §10.g of Appendix Q as "the reasonable value of all services, labor, materials" excluding excavating, painting, or decorating) of the structure. If you're going to use recycled materials you can validly argue that the "cost" of the dwelling is much less than its actual value, and attempt to get your permit fee reduced. (There's no plan-checking fee or doubling of fees for starting construction without a permit under this code.)

The SBC, in §107.4, places the responsibility for setting fees on "the authority having jurisdiction" (presumably the governing body adopting the building code) and not on the building inspector. The standard by which fees are collected is based on the value (defined in §201.2 as "the estimated cost to replace the building in kind") of the construction. If you have underestimated the "value" of the structure on the application, the building inspector does not set his own value, as is done in the other models, but simply denies the permit (§107.5). In that case, you may then have to show detailed estimated costs to support your figures—or submit a new application showing new (higher) estimated costs.

Furthermore, the SBC may require a plan-checking fee of one-half of the building-permit fee for construction valued over $1,000. And the permit fee doubles if you commence construction without a permit (§107.2).

So what you have to do is clear: study your building code to find out how the valuation of the construction is determined for building-permit purposes and get all your best arguments together as to why your owner-built home is lower in value than what the building inspector says it is.

PLANS AND SPECIFICATIONS

Your building code might next require that you present a sketch of the site on which you want to build and the plans and specifications of the house you want to build on that site.

Section 301(b)2 of the UBC indicates that the site plan should:

> Describe the land on which the proposed work is to be done, by lot, block, tract, and house and street address, or similar description that will readily identify and definitely locate the proposed building or work.

But many times that site plan does more than that. As the site plan in Appendix B of this book shows (it's the first drawing in that group), you should also indicate where north is, show the outline of the house and the direction in which it will face, how access will be gained to the property and house, where your water-supply well will be located, and finally where your septic system will be dug. (See Chapter Six of this book for more detail as to how far the water supply should be from the septic tank.) I doubt whether your local building code or inspector will require more information than that—but on second thought, some do want you to show the location of trees over a certain diameter and indicate if those trees will be saved instead of cut or knocked down.

Most building codes have detailed provisions on the plans and specifications that are required, and in some instances don't require plans and specs at all. So when you review the plans and specification provisions of your building code, you should look for two things: (1) whether plans and specs are required at all in order to obtain a building permit for a single-family dwelling, and, (2), if they are required, whether or not the owner-builder can prepare those plans and specs him- or herself.

The BBC, in §113.5, states that two copies of plans and specs must be filed with the building-permit application. "The building official may waive the requirement for filing plans when the work involved is of a minor nature," says this section, but I don't think you'll succeed in arguing that your small one-room cabin is "work of a minor nature." You *can* use this language, however, to argue that repairs which might be extensive enough to warrant a building permit are still of a "minor nature" and therefore don't require plans and specs.

The plans that are mandated by the BBC must be "drawn to scale, with sufficient clarity, and detail dimensions to show the nature and character of the work to be performed." If the building inspector demands more detailed engineering plans (it's his option), the plans must then be prepared and signed by an architect or engineer (§113.7). So if you're governed by a code similar to the BBC, try to keep your construction simple and understandable so that the building inspector will be more likely to let you prepare your own plans and specs.

The NBC has seemingly uncomplicated directions regarding this subject in §102.6:

> Application for permits shall be accompanied by drawings of the proposed work, drawn to scale, showing, when necessary, floor plans, sections, elevations, structural details, computations and stress diagrams as the building official may require.

There is no option under the NBC; you have to submit plans. But there is also no requirement that drawings be prepared by an engineer or architect. On the other hand, the phrase "as the building official may require" means that the building official can elect to demand very precise drawings from you, and reject those not up to his standards.

The SBC is the most liberal and most helpful of all to the owner-builder in terms of application requirements. Section 105.3(a) of this code gives the building inspector discretion to require or not require plans. If the inspector does demand plans, they must be "drawn to scale with sufficient clarity and detail to indicate the nature and character of the work." They don't have to be signed by an engineer or architect. (Section 105.3[c] does say that all structures more than three stories in height or with an area of more than 5,000 square feet have to be designed by an engineer or architect—but specifically exempts one- and two-family dwellings.)

Under the UBC, two sets of plans and specs are required with every building-permit application (§301[c]). And that section goes on: "The Building Official may require plans and specifications to be prepared and designed by an engineer or architect licensed by the state to practice as such." The circumstances under which the building inspector can demand plans are not spelled out. He may as a matter of practice always ask for them or he may not. In other words, the owner-builder is completely at his mercy, and may unnecessarily have to add to expenses and pay an architect or engineer to prepare the plans.

But believe it or not, the UBC does have a specific exception to §301(c), which can be used to the advantage of owner-builders. The exception states that plans and specs need not be submitted—"when authorized by the Building Official"—for one-story conventional wood-stud construction not exceeding 600 square feet, or small and unimportant work. So if you're building small enough (or if you build each room of your dwelling detached from the others with no single room over 600 square feet), you might try to take advantage of this provision.

The Dwelling Code—§R-110—has followed the liberal language of the SBC and gives the building inspector discretion to require or not to require plans. (The Dwelling Code is not very detailed on administration and that's why I have not quoted from its provisions up to this point. I imagine this code assumes that a local jurisdiction that has adopted the Dwelling Code has also adopted one of the other model codes, which are just filled with administrative procedures. For example, §R-109 of the Dwelling Code simply states that you must get a permit and pay a fee set by the building inspector; there are no other administrative regulations.)

If your local building code requires you to submit plans and specifications but allows you to draw them yourself, I've attached a whole set of plans in Appendix B of this book for your study. These plans were prepared by Walter Melvin, an architect who practices in New York City. (Now, I know New York is an unlikely spot for an owner-builder, but it is a great place in which to draft plans that must conform to building codes—and besides practicing in the city, Walter has also designed homes for the rural areas of New York State and New Jersey, in addition to doing some building himself.)

The plans that Walter has drawn do meet the minimum requirements for obtaining a building permit. The plans are sufficient only for obtaining a building permit, because plans from which you can actually construct a dwelling are generally a lot more complicated and detailed. But if you're going to build that house yourself in a code-dominated jurisdiction, you don't need construction plans. All you need is a minimum set of plans that please the building inspector and allow you to get a building permit. So study Walter's plans and the building code you're governed by and determine how detailed the plans you need must be in order to get a building permit.

If you have been reading carefully, you'll have noticed that the plans required under some of the codes "shall be of sufficient clarity" to indicate the nature of the work to be performed. Nowhere in any of these codes is "clarity" or "sufficient clarity" defined or is it stated to whom these plans shall be sufficiently clear. This language must mean, I submit, that the plans have to be clear enough so that the *building inspector* can understand them, and this leads me to the subject—the building inspector—I'll cover in the next chapter.

3. The Building Inspector

This is the individual you'll be dealing with when you apply for a building permit. He's characterized as either the protector of the public safety or the roadblock that prevents you from building your dream house. He's either the unfeeling, freedom-stifling symbol of governmental bureaucracy and red tape, or the knowledgeable, neighborlike expert who helps you over some difficult construction problems. Actually he's all of these things and more.

How do you handle him? What approach should you use in dealing with this man? Should you adopt a tough "he's working for me" attitude, or a meek nonquestioning stance?

Before I answer that question, let's look at the powers and duties of the building official (the codes like to call him "official" instead of "inspector") as they are outlined in the model building codes:

1. He receives the building-permit application and issues permits (BBC §108.2, NBC §4.a of Appendix Q, SBC §105 and §106, and UBC §301 and §302).

2. He conducts required inspections of the different stages of your home's construction to determine whether or not you've conformed to the code and/or to your previously submitted and approved plans and specifications (BBC §108.4, NBC §4.b of Appendix Q, SBC §108.2, UBC §304, and Dwelling Code §R-111).

3. He issues notices to remove illegal or unsafe conditions (BBC §108.3, NBC §4.a of Appendix Q, SBC §103.4; under UBC §203, he has the power to declare unsafe buildings as public nuisances—which in turn triggers rehabilitation or removal action pursuant to laws or statutes other than the building code).

4. He can issue stop-work orders when construction is unsafe or contrary to the code. As its name so aptly states, such an order stops all work on a project until the infraction is removed (BBC §123, NBC §105.3, SBC §103.2, and UBC §202[e]).

5. He can revoke permits if false or incorrect information was used to secure them (BBC §114.6, NBC §102.10, SBC §103.3, and UBC §302[e]).

6. He enforces the code (BBC §108.1, NBC §4.a of Appendix Q,

SBC §103.1, and UBC §202[a]). The UBC even says, in §202(a), that for the purpose of enforcement the building inspector has the powers of a police officer; it's the only model that puts it quite so bluntly!

7. He has the right of entry to your property to enforce the code (BBC §112, NBC §7 of Appendix Q, SBC §103.1, and UBC §202[d]).

8. He initiates necessary legal action to have code violators prosecuted in court (BBC §122, NBC §105). The SBC and UBC have no specific provisions that designate the building inspector as the one to initiate legal action, but both codes, as well as the other two model regulations, do provide criminal penalties for violation of their rules, and (as we have seen) name the building inspector as enforcer.

9. He has discretion to approve alternative materials and/or methods of construction (NBC §100.7, SBC §103.6, UBC §106, and Dwelling Code §R-108; the BBC has a similar provision in §108.5 and §800.4, but the power of the building inspector is not as great in this code as in the other models). The fact that the building inspector has this power to approve alternative materials and methods is vital to the owner-builder's strategy for dealing with him. A complete discussion of these alternate material provisions—together with the BBC's variance procedure allowed for practical difficulties—will be featured in Chapter Nine.

These are just some of the building inspector's explicitly defined functions. He also (as I indicated earlier) decides if your plans and specs are "sufficiently clear," estimates the value of your construction so as to set building-permit fees, and really determines whether your planned repairs of an existing structure are major enough to require a permit. And he also has quasi-judicial and quasi-legislative functions: he determines matters not provided for in the code (BBC §101.3 and SBC §103.5), and can promulgate rules and regulations to interpret and implement the provisions of the code (BBC §109).

Now you know why I stated in Chapter Two that the building inspector *is* the code! The written word as contained in those rules and regulations gets bended, amended, changed, brought to life, made to fit unusual situations—whatever you want to call it—by what this man says. If he goes by the book, you may not see the completion of your dwelling for a long time. If he's practical and understanding, your construction experience can be a real joy.

CODE-READING TECHNIQUE: Whenever the building inspector rules against you in some particular, ask him for the specific section upon which he bases his opinion. Read the language of that provision carefully. If it's a section where the conduct of his action is governed by detailed standards, make sure that the building inspector is correct in his interpretation of those standards and correct in the application of the rules to your project. If, however, the guardian of the code is relying on a provision that gives him discretion, attempt to determine if he's being arbitrary with you. That is, find out if and how he exercised his discretion in a similar situation in the past, and if he is ruling any differently in your particular circumstances. There are ways, which I will discuss in Chapter Nine, to appeal the decision of the building inspector.

On a practical, everyday level, the building inspector is not the tower of strength or authority the codes depict. As reported by Field and Ventre in their survey of building departments entitled "Local Regulation of Building: Agencies, Codes, and Politics" published in the *1971 Municipal Yearbook,* he has a much more difficult, tenuous existence on the job. Seven out of eight building-department heads serve at the pleasure of those who appoint them, and this situation makes them sensitive to political pressure and to the inherent insecurity of their jobs. Many inspectors, therefore, try to maintain a "don't rock the boat" attitude that accounts in large measure for the widespread reputation building departments have for being unduly cautious and conservative.

Field and Ventre also document other interesting facts in their survey: (1) that one chief building inspector in seven is over sixty and half are over fifty years of age, (2) that most building officials are in the twilight of their careers, (3) that the local building department appears to be a place where careers end rather than begin, (4) that many building inspectors come from the construction trades, and (5) that heavy dependence on construction experience may be a factor contributing to a building department's tardiness in accommodating new technology.

Okay. Now with all that background information under our belt, let's discuss how to handle this person whom the codes have almost deified, but whose employment status keeps him teetering on the precipice of the hell of the jobless.

The most important thing to remember is that the building inspector is not (in spite of what the codes say) godlike. He is a human being with the faults, virtues, and frailties that we all have. He's a not-so-well-paid public official trying to hold on to his job. He's a public servant who (unlike mayors, councilmen, and other elected officials) is on the firing line with the general public every day . . . and who comes under intense scrutiny when people are injured or killed in building failures.

So how do you go about dealing with this individual? There are two overriding points that I would emphasize:

1. Try to find out as much as possible about the *person* who is the building inspector—what his personality is like, how he treats people, just how flexible or rigid he is—before you meet him. And don't forget that for some owner-builders a confrontation with the building inspector is really a confrontation between two entirely different life-styles. Try to downplay that aspect of the conflict; it will only defeat your purpose. He has more power at his disposal than you do!

2. Be armed with as much detailed knowledge of (A) the building code (which is what this self-help guide is all about), (B) construction methods in general (which you can learn from the great number of informative how-to books on the market), and (C) the structure you yourself want to build . . . *before* you meet the inspector for the first time. And whatever it is you intend to build, make sure you know *why* the structure is *safe;* this is the most important information with which you can confront the building inspector.

Beyond those two points, I think I can help you best if I briefly present some specific instances of how other owner-builders accomplished what they wanted from their building inspectors. Each tale recounted here is as different as the building inspectors whom each of the owner-builders faced—and different still, no doubt, from your situation and the inspector you'll have to face. But the techniques described should get you thinking of how to deal with your own situation.

Les Scher, in his book *Finding and Buying Your Place in the Country,* relates the following confrontation between his friend Paul and a building inspector:

> Many people in the country deal with the myriad bureaucratic hassles, permits, and fees by ignoring them and hoping they don't get caught. A good friend of mine named Paul chose the exact opposite tactic in dealing with his local Building Inspector, who was one of the toughest I have met. When Paul bought his place the largest structure on the land was a big beautiful red barn which he wanted to convert into his family dwelling. Because a barn in the eyes of the law is not meant to be a house, many problems were involved in meeting the requirements of the building code.
>
> Knowing in advance that he would meet the Building Inspector sooner or later, Paul went to his office and told him what he was going to do. He drew up some fairly sketchy but basic plans, submitted them for approval, and paid the first part of his fees. Then he began to modify the barn and make it his home. The inspector came to make an inspection and then began appearing on a regular basis. Each time he hassled Paul about some aspect of his remodeling job until he really got

on Paul's nerves. So Paul decided to give him some of his own medicine.

Any time he began a new part of his remodeling, like a new wall, floor, beam, ceiling, or fireplace, he called up the Building Inspector and asked him what kind of materials he should use, how much he should buy, what kinds of nails or cement he should get, and how he should do the job. After several weeks of constant phone calls, the inspector had had enough. In complete exasperation he told Paul, "Dammit, I'm not your architect or contractor. Stop calling and bothering me." Paul then sent in the rest of his fees and he never saw the Building Inspector again.

If you don't like this "harass and conquer" method, you might be interested in Rex Roberts's suggestions, as set forth in his book *Your Engineered House:*

> Don't fight 'em, join 'em. The more severe the code, the more lenient the inspector knows he has to be with variations. Your house is going to be loaded with variations, in fact it won't be anything else but.
> You are going to be an asset to the community. You have money to spend and will be able to pay taxes. Your house as planned will beautify the town, not sully it. You will find that the building inspector is a fine source of information on soil conditions, seasonal ground water changes, prevailing winds, and local sources of good quality lumber. You will find the members of the building appeals board most sympathetic with your ambition to put up a fine, big, handsome house by construction methods of your own choosing.
> Don't ever sneak into town and start digging without letting city hall know. City hall will throw the book at you. Smile at city hall, ask its approval, and you'll get it with growing friendship and a lot of good advice thrown in.

River, in her touching book *Dwelling*, recorded some very pertinent conversations with owner-builders and their approach to building inspectors:

> Clancy, *well-known builder of code and non-code dwellings*, says:
> "As a builder, I can't help asking the inspector lots of questions he'll have to look up, or questions he just doesn't know about. Then you can help *him* out by changing the subject. After a time you'll be leaning on the table saying, 'what if I do this?' and he'll be saying, 'I don't know. . . .'"
> *Fil Lewit:* "My initial encounter with the inspector went like this: He drove his truck through my property—there was no gate at the time. There he was, right in the middle of the yard. I was building the cabin and he said, 'What are you doing?' and I said, 'I'm building.' He said, 'You need a permit for that.' And I said, 'You've got to be kidding.' He

said, 'No, but we'll just consider that you didn't know.' So I went in and got a permit to build a studio. And then turned the building into what I wanted. That was the only time they came to the farm. The barn was built before they changed the rules. Now, anything over $100 needs a permit—which is everything.

"I only got mad once. The inspector came in the gate and Barbara met him. He said he wanted to take a look around. Barbara told him he'd have to come back when the owner was there. Angry, I called the inspector and said, 'As far as I'm concerned, you're working for me, not the other way around.' He said he had a complaint about a non-code building and that he could legally check on it any time during business hours. I said, 'The hell you can! Don't come unless you make an appointment.' So my advice is, deal with the building inspector as quickly and efficiently as possible. Never be obsequious. I called them and told them to stay out of the farm unless they were invited in. Nobody can appear at the farm without calling me. Since that call, no one has come.

"It's not that anyone wins or loses. It's just that you have to descend into that game level in order to deal with them. You're jousting with each other. It is interesting to learn that the former head of the building department is now selling Challenger Homes. . . ."

And speaking of women, Alex Wade's approach to the building inspector—in his chapter "Some Problems to Overcome" in the book *Low-Cost, Energy-Efficient Shelter for the Owner-Builder*—presents a neat twist any woman or family can use:

Do your homework carefully before approaching the inspector. Try to locate someone who has dealt with him to find out what he is like. It might also pay to have a friend test the waters by going in and asking questions concerning a mythical small house in another part of town. Friends of mine have used another technique very successfully. Since the husband has a full-time job, his wife has done a great deal of work on both their new homes. Upon finding out that they were faced with a notoriously difficult building inspector, the wife spent several weeks boning up on construction details (for post and beam construction) and confronted the building inspector herself. Dealing with a woman who was knowledgeable on construction matters was such a novel experience that the building inspector was too flustered to be nasty. . . . Finally, remember that you are dealing with a bureaucrat who is near the bottom of the ladder. He needs to feel important. Flatter him, ask his advice. Also bear in mind that it is your tax dollars that are paying his salary, and he is there to serve *you*. . . . Try always to be reasonable and cooperative, as frequently the mood is contagious.

4. Types of Construction, Fire Districts, and Occupancies

We've had a relatively easy time of it so far. We've examined the various construction and repair situations that require a building permit, and taken a look at the functions of the building inspector. And to do so, we've only had to refer to the first chapter or two (the chapters on administration and definitions) in each of the model codes. But once you get beyond those initial chapters, the building regulations cover every conceivable building situation from farms to factories to hotels, and the job of reading and understanding the code becomes horrendously difficult.

In fact, if you're like most people the codes will immediately confuse you with their insistent references to such vague concepts as "types of construction," "fire districts," "fire-resistance ratings," and "classification of occupancies." Worse yet, each code makes unending references and cross-references to other parts of the code, its appendices, and/or even to other books (where, for instance, standards for building materials are provided). Sooner or later you're bound to reach a point where you'll be ready to throw up your hands and whimper, "I surrender." But don't give up! This book is intended to help you! Let's take a look at those "vague concepts" first.

Now, if I didn't have a conscience I could save both of us some work by simply telling you that you, as the owner-builder of a single-family dwelling, need not concern yourself with deciphering the codes' references to "types of construction" and "fire districts"—and that you need only be slightly concerned with "occupancy classifications"—because these don't really apply to your situation; your shelter is only required to meet the minimum standards of the code. But if I did make that statement without explaining to you exactly what "fire districts" and "types of construction" are, and then proceeded to list for you just the minimum standards, you wouldn't truly be prepared to *reason knowledgeably* with your building inspector. Why? Because unless you yourself know which requirements are and are not applicable to your situation—and why—your building inspector will be able to throw some code sections at you that you simply won't know how to handle.

So bear with me as I try to explain how these codes are structured. Once you know *why* you don't have to bother yourself with Type 1 fireproof construction or with the restrictive requirements for building in a fire zone, and can point to specific provisions to support your conclusions, your building inspector won't be able to talk you into doing something you don't have to do. And as an added bonus, you might even be able to convince him or her that those new construction techniques you've ingeniously devised are not prohibited by the code!

TYPES OF CONSTRUCTION

One of the concepts the codes force you to wrestle with is "types of construction." Now, this phrase is misleading because the classification of structures into different "types" has little, if anything, to do with the actual methods (such as post-and-beam or brick construction) that you might use to erect a building.

When the authors of the model codes say "types of construction," they're really referring to the *fire-resistance qualities* of various kinds of structures. For example, the BBC classifies all structures into four fire-resistant groups: Type 1, fireproof (which designates a structure that can withstand exposure to fire for three to four hours); Type 2, noncombustible (a building that has a fire-resistant rating of about two hours); Type 3, exterior masonry wall (which has a fire-resistant rating of one to two hours); and Type 4, frame (which can have either a one-hour rating [called protected] or no rating at all [unprotected]). See BBC §214 through §218, and Table 214.

Each of the other model codes has similar, but not identical, nomenclature and might even have an additional category or two— see NBC §700 to §708, SBC §601 to §610, and UBC §1701 to §2204. But (1) the theory in each code is the same as described here, and (2) the least restrictive category under each code—no matter how designated—does not require any minimum number of hours' fire-rating. (A table that sets forth the specific reference to each such model-code provision follows this chapter.)

As we'll see after a review of fire districts and occupancy regulations (which follows), each code—subject to a certain minimum setback from the property lines and height and area limitations—permits a single-family dwelling to be built according to the least restrictive fire-resistance category (such as Type 4, unprotected, under the BBC). You can, of course, build your shelter to any degree of fire-resistance that you desire. But the important thing to remember is that it's your choice!

FIRE DISTRICTS

A study of your construction ordinance will be a lot easier if you realize first that these regulations are concerned mainly with the protection of buildings from fire and its spread to adjoining structures, and that many restrictive code provisions are formulated on that premise.

Therefore, when a code author refers to a "fire district," he's generally alluding to "areas containing congested business, commercial manufacturing and industrial uses or in which such uses are developing" (BBC §301.2). In other words, these fire zones are places where the high density of people and buildings makes the outbreak of fire a real threat to humans and property. (Don't forget that the first model building code in this country was an attempt by fire insurance companies to help lessen fire-related financial losses.)

Chances are, you'll agree with me when I say that structures used by the public and/or employees should be built only with fireproof or noncombustible material (no unprotected wood-frame construction), and that the rightful purpose of fire districts is to impose stricter regulations on any building within the fire limits.

You might also agree with me when I say that rural land—or any area in which single-family residences predominate—should not (in terms of building codes) be included within a fire district. But it's not always as easy as that, because each individual municipality determines which parts of the town are to be incorporated within such zones—BBC §301.2, NBC §9 of Appendix Q, SBC §301.4, and UBC §1601(a)—and your town fathers, in a moment of optimism as to how the municipality was going to develop, might have placed your vacant property in a fire district. So you'd better check with town hall to be sure your property is outside any restrictive zones.

If your property *is* located within a fire zone, you may be required to build your single-family shelter according to the more stringent fire-resistance requirements demanded of all construction within that zone's limits. I'll assume, however, that your property is located outside a fire district (which is more likely to be the situation) and proceed to examine the code provisions that regulate construction beyond a district's boundaries.

In this area the BBC seems to be more liberal than it probably intends. There are three sections that deal with restrictions outside the fire zone. Section 303.1 provides that

Outside the fire limits, all types of construction except as herein specifically prohibited, or for which special approval is required in connection with high hazard uses and occupancies in Article 4, shall be permitted within the height [2½ stories, 35 feet for a single-family dwelling] and area [4,800 square feet] limitations of Table 305.

Section 303.2 states that a frame-construction building cannot be located less than 6 feet from a property line (unless you use one-hour fire-resistant exterior wall material), and §303.3 provides that roof coverings outside the fire district must conform to the fireproofing requirements of §903 and §926. (See "Roof Coverings" in Chapter Eight for more detail on this subject.)

You can interpret the language of §303.1 in a way that would permit any construction (without code restriction) outside a fire zone with the exception of (1) the height and area limitations contained in Table 305, specifically referred to in §303.1, (2) the 6-foot setback provision in §303.2, and (3) the roof coverings required in §303.3. In other words, my argument is that the rural owner-builder outside a fire zone can erect his dwelling without reference to the other code requirements such as graded lumber, toilets, plumbing, etc.

Now, I realize that's an extreme position to take, but the language of §303.1 does lend itself to that interpretation. The ambiguity, of course, arises from the phrase "types of construction." I'm sure that the building inspector, the municipality that adopted the code, and the authors of the BBC would argue that the phrase only makes reference to the construction classifications we've just examined in §214 through §218 of the BBC (and therefore all the rest of the code requirements control). But §303.1 doesn't define "types of construction" and doesn't make specific reference to §214 through §218. Furthermore, the phrase is not defined in the BBC's chapter on definitions. So the ambiguity does exist.

In order to help you understand more clearly the argument I'm making, look at the language the SBC uses to indicate construction permitted outside fire limits. Section 305 of the SBC says:

Outside the Fire District, all types of construction are permitted provided they comply with the provisions prescribed elsewhere in this Code that apply regardless of location. Roof coverings shall conform to the requirements as defined in Section 706.

Do you see the difference? The authors of the SBC even use the phrase "types of construction," but apparently find it necessary to add that those types of construction must "comply with the provisions prescribed elsewhere in this Code. . . ." There is no doubt under the SBC that all its other code requirements for a single-family dwelling apply, even if your property is located outside a fire district. Whereas under the BBC, none of its provisions would apply (all types of construction being permitted) unless a certain type of construction is specifically prohibited; and most model codes don't generally list what's prohibited.

So, if (1) you're in a jurisdiction that has a provision similar to that of §303 of the BBC, and (2) you own property outside the fire limits of the municipality, you might attempt to present this argument to the building inspector when he or she insists that you must use graded lumber, or meet other code requirements, in order to obtain a building permit. And if the above two conditions exist and (3) your already completed shelter has been red-tagged for demolition due to "noncompliance" with the code, I would definitely argue the point with your building inspector and/or to the court before which you might be forced to appear.

CODE-READING TECHNIQUE: The above discussion of §303 of the BBC is a specific example of how fuzzy language can be interpreted to mean a lot more than the author originally intended, and of how uncertain phraseology can work to your benefit. Always question every word, phrase, sentence, and paragraph of your code as you read it; there may be something hidden away among all that verbiage that can help you.

The NBC handles its "outside the fire limits" restrictions in a way that's different from the two codes just reviewed. There is no mention in the NBC of construction requirements outside a fire district. Section 570 of this code simply imposes additional restrictions on all structures located within such a zone. This, of course, means that the remaining 516 pages of the NBC cover construction both *inside and outside* fire districts.

The UBC is organized differently yet. This code, in §1601(a), requires that all the territory in a jurisdiction, whether it's a county or a municipality, be placed in one of three fire districts. In other words, if your building ordinance is similar to the UBC, your property will not be outside a fire district even if it's in the woods! Rural land, however, will *probably* be classified in Fire Zone No. 3, which—according to §1604—permits "any building or structure complying with the requirements of this Code [to] be erected, constructed, [or] moved within or into Fire Zone No. 3."

OCCUPANCY CLASSIFICATIONS

The model codes employ a third device—called occupancy classifications—that's also intended to prevent fire damage to property and physical injury to people. The idea behind this particular concept is to lump all the possible uses that might be made of buildings into about nine different occupancy categories (business, factory, residential, etc.) and then require more stringent fire-resistant and construction standards for those occupancies—regardless of their location—that pose the greatest threat to property and people.

For instance, a movie theater is generally classified as an "assembly occupancy" and the applicable code provisions require strict fireproof construction, ample means of safe egress, and other tough standards. Under the codes, a structure housing a movie theater would have to comply with the regulations that govern an "assembly use," no matter whether the cinema was located in the middle of a fire district or in a new shopping center erected outside the fire limits.

The code provisions governing a single-family occupancy classification, however, don't impose strict construction or fireproof standards; in fact, this occupancy is generally the least regulated of all the different use categories. So with that basic information, I can probably help you most if I indicate where, in each model code, you can find these minimum requirements for the residential occupancy group.

If your building ordinance is similar to the BBC, you'll find the "Use Group Classification" provisions right after the definitions in Article 2. Section 202 categorizes all buildings and structures into nine different groups and then refers you to other sections for more detailed information on each type of occupancy listed. The standards for residential dwellings are found in §209.

When you turn to §209 in the BBC, you'll note that the residential use group itself is broken down into several subclasses: R-1 (hotels and motels), R-2 (multifamily dwellings), R-3 (one- and two-family houses with not more than five lodgers), and R-4 (all detached one- and two-family dwellings). The R-4 use group is probably the only one that concerns most owner-builders.

The BBC also provides a list at the end of §209 (Table 209.6) that is a reference to all other sections of the code which might be germane to residential construction. This is an extremely helpful guide and the BBC is the only code to attempt to steer you through the entire maze of regulations in such a complete fashion.

There are, however, two caveats to the use of Table 209.6: (1) If the authors of the BBC have by chance neglected to include a necessary reference in that table, the omission doesn't negate the standards of the forgotten section—you're still required to follow all applicable provisions, whether listed in the guide or not. And, (2), the table contains many references that are relevant only to R-1 and R-2 use groups and don't have to be followed for a single-family dwelling in the R-3 or R-4 category.

CODE-READING TECHNIQUE: When reviewing the provisions of this or any other building code, make sure that the section you're referred to (by the building inspector or by another code provision) is pertinent to the kind of residential dwelling you're concerned with. A high-rise condominium is a residential use, but an owner-builder of a single-family shelter does not, obviously, have to meet the construction requirements for a five-story building.

The language the BBC uses to define the R-4 residential subcategory is of interest to the owner-builder:

> 209.5   Use group R-4 structures: This use group shall include all detached one- or two-family dwellings not more than three (3) stories in height, and their accessory structures. . . . All such structures may be designed in accordance with the One- and Two-Family Dwelling Code or in accordance with the requirements of this code for a use group R-3 structure.

What makes this language interesting is the fact that a municipality or county adopting the BBC may—without realizing it—also be adopting the *One- and Two-Family Dwelling Code.* And if your local government has either knowingly or inadvertently adopted this particular building regulation, you're in luck! You'll have a lot easier time reading and understanding the Dwelling Code because it (1) is organized according to a logical construction sequence, (2) contains regulations pertinent only to single- and two-family homes (no classification by occupancy here), and (3) does not confuse you with provisions for "types of construction," "fire-ratings," or "fire districts" (this code's minimum provisions apply both inside and outside a fire zone). So check your building ordinance to see if the reference to the Dwelling Code noted above has been retained.

Now let's look at the usage provisions of the other model codes. Article III of the NBC has over one hundred pages devoted to "Occupancy Requirements." Fortunately for the owner-builder, only a bit more than two of these pages—§382 of the NBC—deal with "Dwellings," which is this particular code's name for residential use. (Section 382 simply lists eight provisions—such as means of egress, doors, windows, stairs, etc.—that the owner-builder must comply

FIRE SAFETY AND BUILDING CODES: A GUIDE

Here—for your use as a checklist—is a guide to the model codes' absolute minim
construction standards (as required by the fire-safety considerations discussed in t

	BBC		NBC	
How single-family residential use is characterized	R-4	§209.5	Dwelling	§3{
Least restrictive type of construction (no minimum no. of hours fire-rating)	Type 4 unprotected (frame)	§218.1	Wood	§70
Minimum setback from property line (no fire-resistant exterior walls required)	6 feet	§303.2 and Table 214	No minimum required	
Maximum height	2½ stories (35 feet)	Table 305	35 feet	Table 51(
Maximum area (in square feet)	4,800	Table 305	6,000 (1 story), 4,000 (more than 1 story)	Table 51(
Roof coverings: A. Minimum requirements	Nonclassified	§926.3.4	Class C	§802.2
B. Definition of requirement	One that has not been tested	§903.3.5	Effective against light exposure to fire	§802.1.a.(3
C. Wood shingles allowed?	Yes, if set back more than 12 feet from another building	§854.8.2	No, but see Appendix G	

icle) for a single-family dwelling located *outside a fire district* (or in Fire Zone No. 3
der the UBC).

SBC		UBC		DWELLING CODE	
esidential	§411	Group I	§1401	No designation (no other use occupancies)	
ype VI nprotected	§607	Type V unprotected combustible	§2201 and Table 17-A	No designation (no other types of construction)	
feet	Table 600	3 feet	Table 5-A	3 feet	§R-203
0 feet	Table 400	40 feet	Table 5-D	3 stories	§R-103
,000	Table 400	No maximum	Table 5-C	No maximum	
ype C	§706.5	Class C	§1704 and §3203(f)	Class C	§R-801
er approved esting gency	§706.4	Not defined		Not defined	
es, if set ack more han 6 feet rom roperty line	§706.6	Yes	§3203(f)	Yes	§R-809

with. I'll review these and similar requirements found in all the model codes in the next chapter.)

The SBC outlines its "Classification of Building by Occupancy" in Chapter IV. The residential-use requirements (designated as *R* in this code) are found in §411. Except for a citation back to "General Protective References" in §402.4 (which contains provisions pertinent to *all* occupancies), there are no requirements in §411 for a single-family detached dwelling. (There are, however, five special fire-protection regulations that are mandated for multifamily, town house, and high-rise residential occupancies.)

Part III of the UBC, Chapters 5 through 15, contains all of that code's "Requirements Based on Occupancy." Residential uses are called "Group I Occupanices" under this code and are found in §1401 through §1413. (Each use group is designated by a letter of the alphabet, starting with *A* and ending with *J*. These assigned letters bear no relationship whatsoever to the first letter of the kind of occupancy being described.)

There is some differentiation made between residential uses in the UBC in that apartment houses and hotels are classified as Group H occupancies, with "Dwellings" and "Lodging Houses" categorized as Group I. The requirements listed for Group I occupancies in §1401 through §1413 are very similar to the ones (such as light and ventilation, room dimensions, etc.) found in the NBC, and are the kinds of regulations I'll cover in detail in the next chapter.

(There are no references to the Dwelling Code in the NBC, SBC, or UBC as there was in the BBC.)

A SUMMARY

After all that, I'm sure you'll comprehend without further explanation the fact that a construction code imposes different degrees of fire-resistant construction on different buildings depending on: (1) the location of the structure inside or outside a fire district, (2) the proximity of the building to its property lines, and (3) the occupancy of the building (movie theater, high-rise offices, residential, etc.).

I'm sure you'll also understand that, under the model codes, a single-family dwelling is the least regulated of the different occupancy categories, because (1) it is generally found outside a "fire district," and (2) it can be—in rural and semirural areas—located more than the minimum requirement of 3 or 6 feet from its property lines. *That's why* the owner-builder doesn't have to concern himself with types of construction and fire districts!

5. "Nonconstruction" Construction Requirements

In the first four chapters I concentrated on the larger framework of the model building codes in an attempt to make those rather formidable ordinances understandable. And in the process I've tried to help you develop the code-reading techniques that are necessary to effectively review and evaluate your own building regulations.

With all that under our belts, we can now begin to shift our emphasis from the general structure of those ordinances to the specific requirements for constructing a single-family dwelling "according to code." In other words, we're finally ready to determine just what the plans you have to present to your building inspector must contain to conform to your building regulations.

Now, as we review these provisions you'll probably notice some standards creeping in that seem to have little, if anything, to do with fire safety or even construction methods. In actual fact, many are outright reflections of society's preconceived concept of how we all should live (without much consideration for alternatives). Others deal with matters that, to my mind, rightly belong in a multifamily housing code and not in a single-family construction regulation. And still others have apparently been instituted simply to satisfy the demands of influential special-interest groups. I call all these kinds of provisions "nonconstruction" construction requirements, and although there's plenty of room for argument against them (which I'll cover later on), the simple fact is they *do* exist. Like it or not, you're going to have to comply with them.

Because the *One- and Two-Family Dwelling Code* puts all of these "nonconstruction" construction requirements in one place (Chapter 2, which is also the only chapter in Part II of the Dwelling Code, both chapter and part being entitled "Building Planning"), and because this code is the easiest model for the owner-builder to use, I will list (and comment on) all these regulations from Part II, Chapter 2, noting—for those of you who are governed by regulations similar to the Basic, National, Standard, or Uniform Building Codes—any similar (and all different) provisions found in those models.

(It's about time that I told you about the indices that are found at the end of each of the model codes. With an index, you can look up any specific topic you're interested in and go right to that subject within the code. I haven't mentioned indices before this because [1] I wanted you to get the feel of the broad organization of the code by thumbing through the pages and working with the table of contents, and [2] your particular local building ordinance may not have an index—and if there isn't an index in your code, then I haven't made you dependent on one. But since we're now getting away from the larger framework of the codes and will start to concentrate on specific requirements, I feel I can tell you about the possibility of your code's having an index and direct you to use it if it's there. In other words, when I start talking about the light and ventilation provisions—as I do immediately—you can go to the index of your code and you should be able to find the specific section on that subject in your code. Then you can compare your code provision on a particular type with my discussion and analysis. If you don't have an index, you'll have to hunt down the various subjects I cover either through the table of contents or by the old speed-read-skim method.)

LIGHT AND VENTILATION

The Dwelling Code, in §R-204, sets forth all of the minimum requirements (and exceptions thereto) for the natural illumination and ventilation of your shelter. The first command is:

> All habitable rooms shall be provided with aggregate glazing area of not less than 8% of the floor area of such rooms. One-half of the required area of glazing shall be openable . . . [and those] required glazed openings shall open directly onto a street or public alley, or a yard or court located on the same lot as the building.

There are two exceptions to this quoted requirement of §R-204—found right in §R-204 itself. The first written exception to this rule in the Dwelling Code is that the windows in habitable rooms don't have to open if you provide a mechanical ventilation system that can produce a complete change of air in the building every thirty minutes. A second written exception is that a glazed opening may face a roofed porch if the porch (1) abuts a street or a yard, (2) is at least 65 percent open and unobstructed on its long side, and (3) has a ceiling height of not less than 7 feet.

Another exception—although it's not labeled explicitly as one—is that the glazing requirement is only applicable to "habitable rooms." Now if you've read the first few chapters of this book carefully, you'll already be turning to the Dwelling Code's definition section to find out if the ordinance defines that phrase. And when you do, you'll discover that the Dwelling Code does indeed give its own particular meaning to those two words. Section R-114 defines "habitable room" as

> any room meeting the requirements of this Code for sleeping, living, cooking or dining purposes *excluding* [the emphasis is mine] such enclosed places as closets, pantries, bath or toilet rooms, hallways, laundries, storage spaces, utility rooms, and similar spaces.

So if you can't or don't want to meet the glazing requirements in a particular room, you can simply mark that space on your plans and specifications as a pantry, storage, or utility room. Then you won't be obligated to meet minimum glazing requirements for that room. (See, sometimes you *can* use building regulations to your own advantage!)

CODE-READING TECHNIQUE: As you'll see later on, most of the other codes' regulations for single-family dwellings also apply only to "habitable rooms." So read each and every provision that attempts to impose restrictions on your dwelling, and find out what kinds of rooms are so regulated. If the regulations apply only to *habitable* **rooms and you simply can't meet some of your code's requirements in one or two rooms, mark those nonconforming areas as something other than "habitable rooms." Better yet, study the regulations before you design your home, and arrange your floor plan to place sleeping, living, and dining rooms in that part of the house where you** *can* **meet the requirements.**

But the real evil that lurks in §R-204 is that there are no exceptions or approved alternatives to the requirements for natural lighting of a habitable room. In other words if you wanted to construct, say, an underground house (to get the energy-saving, temperature-moderating effect of the surrounding earth), you might not be able to meet the Dwelling Code's glazing requirement of "not less than 8% of the floor area" for habitable rooms!

Even though the use of skylights, for instance, is a logical way to provide natural light for an underground home, a literal reading of §R-204 of the Dwelling Code (". . . required glazed openings shall open directly onto a street or public alley, or yard or court located on the same lot as the building") does not seem to allow a window to face skyward! But this last-quoted sentence applies to glazed *openings*, and since you'll probably install a mechanical ventilation system in your underground house, you can argue that this sentence in §R-204 doesn't prohibit a nonopenable skylight to be used to meet the natural-light requirements of the code. Skylights are not, however, expressly permitted in the Dwelling Code as an alternative to natural illumination.

A final mandate for light and ventilation in §R-204 is that bathrooms or water-closet compartments (don't forget, these aren't considered habitable rooms by definition) should have an aggregate glazed area in windows of not less than 3 square feet, one-half of which must be openable. But if a mechanical ventilation system (producing an air change every twelve minutes) is provided together with artificial light, neither natural ventilation nor natural light is required. (Remember: This exception allowing artificial light applies only to bathrooms. There is no artificial-light alternative to natural-illumination requirements for habitable rooms under the Dwelling Code.)

Now let's review the other model codes, all of which, like the Dwelling Code, limit light and ventilation requirements to habitable rooms and bathrooms.

The BBC devotes a whole separate article (Article 5, covering eleven pages) to light and ventilation. And although most of the twenty-one separate sections involved don't apply to single-family dwellings, the requirements that do are similar to those mentioned above for the Dwelling Code—*except:* (1) skylights are specifically allowed to meet natural-light requirements (§506.1), and (2) alternatives for natural light (as well as natural ventilation) "shall be permitted when complying with the approved rules" (§506.4). ("Approved rules" are those which the building inspector has legally adopted pursuant to §109. So if your building inspector has not prescribed such rules, you can show him §109 and §506.4 and ask him to adopt the rules necessary to permit artificial light for your underground house.)

The NBC tucks away its regulations on illumination and airing as a small part of Article VI, and labels them rather nicely—but not quite accurately—as "Environmental Requirements." Section 601.2 (as well as §382.3 in the Article on "Occupancy Requirements") demands *natural* light and ventilation, but §605 provides an alternative: mechanical ventilation of air. As in the Dwelling Code, however, the NBC provides no expressly stated alternative that allows artificial light. Section 604, entitled "Ventilating Skylights," does—in spite of its ambiguous sentence structure and cross-references—allow ventilating skylights in habitable rooms in dwellings. There is a separate section, 807.7, that governs the "how-to" aspects of building a skylight in rooms where those ceiling windows are allowed.

All subterranean builders note: The NBC does *not* permit completely underground houses; §601.4 states that "habitable rooms for residential occupancies shall have not less than 50% of their story height above grade"!

The SBC puts all of its regulations on light and ventilation in §2001. Windows are required by this code, but skylights are a specifically approved alternative "when approved by the Building Official" (§2001.1[d]). In addition, the other provisions of the SBC on light and ventilation—particularly §2001.1, §2001.3, and §2001.5—are generally less rigid than corresponding regulations in the Dwelling Code.

The UBC lists its light and ventilation stipulations for habitable rooms as part of its occupancy standards in §1405. Skylights in general, and the openable variety in particular, are acceptable alternatives to conventional wall-inserted windows. The rest of the regulations of that section are similar to the Dwelling Code, with the exception of one particularly useful provision that allows the windows (and, I assume, skylights too) in one room to satisfy the natural illumination requirements in an adjoining room,

> when one-half of the area of the common wall is open and unobstructed and provides an opening of not less than one-tenth of the floor area of the interior room or 25 square feet, whichever is greater.

An owner-builder can use this half-wall exception very creatively in his room placement and overall design to achieve a uniquely personal shelter while still complying with the code.

I've been trying to show you that there are stated and unstated exceptions to each code's light and ventilation regulations, and that with a little inventive planning these requirements don't have to be the hurdle they might seem to be at first glance. But one of the maddening aspects of working with a building code is that once you think you've found a way to "creatively comply" with a particular section (in order, for instance, to build that underground house), there's almost always another provision—stuck away in an unlikely spot and with an unlikely title—that foils your best-laid plans. And unfortunately the codes' light and ventilation provisions are no exception.

Even though it seems we've reviewed everything there is in the codes about illumination, ventilation, windows, and skylights, there are other sections—notably on the improbable subject of exits—that have a profound effect on your home's design. In the case of that underground structure we've worked so hard to steer through light and ventilation requirements, for instance, those other sections could well prevent construction entirely!

EXITS . . . AND DOORS, HALLWAYS, AND GLAZING

You would think that the "Exits" provision of §R-211 of the Dwelling Code would deal at least in part with doors and their dimensions and placement. But no, that's too logical. All §R-211 states about doors is that not less than one exit conforming to the chapter shall be provided, and leaves it (1) to §R-212—"Doors and Hallways"—to describe a required exit door as being 3 feet in width and 6 feet 8 inches in height, and (2) to §R-209—"Glazing"—to describe the kind of safety glass required for various doors.

What the rest of §R-211 *does* require (and this is where it adds to the window burden that we thought we overcame) is:

> Every *sleeping room* shall have at least one openable window or exterior door approved for emergency egress or rescue. [Emphasis added is mine.]

Section R-211 then goes on to require that those bedroom windows must (1) be openable from the inside without the use of separate tools, (2) have a clear opening of not less than 20 inches in width, 24 inches in height, and 5.7 square feet in area, and (3) have their bottom sash not higher than 44 inches above the floor.

This requirement at first glance seems truly related to the personal safety of occupants, and anyone who attacks it might be accused of being a reincarnated Roman delighting in human bonfires. But at the risk of being thought sadistic, I'll challenge the rule—not because I don't agree with the intent, but because I consider the regulation to be only a halfhearted measure. The regulation does not, as I think it should, require that sleeping rooms *themselves* be on the ground floor (so escape through those openable windows is easy) and prohibit bedrooms (in single-family, frame-construction dwellings) on second or third floors! You see, even if a sleeping room on the second floor does have an openable window, as the rule requires, that window could be 10 or more feet above the ground—which, of course, would make escape extremely difficult and hazardous under emergency conditions. So the intent of the rule is thwarted.

In any event, you will be confronted with the openable-bedroom-windows rule. The BBC in §609.4, the NBC in §382.3, the SBC in §1104.6, and the UBC in §1404 all have nearly identical provisions to §R-211 of the Dwelling Code.

There are, however, two hints that might help you in overcoming the burden of this openable-window regulation for the underground house you might be considering: (1) The requirement is applicable only to sleeping rooms and you might be able to design your subterranean shelter in such a way that the bedrooms are placed in that part of the house where they can meet this stipulation, or (2) if you don't want to redesign the room placement, you can appeal to the building review board (Chapter Nine will give you the specifics of this appeal procedure) for a variance from this requirement.

(Your argument to the appeal board would be that your underground house is made of fireproof masonry material [which is what you would generally use to build such a structure] and therefore the fire-safety *intent* of the rule is satisfied without the openable bedroom windows.)

SMOKE DETECTORS

Since our review of the code sections on exits has led us to the subject of fire safety, we may as well look at another—relatively new—regulation concerning this topic: namely, the requirement, in §R-216 of the Dwelling Code, that each single-family house shall have a "smoke detector sensing visible or invisible particles of combustion."

Obviously, the intent of this section is good and honorable. More people are killed by smoke inhalation than by fire itself, and there is no doubt that early-warning devices usually give sleeping families adequate time to escape. But the codes still allow bedrooms on the second floor. A smoke detector might wake and warn you of a fire, but your chances of getting out *and* avoiding a broken limb or two are limited if your only escape route is out a second- or third-floor window.

So smoke detector manufacturers now have a ready-made market to which to sell their consumer product, while true fire-safety considerations such as limiting bedrooms to the ground level for easy escape have not been accepted by the model-code groups. There are some other disturbing aspects of this smoke detector requirement too.

For instance, the language of the Dwelling Code's §R-216 describes the required smoke detector as "approved, listed, and labeled." Approved, listed, and labeled by whom? And as to what?

The BBC, in §1216.3.4, states that the "approved smoke detector . . . [shall be] installed in a manner and location approved by the authority having jurisdiction." The BBC, therefore, leaves it to the building inspector and/or the local governing body to determine where the device should be located within the dwelling. The UBC, on the other hand, tells you exactly where your warning system should be placed (in §1413). And the SBC, in §1127, requires installation according to "manufacturer's recommendation and listing."

Ah, but I've saved the most controversial code provision for last! Ready? The NBC, in §382.6, requires that a home-builder's approved fire detector "shall have a primary source of *commercial electrical power*." (Emphasis added is mine.)

There it is! You can't comply with the NBC if you power your home with your own self-sufficient hydro- or wind-generated electricity. *You must have commercial utility company power.* You *must* turn control of part of your life over to something over which you have no control. (And in the wake of New York City's brown- and blackouts, I really wonder if commercial power is more dependable.) And what about the family that doesn't want electricity at all? (There *are* some smoke detectors that run on batteries!)

However, in the NBC there is no room for exceptions (such as not requiring smoke detectors if your bedrooms are on the ground floor or if your house is made of fireproof materials), and no room for alternatives (such as allowing battery-operated devices). This is a prime example of how a seemingly well-intentioned rule can be turned into a freedom-stifling straitjacket, just as has been done with so many other rules in our overregulated society.

Enough said! Let's get back to some of the other "nonconstruction" code provisions with which your plans must comply if you want to get that building permit.

ROOM SIZES

Believe it or not, the model codes dictate the minimum size of the rooms in which you and I must live! Now, this kind of provision may be appropriate for a housing code regulating rental apartments, but the rule seems singularly unsuitable for an owner-built single-family dwelling.

The four sentences of §R-205 of the Dwelling Code put it succinctly:

> Every dwelling unit shall have at least one habitable room which shall have not less than 150 square feet of floor area. Other habitable rooms shall have an area of not less than 70 square feet. Every kitchen shall have not less than 50 square feet of floor area.
>
> Habitable rooms except kitchens shall not be less than 7 feet in any horizontal dimension.

There isn't much to be said about this rule, except to remind you that these minimums are applicable only to habitable rooms. So again: Label (on your plans) any nonconforming area as a laundry, utility, or storage room and you won't have to meet these requirements.

At first glance the BBC doesn't seem to have a section similar to §R-205 of the Dwelling Code . . . but it does. If you look, you'll find the BBC's minimum-room-size requirement in, of all places, the *definition* of "Habitable space, minimum size" found in §201:

A space with a minimum dimension of seven (7) feet and a minimum
area of seventy (70) square feet, between enclosing walls or partitions,
exclusive of closet and storage spaces.

Never thought you'd find a code requirement hidden in the definition
section, did you?

CODE-READING TECHNIQUE: I quoted §201 of the BBC to
show you what a rule masquerading as a definition looks like, and
also as a reminder: *Always check the definition section of your code.*
(Remember? I gave you that same tip in the first code-reading technique, back in Chapter Two.) Now that we know that some pur-
ported definitions are regulations in disguise, the importance of
checking to see if your code gives its own meaning to a word or
phrase is doubly underscored. There's just no telling what you'll find
in the definition section of your code. So read it carefully!

Another interesting aspect of the BBC's room-size regulation is
that this code requires a minimum of 70 square feet for a room,
whereas the Dwelling Code's minimum for at least one room is 150
square feet. This difference can be useful to those of you owner-
builders who are governed by the BBC, because (as I mentioned in
the last chapter when I discussed the BBC's occupancy requirements)
the BBC allows you to build according to *either* the Dwelling Code *or*
the BBC. So in such a situation, you can actually choose whichever
code makes it easiest for you to build what you want.

The NBC, in §601.2, has seven subsections, two tables, and a list
of abbreviations in which the rules pertaining to "Habitable Rooms in
Dwelling Units" are laid down. This code has a fluctuating scale of
minimum sizes for single- or multipurpose rooms depending on the
number of bedrooms proposed. For example, a dwelling unit with
one bedroom is required to have a living room with 160 square feet, a
dining room (if you have one) of 100 square feet, and a bedroom of
120 square feet.

I won't go into a tedious five-paragraph explanation of the remaining combinations of bedroom and room sizes under the NBC!
Suffice it to say that any owner-builder who is building under this or
any similar code must study §601.2, particularly subsection b, very
carefully.

You'll find that provisions in §2001.1.1(b) and (c) of the SBC and
§1407(b) and (c) of the UBC are nearly identical to the Dwelling
Code's §R-205.

CEILING HEIGHTS

Yes, the minimum height your ceiling can be from the floor is also regulated. Your plans—in order to be approved—must show a ceiling height conforming to your code's requirements. But these provisions apply only to habitable rooms (and hallways) and, as is inevitable when trying to prescribe requirements on such a trivial subject, there are exceptions.

Section R-206 of the Dwelling Code states:

> Habitable rooms shall have an average ceiling height of not less than 7 feet 6 inches in at least 50 percent of their required area with no portion less than 5 feet in height.
>
> Exception: Beams and girders spaced not less than 4 feet on center may project not more than 6 inches below the required ceiling height.
>
> All other rooms, including hallways and corridors, shall have a ceiling height of not less than 7 feet measured to the lowest projection from the ceiling.

The BBC tucks away its regulation of ceiling height in—you guessed it—the definition chapter, §201, under the rubric "Habitable space, minimum height." This code also requires a minimum 7.5-foot ceiling height, but its only exception is for attic rooms or top-hall stories where "the height shall be not less than seven and one-third (7⅓) feet over not less than one-third (⅓) of the area of the floor when used for sleeping, study, or similar activity."

The NBC, in §601.2c, requires ceiling heights 7 feet 6 inches over not less than 90 percent of the floor area and reduced ceiling heights are only permitted adjacent to walls or partitions.

The SBC, in §2001.1.1(a), and the UBC, in §1407(a), have similar requirements to the Dwelling Code provision quoted above.

SOME MISCELLANEOUS PROVISIONS

We're nearly ready to move on to a discussion of the codes' sanitation regulations—a subject of such importance that I've devoted the entire next chapter to the topic. Before we do, though, there are a few other provisions, admittedly minor, that must be followed if you want your building inspector to approve your plans.

I'll go through these rules quickly, just to let you know they exist. But don't take them too lightly. You must comply with these seemingly insignificant regulations too . . . so study your code provisions on these subjects carefully.

STAIRWAYS. They (1) shall not be less than 3 feet wide, (2) shall have a minimum of 6 feet 6 inches of headroom (measured from the edge of the stair perpendicular to the ceiling), (3) have a maximum rise (the height of the individual stair) of 8 inches, and (4) have a minimum run (the depth of the individual stair) of nine inches. All of these measurements are contained in §R-214 of the Dwelling Code, which also permits spiral stairways according to numerous specifications.

HANDRAILS AND GUARDRAILS. If your stairway has more than three risers, handrails—with a minimum/maximum height of 30/34 inches, respectively—are required. Section R-215 of the Dwelling Code also makes mandatory 42-inch-high guardrails for a porch that's more than 30 inches above floor or grade.

LANDINGS. A minimum 3-foot-square landing is required on all exit doors—Dwelling Code §R-213—except that no landing is required if the exit door does not swing on the stair.

All the other model codes have similar (but not identical) provisions for stairways, handrails and guardrails, and landings: BBC §616, NBC §403 and §405, SBC §1115, and UBC §3305 and §1716.

GARAGES. If you even intend to have one (and I am pleased to announce they are not mandatory under the building code, but may be required under a zoning ordinance), garages (1) can't have a door opening into a bedroom, (2) must be separated from the residence by means of ½-inch gypsum board or equivalent applied to the garage side, (3) must have floors made of noncombustible material, and (4) must have a solid wood (as opposed to the more common hollow variety now being made) door leading to the residence (Dwelling Code §R-210). See also the BBC §413, NBC §391, SBC §412.6 and §403.1(d)1, and Chapter 15 of the UBC for similar provisions.

Please remember: Always check what the code *you* are governed by says about these kinds of provisions. The details might be somewhat different in your particular code, and you are responsible for complying with them.

6. More "Nonconstruction" Construction Requirements: Sanitation

The regulations governing sanitation are the last of the nonconstruction construction requirements found in the building codes. They are not the least, however—not by any means. In fact, it's necessary to devote this entire chapter to the subject in order to provide a complete discussion of (1) all of the various codes' sanitation requirements (and they are numerous), and (2) all the implications of those requirements (and they are significant). It's a big job, so let's get started.

Section R-207 of the Dwelling Code is entitled "Sanitation" and contains three deceptively simple paragraphs. The demands of these paragraphs seem—at first glance—so reasonable and universally acceptable (acceptable, at least, in these United States) that people don't think a great deal about alternatives, much less seriously consider other ways to accomplish similar ends. But these passages (together with others that expand upon, and are related to, these basic regulations) contain requirements that dictate how and in what manner you and I are going to live in our shelters. And they do so in a way that imposes both a kind of social sameness (a kind we seldom know we're being conditioned to) as well as a resource-wasting life-style (a life-style we only now dimly realize is overly consumptive and destructive).

Read carefully the words of §R-207:

> Every dwelling unit shall be provided with a water closet, lavatory and a bathtub or shower.
> Each dwelling unit shall be provided with a kitchen area and every kitchen area shall be provided with a sink of approved nonabsorbent material.
> All plumbing fixtures shall be connected to a sanitary sewer or to an approved private sewage disposal system. All plumbing fixtures shall be connected to an approved system of water supply and provided with hot and cold running water, except water closets may be provided with cold water only.

There it is . . . simple, isn't it? There isn't anything required in those words that we haven't all grown up with, right? But do you see any choices, alternatives, exceptions? I don't! And because of the unbending finality of these regulations, it's important to discuss each of these paragraphs separately (and the other relevant provisions that grow out of these requirements) in the following subsections of this chapter.

WATER CLOSETS, LAVATORIES, BATHROOMS . . .

To repeat, the first paragraph of §R-207 states: "Every dwelling unit shall be provided with a water closet, lavatory and a bathtub or shower."

You can see from the use of the word "shall" in this sentence that you must—there is no choice—have each of these three items. But the code does leave some questions unanswered: Do you have to have these amenities in the same structure that encloses your shelter? And by the way, just what is a "water closet" and what is a "lavatory"?

Let's discuss the last questions first. We all know what's generally meant by "bathtub" or "shower," but there is no definition of "water closet" or "lavatory" in the Dwelling Code, nor are definitions of these two terms found in the other model codes.

"Water closet" is an old phrase no longer in common usage; people don't excuse themselves from cocktail party conversation to go to the water closet nowadays. *Webster's Collegiate Dictionary* gives two definitions for the term. The first is synonymous with a place commonly called a bathroom: "a compartment or room for defecation and excretion into a toilet bowl." The second defines the phrase specifically as a fixture: "a toilet bowl and its accessories."

This same overlapping of concepts (encompassing both places and things) also appears in the definition of the word "lavatory," which has three separate and distinct meanings in *Webster's*: (1) a fixed bowl or basin with running water for washing (a thing), (2) a room for conveniences for washing and also containing toilets (a place), and (3) a toilet (a place *and* a thing).

CODE-READING TECHNIQUE: Now we know that even words with unclear meanings are not necessarily defined in the code. So don't stop at a code's definition section if you don't find there a word or phrase that was used in a code regulation. Check your trusty lexicon. If the ambiguity still persists after you've consulted your dictionary, you can use that uncertainty to argue that what you want to build fits within one of the various possible meanings of the questionable word(s).

For the sake of further analysis, however, I'll go on and give one particular meaning to "water closet" and one to "lavatory." Both are definitions I gleaned by implication from other sections of the Dwelling Code. You are welcome—in fact, you're encouraged—to draw your own conclusions from the wording of other sections of the code and to come up with your own meanings for "water closet" and "lavatory."

It's my conclusion that—because §R-208 of the Dwelling Code is titled "Toilets" and starts with the words "Every water closet, bathtub and shower required by this Code shall be installed *in a room . . .*"—the words "water closet" and "lavatory" as used in §R-207 can't refer to a place (the redundancy is obvious), but must mean a thing. As used in the codes, therefore, a water closet is probably a flush toilet bowl and a lavatory a washbasin. (I must admit, however, that I can't figure out why §R-208 does not specifically mention lavatories. The omission could mean that the washbasin doesn't have to be installed in the same room with the toilet and tub.)

We can now restate §R-207 of the Dwelling Code as follows: Every dwelling unit shall be provided with a toilet (in which to urinate and defecate), a washbasin (in which to wash your hands), and a bathtub or shower (in which to clean the rest of your body).

That's my answer to the question what is a "water closet" and "lavatory," as those words are used in the code. Now let's look for an answer to the first question I posed: Can you locate any of these required fixtures outside the house?

First of all, there are the practical considerations of weather. You may not, if you live in a cold region, want to go outside in three feet of snow on a subzero morning before the sun comes up just to go to the toilet.

But what if the weather is not a factor? Can you, if you want to, locate that water closet—or even your shower—out of doors? My interpretation of the model codes, as I read them, is that outside facilities are not allowed. But in all cases the wording *is* a little unclear. Again, the definition section gives us an answer (not necessarily *the* answer) by the meanings given for "dwelling" and "dwelling unit."

A "dwelling" is defined as

> any *building which contains* one or two "Dwelling Units" . . . to be occupied, or which are occupied for living purposes. [The emphasis is mine.]

A "dwelling unit," on the other hand, is

a single unit providing complete independent living facilities for one or more persons including permanent provisons for living, sleeping, eating, cooking and sanitation.

All of the other model codes define "dwelling" and "dwelling unit"—in their respective definition sections—almost identically to that of the Dwelling Code.

You can combine and paraphrase these two definitions to say that a dwelling is a building *containing* complete living units that provide facilities for, among other things, sanitation. It is from this rephrasing of the definitions that I draw my assumption: Sanitation facilities must be contained in the structure and cannot be located outside it.

On the other hand, you can argue that nothing specifically prohibits these fixtures outside, and if you're persuasive enough to convince your building inspector of your conclusion, you can be the proud owner-builder of your very own outdoor facilities!

However, there are regulations other than §R-207 of the Dwelling Code that you must follow in order to build your water closets, lavatories, and showers/tubs "according to code." I quote in full the provisions of §R-208 so that you can read all of the requirements to which your plans must conform. (I've bracketed my own comments and interspersed them at appropriate places throughout the quote so that I won't have to repeat anything to make an admittedly minor point or two.)

Every water closet, bathtub or shower required by this Code shall be installed in a room which shall afford privacy to the occupant. [I guess a movable curtain won't suffice. The toilet area *must* be enclosed in its own stationary-walled room!]

Each water closet compartment shall be not less than 30 inches in width and there shall be not less than 21 inches clear space in front of each water closet. [Yes, the codes dictate a minimum size for rooms that contain water closets, too.]

Shower compartment floors and walls shall be finished with a smooth, hard and nonabsorbent surface in accordance with Section S-26.208 to a height of not less than 6 feet above the floor. [The mention of S-26.208 is a reference to a construction material standard, which is, in actuality, a reference to another book, and a subject I'll discuss in the next chapter.]

Doors and panels of shower and bathroom enclosures shall be substantially constructed from approved [by whom? see page 70] shatter resistant materials. Glazing in doors and panels of shower and bathroom enclosures shall comply with the requirements set forth in Table No. 2-B [which is part of §R-209, discussed in my last chapter].

64   BUILDING REGULATIONS

What do the other model codes have to say about water closets,
lavatories, bathtubs, and showers? (Before I answer that question, I
must reemphasize a point made in Chapter One: Each of these
model-code groups has a whole separate—and large—book devoted
to the subject of plumbing regulations. So you should therefore realize that a relatively short chapter (or article or part) on plumbing in a
model-code group's *building* regulation is not the final word on the
topic.

(For the purposes of this review, however, I will discuss only
those sanitation/plumbing provisions found in each of the model
building codes [including the Dwelling Code], and not contained in
the more detailed plumbing ordinances. This fact of a separate
plumbing manual makes for some interesting reading in the building
codes themselves—as you will see, next, in the BBC's provisions.)

The Basic Building Code's sanitation rules are found in Article
17, entitled "Plumbing, Drainage and Gas Piping." That part of the
BBC's hygiene provisions in Article 17 which deals with water closets
and lavatories is contained in §1701.1.5, and is peculiarly stated:

> Each dwelling unit abutting on a public sewer or with a private sew-
> age disposal system shall have at least one (1) water closet, one (1) lava-
> tory, [and] one (1) tub or shower. . . .

This regulation states that you need those three fixtures only if
you're abutting a public sewer or have a private disposal system. But
suppose you're not close to a public system and don't want a septic
tank—do you still need those fixtures?

Section 1701.1.16 of the BBC seems to resolve the problem in
favor of requiring these fixtures, but upon closer examination there is
still a doubt. Again, the language is peculiarly stated:

> When water closets or other plumbing fixtures are installed in build-
> ings which are not located within a reasonable distance of a sewer, suit-
> able provisions shall be made for disposing of the building sewage by
> some method of sewage treatment and disposal satisfactory to the ad-
> ministrative authority having jurisdiction.

This regulation does not specifically require flush water closets or
toilets (there are chemical and composting toilets that don't need
water and plumbing for proper functioning). It only states that *if* you
have a water closet or other plumbing fixtures, then a connection to a
septic tank or other type of sanitary disposal system is required. In
other words, if you have a composting toilet you won't be required to
have a septic. The BBC has no direct, affirmative, or unambiguous

language—as there is in §R-207 of the Dwelling Code—that says water closets, lavatories, and showers/tubs are mandatory.

I can come up with four possible explanations for the BBC's failure to specifically require water closets: (1) Section 1700.1 makes reference to a plumbing code, and maybe that's where the requirement for water closets, lavatories, and tubs and showers can be found; (2) the drafters of the BBC have left this requirement to "the administrative authority having jurisdiction" (that is, the local health board and health code); (3) the authors of the Building Officials and Code Administrators (BOCA) code feel that these fixtures are mandated by the definitions of "dwelling" and "dwelling unit" I discussed above; or (4) the code authors couldn't conceive of anyone using anything other than a flush toilet!

It's all very maddening because I just *know* you have to have water closets, etc., to comply with the BBC (§1702.1 of this code even requires a separate plumbing permit for a single-family construction), but I can't point to anything specific within the BBC's regulations to prove the point.

CODE-READING TECHNIQUE: As you can see, you have to look in more than one place to find all the regulations governing hygiene and sanitation. You have to review the building regulations *and* the plumbing code (if your local or county government has actually adopted one) *and* the local health ordinance (which probably has been adopted). Whichever of these manuals or ordinances the building inspector shows you to prove that water closets and lavatories are mandatory, you must review that particular regulation very carefully. The rule may be worded in such a way (as are §1701.1.5 and §1701.1.16 of the BBC) that there is no real requirement for a water closet, simply a statement that if you have a flush toilet, you must connect it to a septic-tank system. (If there is no actual requirement, you could, under these circumstances, legally use a composting toilet.)

If—under the BBC—water closets are required, or if they are not but you yourself want to put in the flush toilet in a jursidiction governed by the BBC, you must place that water closet in a room or compartment that is properly lighted and ventilated (§1701.1.6), and those plumbing fixtures (I'm assuming that the phrase "plumbing fixtures" as used in §1701.1.7 refers to water closets and lavatories, but I will take a closer look at that assumption a little later) should be made of smooth and nonabsorbent material.

The language of the NBC is perfectly clear and unambiguous: "Every dwelling unit shall be provided with not less than one bathroom, containing not less than one lavatory, water closet and bathtub or shower. . . ." Section 607.2.c goes on to say that you must have at least one bathroom that you can get to without having to pass through a bedroom.

The NBC also has an interesting section (§607.3) that describes the kind of room in which you should enclose the water closet: (1) the room must be devoted exclusively to toilet facilities, (2) the walls or partitions encircling the room shall be solid and extend from the ceiling to the floor, and (3) the partitions (if any) within a bathroom can't extend from floor to ceiling but must be constructed to permit air circulation.

(I wonder if the regulations in the NBC are so specifically stated because there is no reference in its regular code provisions to a model plumbing code? Actually, Appendix F of the NBC—which *does* list the four model plumbing codes—suggests to the adopting local government that it amend §607.1.a to incorporate a reference to one of the model plumbing manuals.)

The SBC, on the other hand, has absolutely no direct, or even indirect, statement that requires water closets, lavatories, or showers/tubs. Section 2001.3 does provide that toilet rooms shall not open directly into a kitchen and that every toilet room shall have windows and/or mechanical ventilation (as I pointed out in the last chapter), but nothing mandates exactly what must go into those toilet rooms. Section 808 does, however, proclaim: "All plumbing fixtures and plumbing installations shall conform to the Standard Plumbing Code."

Because of §808, a municipality that adopts the Standard Building Code also adopts—by reference—that code group's plumbing regulations, which is where the water-closet requirements can be found. But what would happen if a local government deleted §808 when adopting the SBC? Without an additional local or state health code, there would not be *any* requirement to have water closets, lavatories, tubs/showers—which means in effect that you have the choice to put in the kind of waste system that you want to (and there *are* excellent alternatives to the 5-gallon flush).

The UBC's sanitation requirements are detailed and explicit. Section 1405(b) states specifically (and without any ambiguity) that "every dwelling unit shall be provided . . . with bathroom facilities consisting of a water closet, lavatory and either a bathtub or shower."

Subsection (c) of §1407 of the UBC requires that "a water closet compartment shall be not less than 30 inches in width and shall provide a clear space in front of the water closet not less than 24 inches." Don't let a building inspector try to impose on you the provisions found in §1711, entitled "Water Closet Compartments and Showers";

that section applies only to "other than dwelling units" and not to your single-family shelter.

. . . AND THE KITCHEN SINK

To continue with our paragraph-by-paragraph analysis of §R-207 of the Dwelling Code, here is the next requirement:

> Each dwelling unit shall be provided with a kitchen area and every kitchen area shall be provided with a sink of approved nonabsorbent material.

This regulation is clear and does not leave much doubt as to what is required. Yes, these codes can, at times, speak straight and to the point! What surprises me is that when the four model-code groups worked together to draft the Dwelling Code, they could all agree on unambiguous language for the various rules governing single-family dwellings, but some of them—such as the BBC—could not achieve similar clarity in their own codes!

For instance, the BBC does not have a requirement for a kitchen area or a kitchen sink; this manual's only mandate is that *if* you have a septic tank you must connect the kitchen sink to that underground receptacle. You can find this peculiarly stated provision in §1701.1.5—the very same ambiguous section I discussed in the previous subsection in this chapter. Of course, all plumbing fixtures, which I will assume at this point includes kitchen sinks, must be made of nonabsorbent material (§1701.1.7).

The NBC, in §607.2c, requires kitchen sinks; and the UBC specifically demands "a kitchen equipped with a kitchen sink" (§1405[b]).

The SBC, on the other hand, does not even mention kitchen sinks or kitchen areas! There are just no requirements for this kind of kitchen fixture in this code. (I assume that the SBC relies exclusively on the reference in §808 to the Standard Plumbing Code to handle the requirement of kitchen sinks, together with water closets, lavatories, etc.)

SEWAGE DISPOSAL

Now we know (1) what water closets and lavatories are, (2) what kinds of material showers, tubs, and kitchen sinks are made of, and (3) where and in what kind of room these fixtures are to be located. But there are toilets and privies and composting toilets; there are lavatories and kitchen sinks hooked up to city water and basins that use hand-pumped or cistern-collected water; and there are built-in plastic showers and portable wooden tubs. Do the building codes go further and dictate which of these alternatives you must have in your "code-built home"?

You bet they do! And the building manuals impose these freedom-stifling conditions by regulating the kind of water system that connects into these fixtures and how and where you dispose of what comes out.

The first sentence of the last paragraph of §R-207 of the Dwelling Code introduces us to the subject of how and where you dispose of what went into your fixtures—in other words, introduces us to the subject of sewage disposal:

> All plumbing fixtures shall be connected to a sanitary sewer or to an approved private sewage disposal system.

The implications of this one sentence are enormous for the owner-builder. It is this requirement to tie into a municipally operated sanitary sewer system or into a private septic/leach field disposal system (this seems to be the major type of private sewage-disposal method that's been approved) that prohibits other alternatives, ones that are: (1) less costly (septic systems can add $1,000 to $2,000 more to the cost of your dwelling), (2) less wasteful (the average American household uses 35,000 gallons of water yearly for toilet flushing), and (3) more ecologically sound (recycling human waste into garden compost is a centuries-old sewage-disposal system used in the Orient). And I won't even mention the high construction, chemical, and energy costs of governmentally built and operated sanitary sewer systems!

The mere use of the words "waste" and "dispose" in the building codes predetermines that excretion is something bad that has to be gotten rid of in the great "away" (of America's consumptive economic system's "throw away" fame) and automatically precludes the thought of excretion as organic material that could be recycled into garden compost and used to build the soil back to its pre–chemical-fertilizer health. I will continue to use, reluctantly, the building codes' words because this book should be helping you to understand the code as it is and not as what it might be.

Without getting any deeper into the criticism of this country's sanitary construction provisions at this time, let's dissect the "all plumbing fixtures shall be connected to" requirement to see if there is any way of bypassing its provisions.

PLUMBING FIXTURES. We first have to find out what plumbing fixtures are. I have, up to this point, interchanged the words "water closets" and "lavatories" for the synonym "fixtures" because I wanted to refer to them collectively as a thing rather than a place. Also, I can make such substitutions (artistic license?) because I'm writing a guide, whereas the authors of the building codes are writing regulations that legally dictate how you and I are allowed to build our own houses. So I expect (but don't always get) a higher degree of precision in the use of terms and phrases in the building codes.

The phrase "plumbing fixtures" is not found in §114, the Dwelling Code's definition section. That doesn't end the search for places to look in the Dwelling Code on this subject, however, because that manual of regulations has a whole separate part—consisting of six chapters—devoted to plumbing, which has its own definition section. But when you turn to the plumbing definitions in §P-2020, you won't find that phrase there either.

(Allow me to digress for a moment . . . again. The model-code groups did incorporate their respective plumbing provisions pertinent to single-family-dwelling construction into the Dwelling Code instead of leaving the subject for another volume as they did in their own building codes. Therefore many of the regulations on plumbing found in the Dwelling Code are not found in the model building codes themselves. The plumbing regulations found in the Dwelling Code are a pretty good indication—and can also be used as a checklist for comparison purposes—of what is in those separate plumbing manuals.)

At any rate, let's go back to the dictionary to find out what "plumbing fixtures" are. *Webster's* does not define the two-word phrase itself, but does give a separate definition for plumbing: "the system of pipes and other apparatus for conveying water, liquid, wastes, etc., as in a building." And a separate one for fixture: "a permanently attached part or appendage of a house, etc.: an electric-light fixture." I conclude, therefore, a plumbing fixture is an appendage permanently attached to a system of pipes for conveying water and wastes.

Are water closets and lavatories, then, plumbing fixtures? I've been attempting to avoid equating plumbing fixtures with water closets because, once you do, you *have to connect*—there is no choice—that toilet up to "an approved private sewage disposal system." But I will have to admit I do think a water closet and a lavatory are indeed plumbing fixtures.

The other provisions of the Dwelling Code in which the phrase "plumbing fixtures" is used confirm this. (This listing will also allow you to become familiar with just some of the requirements in the six plumbing chapters of the Dwelling Code.) For instance, §P-2001 states that "plumbing fixtures . . . used to receive or discharge liquid wastes or sewage [and a water closet certainly discharges liquid wastes and sewage!] shall be connected to the drainage system of the building. . . ." Section P-2013 requires that "fixture connections between drainage pipes and water closets shall be made by means of approved flanges." Section P-2109: "Plumbing fixtures shall be constructed of dense, durable, nonabsorbent materials. . . ." I think, however, that §P-2301 clinches the argument: "Plumbing fixtures shall be approved types and shall be provided with an adequate supply of potable running water, arranged so as to flush and keep the fixtures in a clean and sanitary condition without danger of backflow or cross-connection."

Now we know that a water closet is a plumbing fixture which must have an adequate water supply so as to flush and keep the apparatus clean, and that a water closet—as a plumbing fixture—must be connected either to a sanitary sewer or to an approved private disposal system.

APPROVED PRIVATE DISPOSAL SYSTEM. That phrase is the next ambiguity in §R-207. Just what *is* an "approved private sewage disposal system," anyhow? Well, the Dwelling Code doesn't leave the matter unexplained or ambiguous. Private sewage disposal system is defined in §P-2020 as

> a septic tank with the effluent discharging into a subsurface disposal field, into one or more seepage pits, or into a combination of subsurface disposal fields and seepage pits; or of such other facilities as may be permitted by the authority having jurisdiction.

And the word "approved" doesn't prove to be any loophole either, because the general definition section, §R-114, gives the meaning of that word:

> Approved refers to approval by the Building Official as the result of investigation and tests conducted by him, or by reason of accepted principles or tests by nationally recognized organizations.

(See Chapter Nine, page 147, for a full discussion of all the implications of this building-inspector-approved concept.)

The "accepted principles" for private septic systems that the building inspector is guided by in his determination of whether your system is approved can be found in Chapter 25 of the Dwelling Code.

Chapter 25 is entitled "Sewers and Private Individual Sewage Disposal Systems" and contains ten lengthy sections and four tables. These provisions and the definition of private sewage-disposal system all boil down to the fact that a septic tank and leach field system is *the* major private disposal method approved by the building-code groups. There is nothing in the definition of private sewage-disposal system or in the language of Chapter 25 of the Dwelling Code that would allow you to bypass its provisions and install a composting toilet as an approved disposal system.

Except for the BBC's brief and ambiguous mention in §1701.1, the other model-code groups don't even use the words "private sewage disposal system" in their building codes. But because septics are *the* private waste-removal method favored by the building-code groups in their plumbing regulations (and in their Dwelling Code, as we've just seen), and also favored by state and local health ordinances (in areas that don't have building codes, the health regulations will force you to dispose of your waste in a septic tank), it's important, even though the list is lengthy, that I set forth most of the provisions of Chapter 25 of the Dwelling Code so you can learn how to construct a septic-tank system to plumbing and/or health code standards. You can use the following paraphrased code sections as a checklist either for the construction of your septic system or for the review of your own dwelling, plumbing, or health code. My comments appear in brackets:

1. You can't connect drain spouts or other surface water connections into a sewage-disposal system (§P-2501).
2. You can't get a permit to construct a septic tank if a public sewer is available and, on top of that, you can't connect an already existing septic into a public sewer (§P-2501).
3. Building sewers [that part of the drainage system which comes from the building and connects to the septic tank] shall have a uniform slope of not less than .25 inch per foot and shall be laid on a firm bed of approved materials [generally some kind of gravel] (§P-2502).
4. A cleanout [some means of access to the drainpipe—like a mini-manhole—so that you can clear clogged drains] shall be located at the junction of the building sewer and building drain, at all turns in the building sewer, and at maximum intervals of 100 feet in straight runs of that line (§P-2502).
5. The size of the building sewer is determined by the number of bathrooms, dishwashers, showers, tubs, etc., that you have in the house; generally a pipe 3 to 4 inches in diameter will be required (§P-2502 and Table 22-B).
6. The type of private sewage-disposal system shall be determined on the basis of location, soil porosity, and groundwater level (§P-2503). [There is no indication in the Dwelling Code of what is

meant by the phrase "type of private sewage disposal system" as used in this section. I think the words might refer to the fact that not all soil conditions are conducive to the soil-absorption system which a septic tank and leach field method represents; yet all private disposal systems must be a septic by the code's definition (§P-2020). So I guess the "type" of system means the choice you have of a drainage field, seepage pits, or a combination thereof.

[How a septic system works will help explain why the soil condition surrounding the leach field is so important to the process. (The following is a bastardized version of the definition of septic tank as it appears in the Dwelling Code.) The septic tank, a watertight receptacle, receives the discharge from water closets, lavatories, showers, tubs, and kitchen sinks and is designed (with two or more interior compartments) to separate solids from liquids, to digest (break down and render almost harmless) organic matter such as urine and excrement through a period of detention, and to allow the liquids and small particles of broken-down organic matter to discharge into the soil (which filters out any remaining impurities) outside the tank through a system of open joints, perforated piping, or disposal pits. If the discharge from the septic tank can't filter through the soil—that is, if it just lays there or flows directly into an underground stream— the remaining impurities won't be expunged and other people could come into contact with the unhealthy water.

[There are not many other types of private sewage-disposal systems designed to treat water-carried sewage that are not expensive. In fact, some areas—say, swampy or periodically flooded land—just about preclude the use of a private, relatively "inexpensive" septic tank sewage-disposal system. (These properties could be used, however, if composting toilets were allowed!) So to reiterate a point I made way back in Chapter One, make sure that the soil on the property you propose to buy passes the local percolation test (which I'll show you how to conduct in a minute) *before you buy the land.* If the property can't pass that perc test or the land is swampy and/or periodically flooded, you may have bought a piece of property that you can't use for the construction of your home . . . and that, of course, is the reason you bought your acreage in the first place!]

7. You can't excavate into a water table or to a depth where sewage may contaminate an underground water stratum usable for domestic purposes (§P-2503). [Even if you live miles away from others, if the underground water you might adulterate could eventually be used by others, you can't excavate for a septic tank/leach field.]

8. If "the ground water level extends to less than 12 feet of the ground surface" or where the upper soil is porous and the underlying

stratum is rock or impervious soil, you then have to install a septic tank/disposal field system (§P-2503). [I guess this means that if the surface ground percs properly but the water table is higher (less than 12 feet) you must use a septic system with a leach field instead of seepage pits.]

9. The Dwelling Code sets forth the absorption capacities of five typical soils and the required square footage of leaching field per 100 gallons of septic tank capacity, in Table 25-D, reproduced here:

Table No. 25-D
RATED ABSORPTION CAPACITIES OF FIVE TYPICAL SOILS

TYPE OF SOIL	REQUIRED SQ. FT. OF LEACHING AREA/100 GALS. OF SEPTIC TANK CAPACITY	MAX. ABSORPTION CAPACITY GALS./SQ. FT. OF LEACHING AREA
(1) Coarse sand or gravel	20	5
(2) Fine sand	25	4
(3) Sandy loam or sandy clay	40	2.5
(4) Clay with considerable sand or gravel	60	1.66
(5) Clay with small amount of sand or gravel	90	1.11

[As you can see, as the absorption quality of the soil decreases, the number of square feet of required leach field increases . . . so you need a lot of room for a drain field when the soil has poor absorption qualities.] "In order to determine the absorption qualities of questionable soils not listed [in the above table] the proposed site shall be subjected to percolation tests acceptable to the Building Official" (§P-2503). [This last section really means that if you can prove you do have one of those five soils listed in Table 25-D, you don't need a percolation test.]

10. You've got to design and place your private disposal system in a location that permits the addition of at least a 50 percent increase in seepage pits or subsurface drain fields if later needed [because more bedrooms might be added to the original structure] (§P-2503).

11. And speaking of septic tank location, certain distance factors from buildings, streams, and water-supply wells determine where your private sewage-disposal system may be placed on your property. Table 25-A states:

Table No. 25-A
LOCATION OF SEWAGE DISPOSAL SYSTEM

MINIMUM HORIZONTAL DISTANCE IN CLEAR REQUIRED FROM:	BUILDING SEWER	SEPTIC TANK	DISPOSAL FIELD	SEEPAGE PIT OR CESSPOOL
Buildings or structures	2 feet	5 feet	8 feet	8 feet
Property line adjoining private property	Clear	5 feet	5 feet	8 feet
Water supply wells	50 feet	50 feet	50 feet	100 feet
Streams	50 feet	50 feet	50 feet	100 feet
Large trees		10 feet		10 feet
Seepage pits or cesspools		5 feet	5 feet	12 feet
Disposal field		5 feet	4 feet	5 feet
Domestic water line	1 foot	5 feet	5 feet	5 feet
Distribution box			5 feet	5 feet

[The most important factor here is to stay as far away as possible—and downhill—from water-supply wells; 50 to 100 feet is the minimum.]

12. The minimum size of a septic tank is also regulated, and is directly related to the number of bedrooms proposed for the single-family dwelling. One or two bedrooms requires a 750-gallon-capacity tank, three sleeping quarters demands a 1,000-gallon tank, and four bedrooms mandates a 1,200-gallon tank (§P-2505 and Table No. 25-B). [There must be some kind of assumed ratio between the number of people who use the toilet facilities and the number of bedrooms one has in the house. Since it's possible for a family of six to live in three bedrooms rather than five, the assumed ratio doesn't always make much sense. So instead of regulating the number of people who can live in a house (which would be a rather severe intrusion on the right of private property), the building-code groups get around their dilemma by regulating the size of the septic tank according to the number of bedrooms—together with the already-discussed provision in §P-2503 which requires that the square footage of the original leach field be designed so that it can be increased by 50 percent.]

13. The construction and design of a septic tank is covered in nine long paragraphs of §P-2506. Here's a shortened version (lengthened by my comments):

a. Septic tanks shall be constructed of durable and corrosion-resistive materials [to resist the corrosive effects of the soil surrounding the tank and of the liquid and wastes in the tank itself] and

shall be structurally designed to withstand the surrounding earth
loads.

b. The septic tank shall be installed level on a solid bed.

c. These tanks shall be watertight and designed to produce
clarified effluent, and this is done by requiring not less than two interior compartments. The inlet compartment [which provides the necessary space for sludge and scum accumulations] shall be not less than
two-thirds of the total tank capacity (not less than 500 liquid gallons)
and shall not be less than 3 feet in width and 5 feet in length, with a
liquid depth of not less than 2½, or more than 6, feet.

[It's in the first compartment that most of the organic wastes are
broken down. When they are sufficiently liquefied or particalized,
they're spilled through a compartment partition wall by a baffled pipe
into the second compartment, which has a capacity of not less than
250 gallons, or more than one-third of the total tank capacity. The
water then goes into an outlet pipe (the invert of which shall not be
less than 2 inches below the invert of the inlet pipe) and is filtered
out into the soil through perforated pipes installed in the leach field.
Here's a diagram—which is *not* included in the Dwelling Code—that
illustrates what I'm talking about]:

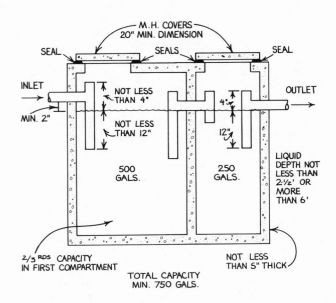

d. Partitions or baffles between compartments shall be
made of durable material and shall extend not less than 4 inches

above the liquid level. [And the pipe between the two compartments must be placed at the same height as the outlet pipe.]

e. The walls, floors, and covers of unreinforced and precast or poured-in-place concrete septic tanks shall have compressive strengths of not less than 2,500 pounds per square inch and a thickness of not less than 5 inches. [It's cheaper to buy and install the precast concrete septic tanks than to pour your own.]

f. Two access manholes or cover slabs shall be provided, one over each of the two required compartments.

g. The upper part of concrete septic tanks shall be protected from corrosion by coating the inside with an approved bituminous coating which shall extend 4 inches below the waterline.

14. The clarified effluent leaves the septic tank through distribution or drain lines to the leach field. These lines shall be constructed of open-joint or perforated tile, or approved perforated plastic pipe, or bituminous fiber pipe having adequate openings for distribution of the effluent in the trench areas. The pipes shall be laid on crushed stone, gravel, slag, or similar filter materials (with voids varying from ¾ inch to 2½ inches) and the crushed stone shall have a depth of 12 inches below and a height of 2 inches above the drains. The upper half of the open joints shall be covered with roofing felt [to prevent dirt from entering the pipes and accumulating, thereby reducing their effectiveness] and the filter material shall be covered with porous material prior to backfill (§P-2508).

15. The drain line trenches themselves "shall be not more than 100 feet in length and have a width of not more than 36 inches or less than 18 inches. The trenches shall be spaced at not less than 6 feet on center and have sufficient depth to provide 12 inches of earth cover over the lines. The clear distance between trenches shall not be less than 4 feet plus 2 feet for each additional foot of depth in excess of one foot below the bottom of the drain line. The slope of the line shall not be more than 6 inches per 100 feet or less than 3 inches per 100 feet" (§P-2508). [You can use seepage pits as an alternative to leach fields; see §P-2509 if you're interested.]

Whew! As you can see, the list of septic tank requirements is long, and not exactly easy for the average individual to decipher. But nevertheless you, as an owner-builder, have no choice but to face the fact that these septic requirements are the law. And until that law is changed—until composting toilets and other less expensive, more ecologically sound alternative methods of sewage recycling are allowed—you must conform, if you don't want your lovingly built shelter to be red-tagged for demolition!

None of the other model codes have any of these fifteen requirements in their respective *building* manuals; these kinds of regulations, as I said previously, have been relegated to their "sister" *plumbing* codes. But the above in-depth review of private sewage-disposal systems as found in the Dwelling Code will give you a very good head start on any health or plumbing code you might confront. In any case, there is one important item that you must always remember when installing plumbing or septic systems in a code-dominated jurisdiction: *You must have all of the work tested, inspected, and approved by the appropriate official before the pipes and/or drain field are covered up and concealed by walls or back-filled dirt.* If you are guilty of a water pipe cover-up (sounds almost political, doesn't it?) before the necessary inspections, be prepared to tear down or dig out those pipes to make them accessible to your building inspector or health officer.

PERCOLATION TEST. As I mentioned earlier, a percolation test is the process used to determine whether or not your soil's absorption qualities are sufficient to meet both practical and legal requirements. It's an important factor to consider when buying land, and can mean the whole ball game when it comes to meeting sanitation codes.

Here's how to conduct a perc test yourself:

First, dig three 12-inch-square holes in the area in which you intend to locate your drain field. Make the holes as deep as the proposed disposal trenches, and take care to keep the holes' sides as perfectly vertical as possible.

Now before you go any further, I should warn you that your building inspector or health official might demand to be present when you conduct your test, and he or she might ask you to thoroughly saturate the soil surrounding and in the holes with water before proceeding with the actual test. Presumably this soaking process creates the kind of conditions that would exist in a leach field in actual operation; but it also, of course, will decrease the absorption-rate results of your test. So if the soil where you want to construct your drain field has questionable absorption qualities, don't wet the earth down more than you have to. (The time of year could also affect the perc reading you'll get from your soil. If you doubt your soil's ability to perc properly, try to conduct an official test during a dry time of year to get the maximum absorption-rate results.)

Anyway, once the test holes are dug (and soaked, if necessary), fill each one with 6 inches of water and clock the time it takes in minutes for all the water to seep away completely from each hole.

Next, calculate how long it took for 1 inch of water to seep away from each excavation. In other words, divide the number of minutes it took for all the water to vanish in each test hole by 6 (the number of inches of water). Then find the average (inches-per-so-many-minutes) rate for all three cavities (add the number of minutes it took all three holes to absorb an inch of water and divide by 3).

If your soil takes more than sixty minutes on the average to perc 1 inch of water, the conditions are not good for a septic tank/absorption-field system (at least not a cheap one). And if that's the case, I would discuss the situation very carefully with the building inspector or health officer (whoever has jurisdiction over sanitation in your area) before I bought the property.

Remember, however, that the over-sixty-minute standard is not absolutely fixed. If you have a lot of low-absorption land and can afford to put in a large leach field, your sanitation officer might allow you to put in such a system. If, unfortunately, your lot is small and you don't have room to spread out the drainage field, you might not be allowed to build!

As you can see, this is another of those "relative" areas—there is no single black-and-white answer to the soil percolation problem.

To make matters worse, not all building or health codes use the same formula to determine how many square feet a drain field should be. The minimum size of the leach area is, however, generally based on some kind of relationship between the percolation rate of the soil and (1) the number of bedrooms in the proposed structure or (2) the capacity of the septic tank (which, as we've seen, is directly based upon the number of bedrooms, anyhow).

The Dwelling Code in Table 25-D (reproduced on page 73) determines the required square footage of the leaching field on the basis of each 100 gallons of septic tank capacity for each of the five different soils enumerated there. (For questionable soils—meaning those not listed in the table—§P-2503 requires a percolation test acceptable to the building official.)

The National Plumbing Code, on the other hand, determines the required size of the absorption area on the basis of the perc rate per 1 inch of water for each bedroom. If it takes thirty minutes for 1 inch of water to be absorbed in your soil, for instance, then you must provide 180 square feet of drainage area per bedroom—the area to be measured at the bottom of your disposal trenches.

Now that you know what septic tanks are, how the tank's capacity is determined, how to conduct a perc test, and the formulas some codes use to determine the size of your drainage field, you should understand why I implore you to read your building, plumbing, or health code *very carefully* on the subject of sewage disposal. The object: To find out whether or not you can even consider using any given piece of property for the construction of your own house. It's that simple . . . and that important!

Incidentally, I have one further suggestion for those of you who dearly (and rightly) want to use some kind of ecologically sound waste-disposal system, but who live in areas where conventional systems are required by code. There *is* an alternative (unsavory though it may be): Go ahead and install the conventional system—to comply with your code—and then put in and use that planet-saving composting toilet you wanted in the first place. It's a good alternative if you can afford it—which, to my mind, makes it a poor alternative overall, philosophically. Why can't the codes accommodate everyone's needs, regardless of their financial status?

WATER SUPPLY

Finally, we've come to the last sentence of §R-207—the Dwelling Code's sanitation provision that originally provoked this long chapter. (I'll review these water-supply regulations from the same point of view I used in the previous subsections of this chapter; I'll point out alternatives while I indicate what the rules require, as written.)

> All plumbing fixtures shall be connected to an approved system of water supply and provided with hot and cold running water, except water closets may be provided with cold water only.

As you can see from this sentence, your water system must include some kind of water-heating device to comply with the requirement that you have cold and *hot* running water at the tap. This requirement doesn't say where that water must come from before it reaches the heater, so it still might be possible to have hand-pumped or cistern-collected water as long as you send some of the H_2O from those sources through a water-heating fixture.

We already know what the terms "plumbing fixtures" and "water closets" mean, and all the other words and phrases of the last sentence of §R-207 are familiar enough. Except, maybe, the phrase "an approved system of water supply." We've previously discussed that "approved" means what the building inspector approves (§R-114), and after a look through the plumbing definitions in §P-2020 we find that a water-supply system

> consists of the building supply pipe [the pipe from the water source to your structure], the water distributing pipes and the necessary connecting pipes, fittings, control valves and appurtenances carrying or supplying potable water [satisfactory for drinking and domestic purposes and meeting the requirements of the health authority having jurisdiction] in or adjacent to building or premises.

There's nothing formidable about that definition (and the others I included in brackets). The requirements these meanings imply and demand don't seem to preclude the use of alternative water-supply sources. We all need healthy drinking water, so requiring potable water is not unreasonable. Obviously, when you're looking at land to buy you should always make sure the property in question has a good water supply—in terms of quality, quantity, and year-round availability.

The "accepted principles" for a water-supply system, that is, the principles your building inspector will follow to determine whether your water system is approvable, can be found in Chapter 24, "Water Supply and Distribution," of the Dwelling Code. The major part of that chapter is §P-2401, where, as you read, you can see all chances of alternatives disappearing. I've italicized the words and phrases in §P-2401 that effectively reduce the number of possible water-supply systems you can use:

> Plumbing fixtures shall be provided with an adequate supply of potable running water, piped thereto *under suitable pressure* and arranged so as to *flush* and keep fixtures in a clean and sanitary condition without danger of backflow or cross-connection.

"Suitable water pressure"—which is defined in §P-2405 as "initial pressure of not less than 30 pounds per square inch and a residual pressure of not less than 15 pounds per square inch after allowing for friction and other pressure losses"—effectively eliminates the choice of hand-pumped or cistern-fed water supplies. Even a gravity-fed water supply from a small spring source 40 or 50 feet above your homestead may not generate enough "head" to meet that "suitable pressure" requirement.

So we must install the energy-intensive water pumps—and our lives are once again dependent on others because we have to purchase our code-conforming equipment and the electricity to run it. Are hand-pumped or cistern- or gravity-fed water supplies—and the life-styles that go with them—so bad that they should be outlawed by the building codes? I think not . . . I think we should have a choice.

And do you see, also, how one questionable regulation can snowball, and lead to more and more questionable regulations? Because we are required to have water closets (a poor regulation because there are no allowed alternatives) we must therefore have a septic tank disposal system, which requires a water-supply system with sufficient pressure to flush human deposits out of the bowl and into the septic system.

If composting toilets were allowed, as they are in the great state of Maine, some owner-builders (not all—the choice is yours) wouldn't have to bear the expense of a septic tank and leach field, or of producing 30/15 pounds of water pressure, and could build on, and productively use, property that has marginal or no absorption capabilities. And you could accomplish all this without taxing the country's natural and energy resources or posing any kind of threat to the public health.

But enough sermonizing—let's get back to the reality of the codes the way they are! Here's a quick overview of some of the Dwelling Code's water-supply provisions that you might confront in your local building, health, or plumbing codes (again my comments are bracketed):

1. "A connection shall not be made to a domestic water supply, or arrangement exist, in a manner which could pollute the water supply or provide a cross-connection between the supply and a source of contamination unless there is provided an approved backflow prevention device" (§P-2402). [You should not only be concerned with cross-connection contamination, as this section correctly points out, but also with keeping the source of supply itself free from contamination by any possible pollutant on your property. You should give consideration to hydrological, geological, and bacteriological factors in placing your water source; ask your knowledgeable neighbors about local conditions.]

2. Codes require a *minimum* of 30/15 pounds of water pressure per square inch and dictate means for handling *too much* pressure. If you have over 100 psi, you must install an approved-type pressure regulator preceded by an adequate strainer to reduce the pressure to less than 100 psi (§P-2406), and a pressure relief valve (§P-2407).

3. Water heaters [which you must have to comply with the hot-running-water provision of §R-207] shall conform to nationally recognized standards and shall bear the label of an approved inspection agency (§P-2408). The Dwelling Code proceeds from there to refer the owner-builder to related water heater provisions, such as Chapter 11 ("General Mechanical Equipment"), and Chapter 19 ("Fuel Supply Systems"). Furthermore, it dictates standards for (1) heater controls (§P-2409), (2) combustion air (§P-2410 and Chapter 12, entitled "Combustion Air"), and (3) vents (§P-2411 and Chapter 15, entitled "Venting of Appliances"). [See how complicated the requirements for hot water at your tap get?]

4. There are two tables in this chapter. Table 24-A sets forth the number of fixture units ("related quantity in terms of which load producing effects on various parts of the plumbing system") for each kind of plumbing fixture [water closets and hose bibs take three fixture

units each—more than any other]. Table 24-B gives the minimum size [from ¾ inch to 1½ inches] of service and supply piping. [Pipe size depends on (1) the water pressure range, (2) the total-feet length of the pipes in the house, (3) the maximum fixture unit loadings for the structure, (4) the difference in elevation between the meter or other water source and the highest fixture or outlet, and (5) the pressure in the street main or other source of supply. You should be aware of all these factors when attempting to determine the size of the pipes for any code—or noncode, for that matter—water system.]

The other model building codes—surprisingly, in light of the absence of any discussion concerning sewage disposal—have a bit more to say about water in their building codes.

The BBC requires potable water in sufficient volume and pressure for flushing, running hot and cold at the taps, conveyed in pipes of sufficient size, with no danger of backflow or back-siphonage (§1701.1.1, .2, .3, .4, and §1705.1).

The NBC demands hot and cold running water, and a water supply in conformance with adopted plumbing regulations (§607.2.a and §607.2.h).

The SBC and UBC are completely silent on the subject of water.

To close this rather lengthy chapter, let me run through a few more of the plumbing provisions found in the Dwelling Code, so that you will be aware of the kinds of areas to which health and plumbing codes address themselves.

Chapter 20 of the Dwelling Code contains "General Plumbing Requirements and Definitions."

Chapter 21's major concern is with "Plumbing Materials" and tells owner-builders the kinds of code-permitted materials you can use for your pipes and fixtures. "Plumbing, Drainage and Venting Systems" is the self-explanatory subject of Chapter 22, and Chapter 23's main concern is "Plumbing Fixtures, Traps and Receptors." (We've already gone into considerable detail on Chapter 24, "Water Supply and Distribution," and Chapter 25, "Sewers and Private or Individual Sewage Disposal Systems.")

So there. That's the end of our discussion on one of the most important "nonconstruction" construction requirements you'll ever find in any building code. Study it carefully!

7. Construction Materials and Methods: Standards

The Dwelling Code's regulations that deal with the actual construction of your home are found in Part III of that code, which part is appropriately entitled "Construction."

There are seven chapters (numbers 3 through 9) in Part III and they are usefully arranged in logical construction sequence. That is, Part III starts with a chapter on "Foundations," and then proceeds to "build" from there with chapters on "Wall Construction," "Wall Covering," "Floors," and "Roof-Ceiling Construction," all the way to "Roof Coverings" and "Chimneys and Fireplaces." The information, charts, and diagrams found in these seven chapters, combined with the almost sixty pages of useful tables in Appendix B, give you a wealth of information and puts it all at your fingertips.

But before we can understand those seven construction chapters in the Dwelling Code, however, we have to thoroughly understand a concept that runs through each and every one of those chapters. That concept is called "standards."

What are these things called standards? How do standards become adopted? How do the model-code groups use them? And, most importantly, what effect do they have on owner-builders? Let's find out.

As you thumb through Part III of the Dwelling Code, you may notice that the wording of the first section in each chapter is almost identical. For instance, here's how §R-401 (from the chapter "Wall Construction") reads:

> Conformity with the applicable grading material, test, construction and design standards specified in *Sections S-26.302 and S-26.401* shall be evidence that *walls and partitions* constructed in accordance with the provisions of this Chapter are reasonably safe to persons and property.

Only the italicized (by me) words and section references change in each section; everything else stays the same. For instance, §R-501 has the same language except that "wall coverings" is substituted for the phrase "walls and partitions" and there is a different reference to §S-26—and so on for §R-601, §R-701, §R-801, and §R-901.

The "material, test, construction and design standards" that are mentioned in each of the introductory sections to these six chapters (§R-301 has slightly different wording) are collected in Chapter 26 of the Dwelling Code. Hence the prefix S, meaning standard, and the number 26, indicating the chapter, both of which are used whenever a reference is made to a standard.

These references and the standards themselves are at the heart of every building code—the nuts and bolts of construction regulation. But they are often controversial, too—not merely to the owner-builder who wants to use unusual or recycled materials, but also to the housing and/or new product manufacturer who develops a new building material or design technique but can't get it approved as a standard.

I'll continue, however, to review these regulations strictly from the point of view of the owner-builder. The shelter manufacturers have enough money and organized power to do their own lobbying!

Okay. Let's turn to the introductory general section, §S-26.000, of Chapter 26:

> Compliance with the applicable standards or publications listed in this Chapter or those approved by the Building Official shall be evidence of compliance with the section of this Code referring to the appropriate section of this Chapter. The digits following the decimal in the section numbers of this Chapter refer to that part of this Code where the standards are applicable.

This is an important section, because it shows that:

1. The building inspector has the power to approve standards. [This is another—quite significant—power given to the building inspector. It is interesting that all four model-code groups agreed to give the building inspector this kind of power in the Dwelling Code, because he or she doesn't have similar authority (at least not stated in those words) in the BBC, NBC, SBC, or UBC!]

2. The last three digits of the section numbers in this chapter (26) refer back to whatever other parts of the code apply to the particular standard in question. For instance, §S-26.208 has to do with shower compartment finishes and refers back to §R-208, the code regulation on toilet, bath, and shower compartments. And §S-26.401 deals with walls and refers back to §R-401, the first section in the Dwelling Code's chapter on "Wall Construction." So, as you can see, you can look up the details of any given standard in either one of two

ways. First, you can read the code text itself to see if any reference is made to a standard, or, second, you can look up a standard and then find the applicable text from the last three digits of that standard's section number.

3. And the most important of all because of the difficulty created, there are really no standards at all in the Dwelling Code but just a *list of titles* of publications in which the standards may be found. The code doesn't provide substantive text on particular standards. You have to refer to other publications to find out what a specific standard requires.

STANDARD-SETTING ORGANIZATIONS

Furthermore, §S-26.001 gives us a greater insight into standards by listing the groups that issue them:

> The abbreviations preceding these standards shall have the following meaning and are the organizations issuing the standards and publications listed.

> AA—Aluminum Association
> 750 Third Ave., New York, N.Y. 10017
> ACI—American Concrete Institute
> P.O. Box 19150, Detroit, Mich. 48219
> AISC—American Institute of Steel Construction
> 1221 Ave. of Americas, Suite 1580, New York, N.Y. 10020
> AISI—American Iron and Steel Institute
> 1200 16th St. N.W., Washington, D.C. 20036
> AITC—American Institute of Timber Construction
> 333 W. Hampden Ave., Englewood, Colorado 80110
> ANSI—American National Standards Institute
> 1430 Broadway, New York, N.Y. 10018
> APA—American Plywood Association
> 1119 "A" St., Tacoma, Wash. 98401
> ASTM—American Society for Testing and Materials
> 1916 Race St., Philadelphia, Pa. 19103
> AWPB—American Wood Preservers Bureau
> P.O. Box 5824, Spartanburg, S.C. 29301
> AWPI—American Wood Preservers Institute
> 1651 Old Meadow Rd., McLean, Va. 22101
> AWS—American Welding Society
> 2501 N.W. 7th St., Miami, Fla. 33125
> CISPI—Cast Iron Soil Pipe Institute
> 2029 K St. N.W., Washington, D.C. 20006

And that's only a partial list! Section S-26.001 reveals that (1) the building-code groups themselves don't produce these standards and that (2) the organizations which do establish standards seem—by their very names, such as the Aluminum Association, or American Concrete Institute, or the American Institute of Timber Construction—to be special-interest groups that have a rather large stake in making sure the standards favor their respective products.

But don't get the wrong impression! These groups are not in all cases the final arbiters in the certification of standards used in the building codes. There are three independent (meaning not affiliated with any particular construction product producer) testing agencies that are responsible for doing the final checking, reporting, and certification of a particular standard. These agencies are the American Society for Testing and Materials (ASTM), the National Fire Prevention Association (NFPA), and the American National Standards Institute, Inc. (ANSI). (In addition, the federal government, through the Departments of Agriculture or Commerce, sometimes also gets into the act of producing standards.)

These three (or four) groups are nonbiased, objective, and really do properly evaluate, test, and report on their findings. But they also receive suggested standards from special-interest groups, and in many cases these "suggested standards" turn out to be—as we shall see—specifications on how to make, or how to use, a particular product (such as Sand-Lime Building Brick) or a class of products (such as grading rules for Western lumber).

In addition, there is a certain unwillingness among materials producers to establish standards that open the market to newcomers. Field and Rivkin point this out quite effectively in their book *The Building Code Burden*. They report that there is a great deal of infighting among special-interest groups to secure a favorable code standard from testing agencies—mainly because it is possible for a technical construction standard to favor one product while actually cutting another out of the market.

These authors go into considerable detail on the subject. For example, on page 37 of their book they cite the controversy created when plastic pipe was considered for plumbing purposes: "In the case of plastic pipe, substantial financial and political resources were brought to bear on the question of code acceptability, because the introduction of plastic pipe meant new pipe producers and potential changes in work hour requirements for organized labor." To say nothing of the fact (and this is me speaking) that laymen, owner-builders, and other novices could do their own plumbing with plastic pipe without all the equipment and expertise that licensed plumbers need—and at a substantial cost savings for the pipe!

If I were to go into all the subtle, and not so subtle, implications of the politics of this subject of standard-setting, I would be writing an exposé instead of telling you—the owner-builder—how to handle what presently exists in the codes. So rather than dwelling on these power struggles any longer, let's get back to the business at hand. Let's look farther into Chapter 26 of the Dwelling Code to see what the owner-builder can do to make the most of his or her situation.

SOME SPECIFIC STANDARDS

We saw back in the beginning of the last chapter that §R-208 contains the following paragraph:

> Shower compartment floors and walls shall be finished with a smooth, hard and nonabsorbent surface in accordance with Section S-26.208. . . ."

When you turn to §S-26.208, here are the standards you find listed:

Glazed Ceramic Wall Tile installed with Portland Cement Mortar—ANSI A108.1-1967
Ceramic Tile installed with Chemical Resistant, Water Cleanable Tile-Setting and Grouting Epoxy—ANSI A108.6-1969
Dry-Set Portland Cement Mortar (for installation of ceramic tile)—ANSI A118.1-1967
Chemical Resistant, Water Cleanable Tile-Setting and Grouting Epoxy—ANSI A118.3-1969
Organic Adhesives for installation of Ceramic Tile—ANSI A136.1-1967 (Type I only in Shower Compartments) Standard Specification for Ceramic Tile—ANSI A137.1-1967
Ceramic Tile installed with Dry-Set Portland Cement Mortar—ANSI A108.5-1967
Ceramic Mosaic Tile installed with Portland Cement Mortar—ANSI A108.2-1967
Ceramic Mosaic Tile installed with Water Resistant Organic Adhesives—ANSI A108.4-1968

Do these titles indicate to you that what you'll find in the text of the standard would be the performance criteria of a smooth, hard, nonabsorbent surface, or will you only find specifications on how to install ceramic tile with Portland cement, epoxy, or organic compounds? I'm afraid that all you'll get are instructions on how to affix ceramic tile to the wall with different adhesives. These titles in §S-26.208 also indicate that the only kind of approved smooth, hard, nonabsorbent material you are allowed to use in shower compartments is ceramic tile—when in fact the new fiberglass tubs and showers are in wide use. So having the titles of standards collected in a chapter in the Dwelling Code doesn't help answer any questions for the owner-builder.

Now that we know the information in Chapter 26—being merely a list of titles—is ambiguous at best and confusing and contradictory at worst, let's see if the language in an actual standard is any help.

I've chosen to quote from one of the standards listed in §S-26.401. This section refers you to more than thirty-five different titles for wall construction standards. (I've already reproduced §R-401, the text of the regulation that refers to this standard section, a while back, so you might want to look it up.) The one particular standard I will quote from is entitled "Classification, Definition and Method of Grading for All Species of Lumber. Standard D 245-70 of the ASTM." If you think the title suggests that a lot of information is covered in the standard, you're quite right, and that's only *one* standard!

In fact, I'll never forget when I first learned how intimidatingly complex and comprehensive these standards and the publications they're in can be. I was just beginning to research this book, and went to the local county library to see if they had any books on building codes. Nancy, the librarian who helped me, pointed to one very large, very heavy, very thick volume crammed with thousands of pages and said: "I'm not sure this is what you want, but no one here knows too much about this book or what it is exactly for. . . . I hope you do!" The tome, as it turned out, was the standards of the American Society for Testing and Materials—the ASTM!

I found D 245-70 on page 957 of the ASTM. This particular standard is eleven pages long, divided into seven sections, a number of subsections, and includes the ever-present tables (thirteen in all). I found it a little more difficult to read and comprehend than building-code lingo, because engineering jargon abounds in great quantity.

I won't quote from the full eleven pages of the standard, but I do want to give you a flavor of what to expect if you ever have to consult a standard at any time. Here are the titles to a few of the sections and subsections of D 245-70 (to show you the scope of the subject matter covered), and the full text of the Foreword (so that you can see what the objective of this standard is and in addition get some insight in terms of what to look for if you use recycled or handmade lumber):

Scope	§1
Foreword	§2
Need for Lumber Grading	§2.1
How Visual Grading is Accomplished	§2.2
Use Classification of Structural Lumber	§2.3
Joists and Planks	§2.3.1.1
Beams and Stringers	§2.3.1.2

2. Foreword

2.1 *Need for Lumber Grading:*

2.1.1 Individual pieces of lumber, as they come from the saw, represent a wide range in quality and appearance with respect to freedom from knots, cross grain, shakes, and other characteristics. Such random pieces likewise represent a wide range in strength, utility, serviceability, and value. One of the obvious requirements for the orderly marketing of lumber is the establishment of grades that permit the procurement of any required quality of lumber in any desired quantity. Maximum economy of material is obtained when the range of quality-determining characteristics in a grade is limited and all pieces are utilized to their full potential. Many of the grades are established on the basis of appearance and physical characteristics of the piece, but without regard for mechanical properties. Other grades called structural or stress grades are established on the basis of features that relate to mechanical properties. The latter designate near-minimum strength and near-average stiffness properties on which to base structural design.

2.1.2 The development of these methods is based on extensive research covering tests of small clear specimens and of full-sized structural members. Detailed studies have included the strength and variability of clear wood, and the effect on strength from various factors such as density, knots, and other defects, seasoning, duration of stress, and temperature.

2.2 *How Visual Grading Is Accomplished*—Visual grading is accomplished from an examination of all four faces and the ends of the piece, in which the location as well as the size and nature of the knots and other features appearing on the surfaces are evaluated over the entire length. Basic principles of structural grading have been established that permit the evaluation of any timber in terms of a strength ratio. The strength ratio of a structural timber is the hypothetical ratio of its strength to that which it would have if no weakening characteristics were present. Thus a timber with a strength ratio of 75 percent would be expected to have 75 percent of the strength of the clear piece. In effect, the strength ratio system of visual structural grading is thus designed to permit practically unlimited choice in establishing grades of any desired quality to best meet production and utilization requirements.

2.3   *Use Classification of Structural Lumber:*

2.3.1   The various factors affecting strength, such as knots, deviations of grain, shakes, and checks, differ in their effect, depending on the kind of loading and stress to which the piece is subjected. Structural lumber is therefore often classified according to its size and use. Four classes are widely used, as follows:

2.3.1.1   *Joists and Planks*—Pieces of rectangular cross section, 2 to 4 in. in least dimension, graded primarily for strength in bending edgewise or flatwise but also frequently used where tensile or compressive strength is important. Lumber 2 in. (nominal) thick is often placed in grades separate from thicker joists and planks.

2.3.1.2   *Beams and Stringers*—Pieces of rectangular cross section, 5 by 8 in. (nominal dimensions) and larger, graded for strength in bending when loaded on the narrow face.

2.3.1.3   *Posts and Timbers*—Pieces of square or nearly square cross section, 5 by 5 in. (nominal dimensions) and larger, graded primarily for use as posts or columns.

2.3.1.4   *Structural Boards*—Lumber less than 2 in. (nominal) in thickness and of any width, graded primarily for use where the principal stresses are in axial compression or tension.

2.3.2   The assignment of names indicating the uses for the various classes of structural lumber does not preclude their use for other purposes. There is need for compressive and tensile values for joists and planks if used in the chord or web members of timber trusses. Posts and timbers may give service as beams. The principles of stress grading permit the assignment of any kind of allowable property to any of the classes of structural lumber, whether graded primarily for that property or not. Recommendations for allowable properties may include all properties for all grades or use classes. While such universal application may result in loss of efficiency in some particulars, it offers the advantage of a more simple system of stress grades of structural lumber.

2.4   *Essential Elements in a Stress-Grade Description*—A stress grade formulated by these methods contains the following essential elements:

2.4.1   A grade name that identifies the use-class as described in 2.3.

2.4.2   A description of permissible growth characteristics that affect mechanical properties. Characteristics that do not affect mechanical properties may also be included.

2.4.3   One or more allowable properties for the grade related to its strength ratio.

I think you can see from this example that the standards outlined in the various publications are not going to make your job of meeting code requirements any easier or less complex—quite the contrary. And if you mulitiply the complexity of this one standard by the more than two hundred (yes, two hundred!) standards incorporated in the Dwelling Code itself, you get an idea of the difficulty involved in figuring out exactly what these standards really say and mean to you.

MANDATORY OR PERMISSIVE?

I think the key question for the owner-builder boils down to this: Are the standards listed in the Dwelling Code mandatory rules that you must follow without deviation, or are they just examples of acceptable practices which would allow you to come up with comparable—but different—solutions? The answer to that question is yes . . . and no . . . and an emphatic I'm not sure!

The reason for this definite indefiniteness is the uncertain way the Dwelling Code handles the subject.

On the one hand there is the strict language of §R-208. To quote that section again, this code provision says that shower compartments "*shall be finished* with a smooth, hard, nonabsorbent surface *in accordance with* Section S-26.208. . . ." (Italics mine.) The words don't say that the surface should be *like* or similar to those described in §S-26.208, but "shall be . . . in accordance with" that section. This certainly sounds as though the reference must be complied with.

On the other hand there is the permissive language of §R-401 (and the similar provisions in §R-501, §R-601, etc.) which says that "conformity with the applicable grading material, test, construction and design standards . . . *shall be evidence* that walls and partitions constructed in accordance with the provisions of this Chapter are reasonably safe to persons and property." (Italics mine.)

The words "shall be evidence" indicate that (1) if you follow the standards, code approval is automatic, but that (2) there are other methods that might be used—even though there is no specific indication in this section of how those other methods can be approved.

ALTERNATE MATERIALS AND DESIGNS

Also, there is the provision of §R-108, which—since it is so favorable to owner-builders—I feel takes precedence over inconsistent, restrictive sections (such as §R-208). Section R-108 provides:

> The provisions of this Code are not intended to prevent the use of any material or method of construction not specifically prescribed by this Code, provided any such alternate has been approved.
>
> The Building Official may approve any such alternate provided he finds that the proposed design is satisfactory and complies with accepted design criteria.
>
> The Building Official may require that evidence or proof be submitted to substantiate any claims that may be made regarding its use.

This provision is crucial for any owner-builder who wants to do things his or her own way. Sure, there are some rough spots in the requirements of this section. For instance, (1) the building inspector may—but isn't required to—approve alternatives; (2) the proposed design must be satisfactory and comply with "accepted design criteria" (whatever that is); and (3) the building official may require evidence or proof to substantiate its use. But the important part of this section is the first paragraph—which bears repeating:

> The provisions of this Code are not intended to prevent the use of any material or method of construction not specifically prescribed by this Code, provided any such alternate has been approved.

This is the provision you can use when you want to employ a building material or technique that was not originally envisioned in the straight code standards. Of course, you'll have to do some research first to take advantage of this alternative-material-and-method section; you'll have to take the time to read, study, and learn (1) the applicable code section that you may be violating, (2) the applicable standard (if you can find it in your local library or building inspector's office) that you don't want to follow, and (3) the qualities of the material you want to use and/or the inherent features of the design you propose. With that information, you can proceed to prove to the building inspector how and why your materials and/or design are "reasonably safe to persons and property." It's the *best* argument you can make! Difficult, yes, but it can be done.

In spite of the profile of the building inspector that I painted in Chapters Two and Three (I said s/he was usually not well versed in code-reading and interpretation), don't ever take the building inspector for granted. Don't ever be unprepared in your knowledge of the alternative design or material you want to use. Make your very best possible argument to him or her, and back it up with solid facts. One of the services all building-code groups provide their inspectors with is a question-and-answer referral system. Each group has a whole engineering department geared to answer any and all questions a building inspector (in a locality that has adopted that code group's building regulation) might have.

So the building inspector to whom you are presenting an argument under the auspices of §R-108 might very well pass the question on to an engineering department of a model-code group for consideration. Any information you fail to provide will reduce the chances of an affirmative decision on your project. (By the way, no individual other than a building inspector can directly take advantage of the code groups' question-and-answer service.)

If your particular code does not have an alternate materials provision similar to §R-108, there is still some help I can suggest. The best way to explain this one is by example, and to do that I have to discuss two provisions that I've used before.

I'm sure you're already sick of reading about §R-208 and §S-26.208, but here we go again anyway. As we've discovered, §R-208 says that shower compartment finishes must be smooth, hard, and nonabsorbent in accordance with §S-26.208. But when we turned to that standard, all we saw was a list of instructions concerning how to attach ceramic tile to a wall with various kinds of adhesives. Does the reference to those ceramic tile standards mean that the new one-piece molded fiberglass tub and shower units (or the shower compartments alone) do not meet the criteria of §R-208 and §S-26.208 because the molded shower units are not made of ceramic tile? And if the fiberglass units are code-approved because they meet the smooth, hard, and nonabsorbent qualities listed in §R-208, then what is the use of the ceramic tile standards in §S-26.208?

CODE-READING TECHNIQUE: You should look for and note all conflicts you find between the more general performance criteria found in the building regulations of your code and the actual specifications for materials that you might find in the standards section of your construction ordinance. You can take advantage of these differences by arguing to the building inspector or board of review that the only way to resolve the apparent conflict is to hold that the performance standards (smooth, hard, and nonabsorbent, in the above example) control and that the specification criteria (the "how-to" list about ceramic tile in the standards) come into play only if you decide to use the kinds of materials mentioned in the specification. This does, of course, leave the burden on you to prove that the nonspecified material you intend to use meets the general performance standards in the building code. In the example of molded shower units, you would have to show to the building inspector's satisfaction that such units meet all the performance criteria of smooth, hard, and

nonabsorbent in §R-208, even though the product is not specifically mentioned in §S-26.208.

STANDARDS (AND ALTERNATE MATERIAL PROVISIONS) IN THE BBC, NBC, SBC, AND UBC

The other model codes, of course, also contain standards. Each model-code group, however, uses these standards—and alternative material requirements—in different ways. But once we've reviewed each of them, you should be able to find similarities between them and whatever code you must follow.

THE BBC. Most of the BBC's references to standards are found in Article 8, which has three separate chapters or parts: "Materials and Tests" (Article 8–Part A), "Steel, Masonry, Concrete, Gypsum and Lumber Construction" (Article 8–Part B), and "Building Enclosures, Walls and Wall Thickness" (Article 8–Part C). The section numbers are consecutive through all three parts of Article 8. For instance, §825.2.1 is the last section of Part A and §826.1 is the first provision of Part B.

Article 8 is the very heart of the BBC because, as explained in §800.1 (the very first section),

> The provisions of this article shall govern the quality, workmanship and requirements for all materials and methods and the minimum specifications for enclosure walls and wall thickness hereafter used in the construction of buildings and structures. All materials and methods of construction shall conform to the approved rules and the standards for materials and tests and the requirements of accepted engineering practice as herein listed.

This is a definite command. *All* the materials and methods of construction *shall* conform to "approved rules and standards for materials and tests." The wording is much harsher and stricter than the Dwelling Code's language, which says that conformity with these standards evidences safe construction.

The severe language of §800.1 goes contrary, however, to the intent of the BBC's introduction (entitled "General Notes Concerning Standards Cited in Basic Building Code") to the appendices where the standards are collected:

> The standards issued by the accredited authoritative agencies listed herein are intended to serve as criteria for accepted safe practice for various materials, products, systems of construction, or specific uses as required or used under the provisions of this code. The text of the code

referring to any standard indicates whether conformance with that standard is mandatory or permissive.

Reading the first sentence of this quote would lead you to believe that the standards are considered only *criteria* for construction design or materials, which would then lead you to believe that the "standards" are really just examples of building construction techniques and are therefore not mandatory. But the last sentence of this introductory paragraph tells us that the text of each code section itself indicates whether the standard is permissive or mandatory.

Section 800.1 is, I guess, one of those mandatory code regulations, and since it covers "all materials and methods of construction," I don't know what can be left that the BBC could make permissive! Besides the fact tht I couldn't find any permissive code sections, the "General Notes" themselves precede the appendices containing the standards and are not a binding code regulation, whereas the mandatory §800.1 is very definitely and positively part of the BBC's requirements.

CODE-READING TECHNIQUE: Watch out for explanatory and other (sometimes self-serving) statements found in prefaces or introductions to a code. These kinds of remarks may not be part of the code's binding regulations. And if there is an inconsistency between the intent of a particular regulation as expressed in the introduction and the language of the code section itself, the code provision always prevails. The courts (and therefore administrative agencies and, sometimes, building inspectors) would only consult the intent expressed in the preface if there was an ambiguity in the text of the code requirement itself. If there is no ambiguity (which of course is different from an inconsistency), the code provision prevails—even if the text contradicts the intent expressed in the introduction. So don't, if you can help it, base any of your arguments to the building inspector on statements made in prefatory comments; use those statements only to back up what is already apparent in the text of the code. If there are no other sections you can use, refer to the introduction, preface, or anything else you can find to make your argument.

The titles of the appendices that contain the standards in the BBC are also informative. They show the standards to be organized in a completely different way from anything we've seen so far:

Appendix B   Accepted Engineering Practice Standards
Appendix C   Material Standards

Appendix D   Structural Unit Test Standards
Appendix E   Structural Assembly Test Standards
Appendix F   Durability Test Standards
Appendix G   Fire Test Standards
Appendix H   Standard Time-Temperature Test Controls
Appendix I   Fire Protection Standards

These titles indicate that the BBC attempts to arrange its standards according to tests—or performance criteria—for a particular *function* rather than specify an actual construction *technique* for, say, a wall or foundation.

Furthermore, each of the appendices is itself organized according to performance subjects, such as concrete, heating, fire protection and safety practices, masonry, wood and wood products—to name just a few. These standards are not, however, numbered with a system of cross-references to the applicable code provisions. In fact, there are no section numbers found there at all!

Another difficulty with this method of organization is that a particular performance standard may be pertinent to both an engineering practice and a material specification, or other such combinations of subject matter. The BBC provides for this by listing the standard in every appendix and in every subject heading within an appendix to which it is applicable.

(For those of you who are governed by the BOCA code, read carefully the full eleven paragraphs of the "General Notes . . ." preceding the standards appendices. Even though these comments are nonbinding, they do contain much good and pertinent information which the owner-builder can use to his or her benefit—as explained in the last Code-Reading Technique.)

By the way, Appendix A, though not mentioned in §800.1, has a long list of the names and addresses of "Accredited Authoritative Agencies"—the same kinds of organizations I listed from §S-26.001 of the Dwelling Code—from which the standards come. Not all the model codes have such a complete catalog of names and addresses, and that's a shame, because with the BBC you can write away to the various standard-setters and get a wealth of construction information—most of it free!

The BBC also provides for new materials in §800.4:

> All new building materials, equipment, appliances, systems or methods of construction not provided for in this code, and any material of questioned suitability proposed for use in the construction of a building or structure, shall be subjected to the tests prescribed in this article and in the approved rules to determine its character, quality and limitations of use.

The wording of this section is not as liberal as you might, on first reading, think. The key to this section is that this alternate material provision only comes into effect if the particular material, equipment, appliances, systems, or methods of construction are *not* regulated in the BBC. If the material, equipment, etc., are already mentioned in the code (and there is little that this model has left out of its four-hundred-page regulatory scheme), you must follow the code. Your first difficulty, therefore, will be to convince the building inspector that your material or method of construction is not covered by the code—even though there may be a distinct similarity!

After you've overcome that hurdle, you still have to submit your new creation to the test procedures set forth in §800.6:

> In the absence of approved rules or other accepted standards, the building official shall make or cause to be made the necessary tests and investigations, or he shall accept duly authenticated reports from recognized authoritative sources in respect to the quality and manner of use of new materials or assemblies as provided in Sections 108.0 and 109.0. The cost of all tests and other investigations required under the provisions of this code shall be borne by the applicant.

Here again, as you can readily see, the cost of all testing is to be borne by the applicant—meaning you, the owner-builder. I think this requirement may be fair when applied to construction firms or new product manufacturers, who will get their money back in the price they charge for the house or product. But it's unfair for the owner-builder, who simply wants to exercise a little control over his or her own life and build his/her own shelter. Fair or not, however, the end result of this requirement is that you have to determine if your self-made product or unique method of construction is really worth the time and money you'll have to spend to get it approved.

And finally the BBC—in accordance with its predisposition to attempt to be a performance code—has a ten-subpart section on "Tests" to be used "to check the adequacy of the structural design of an assembly when there is reasonable doubt as to its strength or stability. . . ." Section 802 contains all kinds of different procedures to conduct strength tests for glass (§802.2.1), durability and endurance tests (§802.3), maintenance tests (§802.4), and workmanship tests (§802.5), to name just a few.

(Even if you aren't governed by this code, you should find a copy at your local library or elsewhere and study some of the test procedures. If your personally built shelter can pass these tests, you'll have a very strong argument to make to your building inspector—no matter what code you're governed by—that your dwelling is safe to persons and property.)

The building inspector under this code has objective "conditions of acceptance"—set forth in §803—by which to evaluate new materials or designs. So be aware of these criteria before you present your new method of construction to the building inspector. And after you've made your presentation, the building inspector's approval "shall be . . . in writing within a reasonable time after satisfactory completion of all required tests and submission of required test reports" (§804.1).

I will leave it to you to evaluate—after your own study of the BOCA code—whether this manual lives up to the statements made in the Preface:

> The *Basic Building Code*, now in its 25th year, states regulations in terms of measured performance rather than in rigid specification of materials and, in this way, makes possible the acceptance of new materials and methods of construction which can be evaluated by accepted standards, without the necessity of adopting cumbersome amendments for each variable condition.
>
> By presenting the purposes to be accomplished rather than the method to be followed, the *Basic Building Code* allows the designer the widest possible freedom and does not hamper development. It accepts nationally recognized standards as the criteria for evaluation of minimum safe practice, or for determining the performance of materials or systems of construction. The application of these standards is stated in the text of the code requirements, and the standards are listed and identified in the appendices of the code, making it practical and convenient to update any standard as it is revised or reissued by the sponsoring agency.

THE NBC. The NBC is organized similarly to the Dwelling Code in that each standard—collected in Article XVIII, entitled "List of Standards and Publications" (a part of the regulations themselves as opposed to an attached appendix)—is designated by the same section number that is used to label the text of the applicable code provision. So you can look up (1) the standard by reading the code regulations, or (2) the text of the appropriate code section by reviewing the standards.

Section 1800 of the NBC—the initial paragraph in Article XVIII—contains language that would indicate these standards are permissive rather than mandatory:

> Compliance with the standards or publications listed under the section numbers of this Code in this Article XVIII shall be evidence of compliance with the Section of the Code referring to this Article.

But, as always, you should check the text of each code provision that makes reference to a standard to determine whether compliance with the standard is required or not.

Most of the references to standards are found in Article IX of the NBC, entitled "Structural Design Requirements of Buildings and Structures." Section 912.1a, besides being the introductory provision to the subject of "Pile Foundations" in this code, also contains a truly excellent statement that shows how rules and regulations found in the codes—and the standards to which the rules refer—can be worded to set forth a performance criterion rather than a strict and limiting "how-to" specification:

> Piles and pile foundations shall be designed and installed to be reasonably safe to persons and property. Piles and pile foundations designed and installed in conformance with the applicable provisions of this Code shall be deemed to be reasonably safe to persons and property; on matters not detailed in this Code, piles and pile foundations designed and installed in conformance with the provisions of the standards listed for this Section 912.1a in Article XVIII of this Code shall be evidence that piles and pile foundations are reasonably safe to persons and property.

The main and overriding criterion for acceptability in this section is not conformance to a set of preexisting requirements, but that the piles be "designed and installed to be reasonably safe to persons and property." If you design according to the applicable rules, regulations, and standards set forth in the NBC you'll have, of course, irrefutable proof that your foundation piles will be code-approved.

But as implied by §912.1a and stated specifically in §912.li, there's another choice open to you:

> The use of types of piles not specifically mentioned herein, and the use of piles under conditions not specifically covered herein, is permitted, subject to the approval of the Building Official, upon the submission of acceptable test data, calculations and other information relating to the structural properties and load-carrying capacity of such piles. Prior to giving such approval, the Building Official shall require any information or demonstrations which he deems necessary for the determination of the adequacy of the design or the suitability of the method of installation. In no case shall the allowable design load exceed that determined in accordance with the provisions of this Section 912.

This language is much more liberal than similar provisions of the BBC (and even of the Dwelling Code, for that matter), because this code section is not limited to "new" use of piles (as in the BBC) but any use of piles not specifically mentioned (whether an old, new, or "recycled" method). You should, to repeat, read carefully each section containing a reference to the standards in order to determine just how permissive it really is.

Section 100.7 of the NBC confirms the liberalness we've already seen in the other sections of this code:

> Nothing in this Code shall be construed to prevent the use of any material or method of construction whether or not specifically provided for in this Code if, upon presentation of plans, methods of analysis, test data or other necessary information, to the building official by the interested person or persons, the building official is satisfied that the proposed material or method of construction complies with specific provisions of *or conforms to the intent* of this Code. [Emphasis added is mine.]

And §101, entitled "Tests and Approvals," allows the building inspector (1) to require tests (at the expense of the applicant) whenever he or she has reasonable doubt as to the quality of a material or method of construction (§101.1), (2) to prescribe the test when none is provided for in the code (§101.2), (3) to supervise the test (§101.3), (4) to approve "any material or method of construction meeting the requirements of this Code . . . within a reasonable time after completion of the tests" (§101.4), and (5) to keep the test results on file, open to the public (§101.4).

THE SBC. The Standard Building Code uses still another method to make references to standards. This code group sets forth the title of the applicable standards right in the text of the code provision itself and only lists in Appendix M the section reference (where the standard is mentioned in the code) and the "Standard Designation" (for example, ASTM D245-70).

Even though §1700.1(d)—found in Chapter XVII on "Wood Construction"—implies a permissive approach when it states that

> The detailed requirements contained in this Chapter are based on sound engineering principles such as those in the Standards hereunder and are intended for light frame construction in general use for structures having light loads and closely spaced framing. Where additional structural requirements should be applied because of the nature of the structure, the Standards hereunder shall be accepted as good engineering practice.

you'll find—when you read the specific sections of this code that incorporate a standard—that most of the references use the words "shall conform to" or "shall be in accordance with" a particular listed standard. This language connotes more of a mandatory, rather than a permissive, reference.

The SBC also has a provision for alternative materials and methods of construction. Section 103.6 gives the complete details:

> The provisions of this code are not intended to prevent the use of any material, or method of construction not specifically prescribed by this code, provided any such alternate has been approved and its use authorized by the Building Official. The Building Official shall approve any such alternate, provided he finds that the proposed design is satisfactory and complies with the provisions of Chapter XII [entitled "Minimum Design Loads"], and that the material, method, or work offered is, for the purpose intended, at least the equivalent of that prescribed in the code in quality, strength, effectiveness, fire-resistance, durability, and safety. The Building Official shall require that sufficient evidence or proof be submitted to substantiate any claim that may be made regarding its use. If, in the opinion of the Building Official, the evidence and proof are not sufficient to justify approval, the applicant may refer the entire matter to the Board of Adjustments and Appeals as stipulated in Section 111.

I have a few comments to make on this provision:

1. The alternate allowed here is not limited to "new" materials or designs (as in the BBC), but is applicable to "any material or method of construction not specifically prescribed" (as in the NBC). In other words, the SBC gives you extra latitude when it comes to *possible* alternatives . . . but each is still subject to approval.

2. The criterion as to what constitutes actual approval under the SBC is more detailed and stricter than the other codes'. Here the material or method of construction has to be equivalent to that prescribed in the code for quality, strength, effectiveness, fire resistance, durability, and safety.

3. A new twist in these alternate material provisions that we haven't found in the other model codes is contained in the last sentence of §103.6. I'm referring to the phrase that allows the applicant to bring the entire matter to the Board of Adjustments and Appeals. I'm not sure why this code group found it necessary to put that statement in, because in almost all cases an applicant who disagrees with a decision of the building inspector can appeal *any* matter to the Board of Adjustment or Appeals—not just when the building inspector doesn't approve the new material or method. (I'll be discussing this appeal procedure in full in Chapter Nine.)

There is in the SBC—as in some of the other codes we've reviewed—a provision, in §104, that authorizes the building inspector to require tests. The tests authorized here are directed to show "proof of compliance" (whether the floors hold sufficient weight, etc.). The building inspector may also require that these tests be performed by "an approved laboratory or other approved agency"—at the applicant's expense, of course.

THE UBC. This code has yet another method of organizing standards. This code group has published all the standards to which it refers in its own separate book, entitled *Uniform Building Code Standards,* and uses—at least in the text of the code regulation itself—its own designated numbers. Now, before you jump to the conclusion that the International Conference of Building Officials went out and did their own testing and drafted their own standards, please restrain yourself. Most, if not all, of the standards contained in Part XII, Chapter 60, §6002, are the same ones used, and made reference to, by the other model-code groups.

Many of the references to standards are found in Part VI of the UBC, entitled "Engineering Regulations—Quality and Design of Materials of Construction." This part is further broken down into chapters on different building materials: "Masonry" (Chapter 24), "Wood" (Chapter 25), "Concrete" (Chapter 26), "Steel and Iron" (Chapter 27), and "Aluminum" (Chapter 28). In almost all of these chapters there is a reference to standards similar to that found in §2501(a):

> The quality and design of wood members and their fastenings shall conform to the provisions of this Chapter, and to the following Standards:

Materials or Design	UBC Designation
All Species of Lumber	25-1
Balsam Fir	25-5, 25-8
California Redwood	25-7
Douglas Fir–Larch	25-2, 25-3, 25-4
Douglas Fir South	25-4

Here, not only is the use of the prescribed standards required, but you also have to follow this code's nailing schedule (found in Table 25-P).

And how you locate the standard designated by the UBC's very own numbering system is easy. Say, for example, you want to find out what Standard 25-1 is. All you have to do is turn to Chapter 60 of the UBC, look through the headings there until you locate the caption "Chapter 25," find the UBC designation you're interested in (25-1, in this case), make sure that the number which follows that designation corresponds to the section number of the code provision you were reading in the first place (§2501 in the example we're following), and finally you'll find the title of the standard you are looking for. (See, I told you it was simple!) UBC Standard 25-1 turns out to be an old friend in disguise: "Classification, Definition and Method of Grading for All Species of Lumber," based on Standard D 245-70 (from which I took a long quote starting on page 88).

The alternate materials provision in the UBC, found in §106, is almost identical to that in the SBC. But I will quote the UBC version anyway, for those of you who are governed by this code. By all means, go back and read my comments in this chapter on the SBC's regulation, because those remarks are applicable here too.

The provisions of the Code are not intended to prevent the use of any material or method of construction not specifically prescribed by this Code, provided any such alternate has been approved.

The Building Official may approve any such alternate provided he finds that the proposed design is satisfactory and complies with the provisions of Chapter 23 [entitled "General Design Requirements"], and that the material, method, or work offered is, for the purpose intended, at least the equivalent of that prescribed in this Code in quality, strength, effectiveness, fire resistance, durability, and safety.

The Building Official shall require that sufficient evidence or proof be submitted to substantiate any claims that may be made regarding its use.

The provision authorizing tests in the UBC specifically refers to alternate materials. Section 107 reads as follows:

Whenever there is insufficient evidence of compliance with the provisions of this Code or evidence that any material or any construction does not conform to the requirements of this Code, or in order to substantiate claims for alternate materials or methods of construction, the Building Official may require tests as proof of compliance to be made at the expense of the owner or his agent by an approved agency.

Test methods shall be as specified by this Code for the material in question. If there are no appropriate test methods specified in this Code, the Building Official shall determine the test procedure.

Copies of the results of all such tests shall be retained for a period of not less than two years after the acceptance of the structure.

FURTHER COMPLICATIONS. Now if all this information isn't snarled enough, yet another factor confuses the subject of standards even more. And that monkey wrench is that each municipality or county can disregard the national standards and draft and adopt its own. Many local governments do just that, even though it is an expensive proposition. And the standards that are locally devised and developed sometimes differ significantly from the more widely accepted ones.

All of this means, of course, that you have to study *your* particular code to determine (1) how standards are used (whether mandatory or permissive), (2) what those standards are (whether nationally or locally developed), and (3) if alternate materials are allowed and, if so, under what circumstances and conditions. Finally you have to determine (4) what the building inspector you're dealing with knows about standards. How this public official interprets your code's standards and the engineering lingo found in them will determine how easy or difficult it will be for you to use your new construction technique or unusual building material.

Don't forget, by the way, the experiences of the owner-builders I quoted way back in Chapter Three of this book. Ask questions, propose some tentative answers, show the building inspector you're knowledgeable and you're as concerned with safety as he or she is. In this atmosphere of mutual respect, the building inspector will be much more likely to resolve any doubts he may have about your project in your favor.

8. Construction Materials and Methods: Code Requirements

Now that my long (but necessary) dissertation on standards is over, we can move on to examine the construction chapters of the Dwelling Code (numbers 3 through 9). Let's see what evils, if any, lurk in the heart of these building regulations.

First, though, let me point out that I'll be organizing this review in checklist form only (adding, as you may now expect from me, a comment or two on provisions that might cause general misunderstanding or confusion, or provisions that are particularly burdensome to owner-builders). In other words, I'll just list the topic and point out where to find that subject in the Dwelling Code and the other model regulations. I won't go into fine details on how to build a house; there are already plenty of good books on the market on that subject. I will, however, continue to concentrate on *how to read the code* and on the various provisions that owner-builders need to look for in their own construction ordinances in order to build their homes "according to code." If you don't find all of the requirements I list here in your code, you'll at least have the satisfaction of knowing that you're not as confined in your building project as you might be.

One further point of explanation before starting the checklist. As I said in Chapter One, the Dwelling Code titles its construction chapters according to the *specific construction steps necessary to build a house:* "Foundations," "Wall Construction," "Roofs," to name a few. The remaining model codes, on the other hand, generally organize and title their chapters according to the *different design specifications and various building materials,* such as "Wood," "Masonry," "Steel," etc.

I will, in spite of these organizational differences, cite provisions from the other models—wherever those provisions may be found— that are similar to the regulations we discuss in the Dwelling Code. It will be up to you to determine how your own code is organized and to follow my discussion of the particular model that is most similar to yours.

FOUNDATIONS

This subject is covered in Chapter 3 of the Dwelling Code, where §R-301 states that "foundations, footings, and basement walls *shall be* constructed in accordance with the requirements of this Chapter." (Emphasis added is mine.) As I discussed in the previous chapter of this book, that language suggests that the requirements are mandatory.

MATERIALS. Section R-302 makes reference to Chapter 26 of the Dwelling Code, where all standards on foundation materials are found. That section states that when all materials used for foundations, footings, and basement walls conform to these standards, they shall be found to be reasonably safe to persons and property. If your code has similar language, you can argue (it's your burden) that the materials you plan to use, even if not listed as a standard, are satisfactory because they are equally safe!

FOOTINGS. Footings are discussed in §R-303 of the Dwelling Code. In addition to supplying technical information about the depths of footings in relation to the frost line, this provision states that the foundation "shall be of sufficient design to support safely the loads imposed as determined from the character of the soil. . . ." The Dwelling Code doesn't go any further into the topic, and that's too bad, because it should. So I'll pick up where it leaves off.

The kind of soil you build on will determine the kind of foundation you can construct. And, even more important, the character of your soil might very well have a large influence on the overall design of the house you can build. So study the nature of the soil very carefully *before* you buy that piece of property—make sure you can build the kind of house you want to build on it.

The other models cover this subject in more detail than the Dwelling Code. The BBC covers the general subject in Article 7, entitled "Structural and Foundation Loads and Stresses." Section 722, named "Bearing Value of Soils," states that all applications for building permits "shall be accompanied by a statement describing the soil in the ultimate bearing strata, including sufficient records and data to establish its . . . load-bearing capacity." The difficulty here for owner-builders is that the BBC requires this information to be certified by a licensed professional engineer or architect. (Here's a tip on how you might save that expense: If other people have built on adjacent properties, you might review their soil reports—you'll find them in the building inspector's office—and use those reports as evidence of what your soil is like. It can save you some money, so it's certainly worth a try.)

The BBC goes further and actually lists satisfactory soils and their load-bearing characteristics. Because this concept is so important and can so easily be overlooked, I want to quote §722.2 and reproduce Table 722, which gives the presumptive surface-bearing values of soils upon which foundations can rest:

> Satisfactory bearing materials for spread footings shall include ledge rock on its natural bed; natural deposits of sand, gravel or firm clay, or a combination of such materials, provided they do not overlie an appreciable amount of peat, organic silt, soft clay, or other objectionable materials.

Table 722
PRESUMPTIVE SURFACE BEARING VALUES OF FOUNDATION
MATERIALS

CLASS OF MATERIAL	TONS PER SQUARE FOOT
1. Massive crystalline bed rock including granite, diorite, gneiss, trap rock, hard limestone and dolomite	100
2. Foliated rock including bedded limestone, schist and slate in sound condition	40
3. Sedimentary rock including hard shales, sandstones, and thoroughly cemented conglomerates	25
4. Soft or broken bed rock (excluding shale), and soft limestone	10
5. Compacted, partially cemented gravels, and sand and hardpan overlying rock	10
6. Gravel and sand-gravel mixtures	6
7. Loose gravel, hard dry clay, compact coarse sand, and soft shales	4
8. Loose, coarse sand and sand-gravel mixtures and compact fine sand (confined)	3
9. Loose medium sand (confined), stiff clay	2
10. Soft broken shale, soft clay	1.5

The BBC also requires soil-bearing investigations in the absence of satisfactory data (§723), outlines a soil test procedure (§724), and sets forth footing requirements (§726 through §731). Owner-builders note: Timber footings, wood foundations, and pole buildings are specifically approved in §728—subject, of course, to some limitations, but nevertheless approved.

The National Building Code covers the subject of footings in §909.3 in its chapter on "Structural Design." Soil characteristics for footings and foundations are discussed in §911. This section also has a table, 911.2a, which contains information on soil-bearing capacities similar to Table 722 of the BBC reproduced above. The NBC also permits wood foundations (§909.4) and timber piles (§912.2).

The SBC's regulations concerning the bearing capacity of soils is found in §1302.2. Section 1302.3 deals with footing design, while §1302.6 permits timber footings.

The footing and soil .characteristic rules of the UBC are found in Chapter 29, "Excavations, Foundations, and Retaining Walls." Section 2904 deals with soil classification and expansive soils, while §2905 covers the subject of foundation investigation. The requirements for footings are found in §2907.

Round wood piles are specifically allowed under the UBC in §2909 . . . and there is even an exception to the requirement that the poles be pressure treated "when it has been established that the cutoff will be below lowest ground water level assumed to exist during the life of the structure."

BASEMENT WALLS. Section R-304 of the Dwelling Code covers the subject of basement walls, including diagrams of six different construction methods for foundations. These drawings deserve some study by owner-builders who are new to dwelling construction; the information is basic and highly useful.

The most important question that this section addresses is whether the basement walls must be of reinforced or unreinforced masonry. The answer depends largely on whether or not you're building on unstable soil or in a seismic-zone area where earthquakes are a possibility. (Watch out, California owner-builders!) Section R-304 also covers such details as the proper time to backfill (only after the walls have achieved sufficient strength), and requires that the walls be drained (according to the provisions of §R-305) and dampproofed (according to the provisions of §R-306).

Drains are often required in areas where natural drainage is not sufficient. The dampproofing methods you can use are found in §R-306, and vary according to soil conditions and the type of house you want to build. If you plan to have habitable rooms below grade, for instance (remember that underground house we discussed in Chapter Five of this book?), the dampproofing methods are quite strict: a membrane of two-ply hot-mopped felt, six mil polyvinyl chloride, 55-pound roll roofing, or equivalent material, is required.

Alternate methods of dampproofing are specifically allowed when approved by the building inspector.

The Basic Building Code's provisions for similar requirements are found in §869 ("Foundation Walls") and §872 ("Waterproofing and Floodproofing"). If the basement rooms are occupiable, the standard for waterproof basement walls in this code is that they "shall be made watertight and . . . reinforced to withstand water pressure."

The NBC's requirements for foundation walls are found in §910.1 ("General") and §910.2 ("Thickness of Foundation Walls"). The water- and dampproofing requirements of the NBC are found in §933.1.

Section 1302.5 contains the Standard Building Code's regulations for foundation walls. After an extensive search, I could not find any requirements in this code for dampproofing or waterproofing basements.

In the UBC, the requirements for foundation walls—their thickness and load-bearing capacity—are found in §2907(b) and Table No. 29-A. I wasn't, however, able to locate any water- or dampproofing requirements in the UBC.

FOUNDATION STUDS. One particular building technique uses 2 by 4 wood studs for foundations walls, and is specifically permitted by the Dwelling Code in §R-307. A minimum stud height of 14 inches is required if you use this method, and if you use foundation studs exceeding 4 feet in height, they "shall be of the size required for an additional story."

I could not find a specific provision for this type of foundation in the BBC. The NBC in §909.4 and the SBC in §1302.7 both allow wood-frame foundations, and refer to specific standards in the back of their respective manuals. There is a §2518(f)6 of the UBC entitled "cripple walls." I could not find a definition of that term in the UBC, but after some investigation I can tell you that the phrase refers to foundation studs. The requirements there are very similar to those found in the Dwelling Code.

PROTECTION AGAINST DECAY AND TERMITES. The objective of this provision is obvious. The Dwelling Code's specific requirements—such as the use of treated wood at certain ground-level locations—are gathered in §R-308.

Not every locality, of course, has termite problems and therefore local officials adopting a building code can choose whether or not to make termite-protection provisions mandatory. Even if your code doesn't require special measures against these pesky wood-eaters, however, you might—if you think you'll have a problem with the critters—look at this provision of the Dwelling Code to determine a recommended course of action for yourself.

Unfortunately, the major code-prescribed methods for preventing termite infestation present problems for owner-builders who want to do everything themselves. The method allows you to use pressure-treated lumber to defeat the termites, but of course the treatment process requires machinery and equipment that the ordinary owner-builder doesn't have. One way to get around this is to use certain decay-resistant species of wood; you'll find them listed in the Dwelling Code.

The BBC has similar termite provisions—including the statement that its requirements are not applicable in all areas—in §874. The NBC's requirements, which are also similar, are in §927.8.

In the South, termite infestation is a serious problem, and as a result the SBC provides rather extensive requirements in §1702. In fact, SBC's provisions are not only more extensive, they're more stringent. Section 1702.12 goes so far as to require you to install floor framing of termite-resistant wood if the building inspector feels that the hazard of termite damage in your area is particularly heavy.

The UBC's termite provisions—which call for the use of treated wood—are found in §2517(c).

UNDERFLOOR SPACE. Section R-309 of the Dwelling Code prescribes regulations for the area between the ground and the bottom of the floor joists. You'll find such topics as ventilation and access crawl holes discussed here.

The BBC's requirements for crawl spaces are in §507.3, the NBC's in §933.2, the SBC's in §1302.5(e), and the UBC's in §2517(c)2.

WALL CONSTRUCTION

Chapter 4 of the Dwelling Code covers the topic of wall construction. Unfortunately, it doesn't include discussions on building walls with poles, logs, or other alternative materials and methods. This doesn't mean that these techniques are prohibited, however; it just means that you'll have to convince your local building inspector that a given alternative construction technique is as safe as the standard, stud-frame construction that the codes seem to venerate.

If your building inspector is hard to convince, show him or her §R-401 of the Dwelling Code, where conformity with the standards and requirements in the chapter on wall construction is deemed only as *evidence* that the walls are "reasonably safe to persons and property." As I pointed out in the previous chapter of this book, language like this suggests that it is not mandatory for you to follow exactly the related provisions and standards of the code as long as you can prove what you're doing is safe.

If your building inspector is still not convinced, (1) turn to the standards listed in §S-26.401 of the Dwelling Code, where you'll find such titles as "Wood Poles" (Specifications and Dimensions for Wood Poles, ANSI 05.1-1963) and "Plank-and-Beam Framing" (Wood Construction Data No. 4, National Forest Products Associations), and (2) refer him or her to §R-108 of the Dwelling Code (and the corresponding sections from each of the other model codes), which specifically permits alternative methods of construction not expressly prescribed by the code.

And, finally, back up your whole argument by pointing out to your building inspector the following quote from the Preface of the Dwelling Code. (Remember, as I told you back on page 95 of the last chapter: You shouldn't use statements from nonbinding prefaces and introductions as a main argument, but only to substantiate code provisions located in the body of the code.)

> All of the nationally recognized model codes upon which this Code is based are comprehensive and flexible and make provision for the use of all safe materials or methods of construction. Consequently, there are construction materials and practices other than listed in this Code which are adequate for the purposes intended. These other methods represent either seldom used systems or performance type systems which require individual consideration by the professional architect or engineer based on either test data or engineering analysis and are therefore not included herein. The construction methods covered in this Code are time tested and therefore do not need additional substantiating data to justify their adequacy.

The Dwelling Code divides its chapter on wall construction into the different code-approved materials that can be used to build walls, and then sets out the requirements applicable to each of those construction materials.

WOOD. Section R-402 of the Dwelling Code has no less than six separate subsections for this topic.

The most damaging requirements for owner-builders who make their own lumber are in subsection one, entitled "Identification" (§R-402.1). This provision requires that

> All load-bearing lumber, plywood and particleboard shall conform to applicable standards or grading rules and shall be so identified by the grade mark, or certificate of inspection issued by an approved grading

or inspection bureau or agency. The grade mark for such load-bearing
lumber shall provide adequate information to determine the "f" [the allowable stress in bending] and "E" [the modulus of elasticity] values.

This means that in a code-dominated locality you can't use
timber you've cut and trimmed yourself from your own property to
build your own house. In fact, according to this rule, it doesn't even
matter if your wood happens to be better than the mass-produced,
lumberyard-bought variety. If there is no official inspection or grade
mark on the wood product, you can't use it!

Of course, the intent of the grading system is to ensure that the
quality of the wood you buy from commercial sources is sufficient for
the purpose intended. And yes, if I go out to buy wood from a lum-
beryard, I do want the assurance of an inspection or grade stamp on
that product.

Nevertheless, there should be an allowed alternative for someone who cuts and trims his or her own lumber for a house he or she
will build and live in. To my mind, a building inspector should be
required to do visual grading—in accordance with the methods prescribed in the standard I quoted on pages 88 to 90 of this book—
of homecut lumber that is to be used in an owner-builder's dwelling.
(Incidentally, if you're into producing your own lumber, you might
want to read Larry Hackenberg's book, *The Green Wood House*
[Charlottesville: University Press of Virginia, 1976].)

All the other codes have similar grade and inspection requirements for wood products: the BBC in §852.1, the NBC in §927.1.d,
the SBC in §1700.3, the UBC in §2505.

The five remaining subsections of §R-402 of the Dwelling Code
are: "Grade" (requires No. 3 Standard or Stud Grade Lumber for
headers and studs); "Construction" (refers to figures and diagrams
which show stud-frame construction methods, including a very detailed nailing schedule that tells you how to nail and what kind of nail
to use); "Cutting and Notching" (details the procedure on how
plumbing, heating, and other pipes are to be framed into the walls);
"Headers"; and "Firestopping."

The BBC's regulations on wood-frame construction are found in
§854.1 and §854.2. Some of the topics covered here are "Bearing
Walls," "Bracing," and "Mortise and Tenon Framing." (The firestopping provisions are found in §875.) By the way, post-and-beam construction is specifically approved as an acceptable framing method in
§854.2.4 ("Mortise and Tenon Framing").

The NBC's requirements on this topic are set forth in §708.
Some of the subjects mentioned above are included, but so are rules
on "Beams, Girders, and Joists" and "Wood Columns." This code also

has "Supplementary Provisions for Wood Frame Construction" in Appendix A, and adds explanations and requirements to the topic found in §708. Section 708.11 of Appendix A permits post-and-beam framing (while §927.7 specifically allows pole buildings).

General wood construction is detailed in §1700 of the SBC and the requirements for vertical (or wall) framing are outlined in §1706. Post-and-beam framing is specifically permitted in §1706.4.

There's a whole chapter (25) devoted to wood construction in the UBC. The actual building requirements for wood are in §2517 and wood wall framing in §2518(f).

As you design and build your house, you should make regular reference to the wood construction regulations in your building code—you'll find 90 percent of your questions answered there. I myself will be mentioning these sections frequently when discussing the code requirements for constructing the remaining parts (floors, roofs, etc.) of your house.

METAL. I'm not sure very many people would want to build their home's walls out of steel, but there is a small section on that subject—§R-403—in the Dwelling Code. Each of the other codes, in fact, have rather lengthy and detailed chapters devoted to steel construction. (Don't forget, however, that these other model codes cover factories and high-rise construction—which require this type of building material.)

Since steel is not a favorite owner-builder construction material, I'll just list the sections where this topic can be located in the models, with no further comments: BBC §826 to §832, NBC §921 to §926, SBC Chapter XV, and UBC Chapter 27.

GENERAL (AND SPECIFIC) MASONRY CONSTRUCTION. Section R-404 of the Dwelling Code has ten subsections, a few tables, and numerous diagrams that contain all the different provisions which relate to masonry construction. Here are the topics covered: (1) "Corbeling," (2) "Combined Units" (when you use different kinds of materials, the maximum stress shall not exceed the allowable stress for the weakest member), (3) "Piers," (4) "Chases," (5) "Stack Bond," (6) "Unsupported Height" (where the limits of which are set forth in Table 4-C), (7) "Lintels" (the reinforcement needed over door, window, and other openings), (8) "Anchorage" (masonry walls are required to be anchored to floor and roof systems), (9) "Reinforcement" (needed in certain seismic zones and in locations where wind velocity is high), and (10) "Beam Supports."

If you're considering building with masonry, you should check out the similar provisions in your own building code. And if your building code doesn't give the definitions of the terms I've just listed above, don't worry—neither do the model codes. Most, if not all, of these terms are common construction words and phrases. You'll probably find them in any building books you might consult.

The specific masonry construction techniques that the Dwelling Code prescribes are: "Hollow Unit" (§R-405), "Solid" (§R-406), "Cavity Wall" (§R-407), "Grouted" (§R-408), "Reinforced Grouted" (§R-409), and "Reinforced Hollow Unit" (§R-410). Choose the technique and method best suited for you, your situation, and your finances.

The other model codes have integrated their masonry wall construction provisions with their general masonry regulations. So I'll cite all the regulations (not just the wall construction requirements) dealing with masonry from each of the model codes.

The BBC's masonry rules are spread out among the three parts of Article 8: Sections 805.1 through 817.3 discuss the various masonry materials (Part A); §834 through §851.1 contain the rules on actual masonry construction techniques (Part B); while all of Part C (entitled "Building Enclosures, Walls, and Wall Thickness") deals with the full subject of walls in general, regardless of the materials used.

The NBC's rules on masonry construction are found in §913 in that manual's chapter on "Structural Design." Sections 914 through 920 contain provisions on some of the more sophisticated masonry techniques that are of no real consequence to owner-builders.

The SBC devotes an entire separate chapter—Chapter XIV, entitled "Masonry Construction"—to the subject. It's quite complete and provides a handy all-in-one-place source of useful information.

The UBC also devotes a complete chapter to masonry construction: Chapter 24. It's rather long and contains many more engineering formulas than I've seen in the other codes, but then the UBC is published in California, where buildings must be engineered to withstand the periodic earth tremors that occur there.

Not incidentally, I want to mention that there are two alternative masonry methods that owner-builders are often interested in. One, of course, is the use of natural stone (using the slip-form method of construction popularized by Helen and Scott Nearing) and the other is the use of homemade adobe brick. Because of the relative popularity of these methods, I want to make sure that I specifically point out the sections in each of the codes that cover them.

STONE. I must have read and reread the Dwelling Code at least five times to see if stone was an allowed building material. Despite my efforts, I couldn't find the word mentioned even once in the eleven pages of text on the subject of masonry construction, and the index wasn't any help either. So I decided to check those pages over one final time and—eureka!—there, tucked away in Table 4-C (entitled "Allowable Span for Masonry Walls Between Lateral Supports"), was a reference to stone as a building material for a wall!

CODE-READING TECHNIQUE: This is an example of how difficult it sometimes is to find a particular subject in the building codes. If you can't find the topic in which you're interested in the section where you think it should be, follow this procedure: Review the table of contents and skim-read the chapters where you think the subject might be discussed (not just the obvious chapters, either; read the not-so-apparent chapters too). Then, consult the index. Don't look up just a single word and then give up if you fail to find it; try to think of every possible related topic and subtopic, and look those up also. Read through the tables and diagrams in the chapters where you think the subject might be located, turn to the standards that are collected in the back of the code (and check the titles in those sections that are most applicable), and—finally—go through all the appendices that are attached to your building code (you just might find what you're looking for there). As a last resort, ask the building inspector. I say "as a last resort" because if you can locate the subject yourself, then *you* will probably know more than he or she, and that's always a good position in which to be!

If your building inspector then gives you a hard time about building your home's walls of stone in a Dwelling Code–dominated jurisdiction, just point to the word "stone" in Table 4-C as proof that natural stone *is* a code-approved material.

The Dwelling Code's failure to mention stone more prominently as a code-approved building material is especially puzzling to me because most of the other model codes specifically and very visibly approve natural stone in the text of a section or two.

The BBC gives its blessing to natural stone as a building material in §813:

> Natural stone for masonry shall be sound and free from loose or friable inclusions; and shall meet the strength, fireresistance, durability and impact resistance for the intended use in accordance with accepted engineering practice.

This code also requires that rubble stone walls be at least 16 inches thick when used for foundation walls (§869.2.4).

The NBC, like the Dwelling Code, hides its reference to natural-stone construction in a table—Table 910.2a. This "Table on Foundation Walls" (the reference seems to be limited to that kind of wall) states that "rubble stone [foundations] shall not be less than 16 inches in thickness" nor can they "be used as foundations for walls exceeding 35 feet in height."

Natural stone is also an approved building material under the SBC (§1402.7). Table 4 makes another reference to stone in its regulations on "Allowable Compressive Stresses in Unit Masonry." Section 1404.2(j) gives the same 16-inch minimum thickness requirement that the other codes do, but here the use of natural stone is not limited to just foundation walls; the SBC specifically indicates that stone may be used for any kind of wall.

The UBC, too, specifically approves the use of natural stone for masonry construction, in §2403(j). In fact, this code devotes an entire separate section to the rules for using this material—§2409—and *does not* limit the use of stone to foundation walls only.

ADOBE BRICK. The other masonry material that owner-builders might be inclined to use is known in building-code lingo as "unburned clay masonry units." (See Eugene Boudreau's book *Making the Adobe Brick* [New York: Bookworks (dist. by Random House), 1972] for complete "how-to" instructions on this fascinating construction material.) Unfortunately, I could find no reference to this homemade "masonry unit" in the Dwelling Code, and I looked very carefully in the list of standards in §S-26.302 and §S-26.401. I'm at a loss to understand why the Dwelling Code does not specifically mention that material because at least two of the other models do.

The BBC, in §806, indicates that unburned clay brick is okay to use, but not for isolated brick piers or for any part of a building—such as exterior walls—that will be exposed to the weather or for a wall exceeding 40 feet in height.

Neither the NBC nor the SBC makes provisions for the use of unburned clay brick in either the main text or the standards section of their respective codes.

The UBC, on the other hand, not only defines the term—in §2403(i)—but also has its very own section devoted to the necessary construction techniques for this alternative material (§2405; 16 inches thick and not more than one story high), as well as a standard covering the composition of the homemade brick—Uniform Building Code Standard 24-15, which requires not more than 25 percent soil, not more than 45 percent material passing through a No. 200 mesh sieve, plus clay and stabilizer. For those really interested, the UBC standard can be found quoted in Boudreau's book.

WALL COVERING

The Dwelling Code devotes a whole chapter (5) to both interior and exterior wall coverings. The oft-appearing reference to the standards is found in §R-501, the first section of the chapter.

INTERIOR COVERINGS. Section R-502 has seven subsections for interior coverings. Detailed instructions on such methods as "Vertical Assemblies" (§R-502.2), "Gypsum Wallboard" (§R-502.5), "Shower and Bathroom Compartments" (§R-502.6, which contains a reference back to §R-208, the provision I beat to death a few chapters back!), and "Other Interior Finishes" (§R-502.7) are included, together with the ever-present (but useful) tables.

The other model codes don't have separate chapters on this subject. The only way to find their provisions is to look in the index of the code you're governed by and hunt for the topic.

In the Basic Building Code, the requirements on interior lath and plaster can be found in §819, and on gypsum wallboard in §822, §823, and §825. Also, there is a whole separate discussion of interior finishes in §918 through §921, found in a chapter entitled "Fireresistive Construction Requirements."

The National Building Code's requirements for "Lath, Plaster and Gypsum Wallboard" are set forth in §931.1. But you should also review §810, where interior-finish material is discussed.

The SBC has a whole chapter (XVIII) on "Lathing, Plastering, and Gypsum Wallboard." It's not very long and even contains regulations for exterior work, but at least all the requirements are in one place.

The UBC has a chapter (47) entitled "Wall and Ceiling Coverings" that is similar in concept and content to the Dwelling Code's treatment of "Interior Coverings." There are sections on vertical assemblies (§4703), interior lath (§4705), interior plaster (§4707), and gypsum wallboard (§4711).

EXTERIOR COVERINGS. Section R-503 of the Dwelling Code has not less than ten subparts that give the rules, regulations, and requirements on: "Exterior Lath" (§R-503.2), "Exterior Plaster" (§R-503.3), "Masonry Veneer" (§R-503.4), "Weather Protection" (§R-503.5), "Weather-Resistant Siding" (§R-503.6), "Weather-Resistant Membrane" (§R-503.7), "Flashing" (§R-503.8), "Plywood Application" (§R-503.9), and "Attachment" (§R-503.10).

Some of the useful tables found in this section are "Maximum Spacing of Supports for Lath" (Table No. 5-A), "Thickness of Plaster" (Table No. 5-C), "Gypsum Plaster Proportions" (Table No. 5-D), and "Weather-Resistant Siding Attachment" (Table No. 5-G).

118   BUILDING REGULATIONS

In the BBC's §820, you'll find the requirements for "Exterior Lathing and Stucco." Section 854.4 details the provisions for "Exterior Weather Boarding, Veneer, and Condensation"; §854.9, "Flashing"; §861 through §865, kinds of veneer; while §924 sets forth the "Exterior Trim Restrictions."

The NBC does not cover all of these topics in the main text of its manual. Those that *are* there are: "Exterior Walls" (§708.4), "Plywood" (§928.1), and "Masonry Veneer" (§929), which, by the way, has an alternative methods section in 929.7. There is much information in Appendix A of the NBC on this topic; see §708.4d through s.

The Standard Building Code has more complete regulations on exterior coverings. Section 1803 deals with "Application of Exterior Lathing and Plastering," §1414.16 with "Flashing," and §1706.7 with plywood, weatherboarding, and other exterior coverings.

The Uniform Building Code's rules on this subject are found in Chapter 47 (which also has regulations on interior walls and ceiling coverings). Veneers have their own separate chapter (30) and also you can find some general rules for exterior wall coverings in §2517(g), including the prescribed use of plywood, shingles and shakes, and weatherproofing.

FLOORS

The next major construction chapter in the Dwelling Code (6) gives all the requirements for building floors. As you'll see, this chapter follows the same structure and outline that the other chapters on construction do.

WOOD. The first substantive section after the general opening section, §R-601 (which makes the usual reference to standards), is entitled "Wood." Section R-602 contains six subparts; the first two are "Identification" and "Grade" (§R-602.1 and §R-602.2), which contain the same identification and grade requirements that I mentioned in the discussion of wall construction on pages 111 to 112 of this book. My cry of outrage and plea for an alternative for do-it-yourselfers who produce their own lumber is as valid here as it was there! The next subpart is "Allowable Spans" (§R-602.3; here the calculations get complicated and there is a reference to four pages of closely packed tables in the appendix—which all boil down to the fact that if you use 2 by 10 or 2 by 12 inch joists at 16 inches on center, you should be okay). The remaining subparts are: "Bearing" (§R-602.4—which details how much of the ends of each floor joist must rest on a wall or other support); "Lateral Support" (§R-602.5—including both solid blocking and diagonal support); and "Notching" (§R-602.6—where you find that you must be very careful where and how you notch or bore holes into joists, so as not to destroy the load-carrying capacity of the wood).

Similar provisions in the other model codes are found scattered throughout their respective manuals.

The BBC puts its requirements for floor loads in §701 through §707. For a discussion of other aspects of wood floor construction, see "Lumber and Timber Construction" (§853) and "Wood Frame Construction" (§854; particularly §854.7, which deals with floors and flooring).

The NBC's rules on floor requirements for heavy-duty construction are found in §706.3; for ordinary construction, §707.3; for wood-frame construction, §708.3 and §708.8c and in Appendix A; and for general structural and stress provisions, §927.

All of the SBC's floor requirements are found in §1705, "Floor Framing," except that §1408.3 has all the information on how to anchor wood floor joists on masonry walls.

Check the UBC's §2517(c) for general construction requirements for floor framing. Section 2517(h) deals with structural floor sheathing, §2517(j) covers joist hanging and framing anchors, and §2518(d) has the general construction provisions for floor joists.

CONCRETE FLOORS (ON GROUND). If you plan to lay a concrete floor directly on the ground, you definitely should consult the Dwelling Code's informative §R-603. Here you find that the most important step in the process is site preparation: ". . . the area within foundation walls shall have all vegetation top soil and foreign material removed . . . [and] the fill shall be compacted to assure uniform support. . . ." Another requirement that you should pay special attention to is the provision that a vapor barrier—usually a thin plastic sheet—be placed between the base course of gravel and the concrete slab. This vapor barrier can be a temperature-regulation and energy-conservation device in your home-construction plans! I do not, however, see any requirements for reinforcing rods in the poured concrete floor. I would recommend that you inquire about (or read up on) the use of these rods when pouring a large slab of concrete. The added initial cost can save you needless headaches, because an *un*reinforced concrete slab will often crack.

The BBC's provision on reinforced concrete slabs is found in §841.2. The NBC's requirements for "Floors on Soil" are found in §933.3 (a vapor barrier is required here). The SBC provides in §1603 for a minimum 3½-inch concrete slab on the ground over an approved vapor barrier. You can find the UBC's provisions on this subject in §2603.

It was difficult for me to find the requirements in the various model codes on this subject because the index of each code did not contain the specific words "concrete floors (on ground)," as did the Dwelling Code. You might look for such key words as "concrete," "floor," "reinforced concrete," "concrete construction," as well as "floors on soil."

METAL. The Dwelling Code sets forth the requirements for the use of structural steel in floors in §R-604. The other models devote whole chapters to the subject: BBC Article 8, Part B; NBC §921; SBC Chapter XV; and UBC Chapter 27.

PARTICLEBOARD. I'm not sure why the Dwelling Code devotes a whole separate section, §R-605, to the use of particleboard in floor construction and then fails to mention it so prominently as a construction material for other parts of the building. Whatever the reason, the Dwelling Code requires that—no matter what you use it for—particleboard must be inspected and graded (as wood must) by an approved inspection agency.

Except for the SBC and the UBC, the other model codes don't have the word "particleboard" in their indices. The SBC's provisions on this building material are found in §1700.3(g) (for under floors) and §1706.7(f) (for exterior siding). The UBC's mention of particleboard is found as a subclassification of the word "wood" in its index, and §2517(g) gives the requirements for the use of particleboard for exterior siding. Though the BBC does not list the word in its index, it does mention the material in a list for exterior weatherboarding (§854.4) and for wall sheathing (§854.3), while the NBC mentions particleboard in §708.4.o, found in its Appendix A.

ROOF-CEILING CONSTRUCTION

All the details of roof-ceiling construction for your home are found in Chapter 7 of the Dwelling Code. After the introductory section—R-701, which makes reference to the ever-present standards in §S-26.701—the first substantive provision deals with:

WOOD. As always, when wood is mentioned in the Dwelling Code, grading and inspection requirements rear their ugly heads. Section R-702.1 and §R-702.2 require that all wood used for roof-ceiling construction be properly identified and graded by an approved lumber-grading bureau or agency. (See pages 111 to 112 for my remarks on this subject.)

The allowable spans of the rafters and ceiling joists—mentioned in §R-702.3—are set forth in no less than *twenty* tables found in Appendix B of the Dwelling Code. General framing details for this part of your house are given in §R-702.4. The other models don't lump together roof and ceiling construction. The BBC's provisions for floors are at §854.7 and for roofs at §854.8. You should consult §710, §711, and §712 for roof loads, snow loads, and wind load, if you are affected by any of these problems. The NBC's roof requirements are found in §706.4, for heavy timber construction; §707.8, for ordinary construction; and §708.8c, for wood-frame construction. (Don't forget to check Appendix A in this code, because §708.11, found there, gives details on ceiling joists and rafter framing, and §927.12 in Appendix A gives the requirements for subflooring and roof sheathing. See also §904.2 for the NBC's roof load requirements.)

The SBC's regulations on roof and ceiling framing are found in §1707.

The UBC has its provisions for roof loads in §2305 and §2308, structural roof sheathing in §2517(i), roof and ceiling framing in §2518(g), and roof construction in §3201 and §3202.

METAL. The provisions of §R-703 of the Dwelling Code specifically detail the use of metal in roof construction. In the other model codes, you'll have to read through their chapters on general metal construction: BBC Article 8, Part B; NBC §921, §923, §926; SBC Chapter XV; UBC Chapters 27 and 28.

CEILING FINISHES. The Dwelling Code, in §R-704, simply says that ceiling finishes shall be installed in accordance with the requirements of "Wall Coverings," found in Chapter 5 of that code. I refer you to page 117 of this guide for a complete discussion of the requirements for interior finishes.

VENTILATION. By virtue of the provisions of §R-705 of the Dwelling Code, the building inspector has the authority to choose whether or not to require ventilation of enclosed attic spaces, depending on "atmospheric or climatic conditions." Exactly how the attic should be ventilated, if ventilation is required, is also set forth in §R-705. The BBC's attic ventilation provisions are mandatory (§507.2), the SBC's mandatory requirements are found in §1707.8, and the UBC's optional attic ventilation provisions are in §3205(c) of that code. The NBC has no provisions for attic ventilation.

ATTIC ACCESS. The Dwelling Code requires that all attic areas which have a clear height of over 24 inches must have a "readily ac-

cessible attic access opening not less than 22 inches by 30 inches"
(§R-706).

The BBC and NBC have no comparable provisions. The SBC in
§1707.7 and the UBC in §3205 have almost identical requirements to
those found in the Dwelling Code.

ROOF COVERINGS

This subject is found in Chapter 8 of the *One- and Two-Family
Dwelling Code*. The topic is important to owner-builders because
roofs and their coverings can be definite fire hazards and thus their
construction is highly regulated.

We saw in Chapter Four of this book that the model codes establish and define three different classes of roof coverings—coverings
that, respectively, protect from severe, moderate, or light fires. (You
might review Chapter Four of this book, together with the chart at
the end of the chapter, for full details on these concepts.)

You may also remember (from the same chapter) my statement
that single-family residences are the least regulated buildings in the
model codes. That statement is borne out again here; the Dwelling
Code itself only mentions the various classes of roof coverings briefly,
and then goes on to set forth the construction requirements for the
different kinds of roof coverings that you might want to use. The
other model groups, however, organize their codes quite differently.

Therefore, I'll review first the kinds of roof materials the Dwelling Code permits (and the sections where the requirements can be
found). Then, when our review of the Dwelling Code is complete, I'll
discuss how the other models organize their regulations on this subject.

THE DWELLING CODE. Section R-801 contains the reference to
the applicable material standards found in §S-26.801. This section
goes on:

> Roofs shall be covered with Class A [effective against severe fire ex-
> posure], B [effective against moderate fire exposure], or C [effective
> against light fire exposure] roof covering.
> Exception. The roof coverings set forth in Sections R-803 [composi-
> tion asphalt organic felt shingles], R-808 [built-up roofing], R-809
> [wood shingles], and R-810 [wood shakes] may be used provided the
> building is located in areas designated by law as permitting their use
> [meaning that your property should be located outside the fire district].

As you can see, this section is especially helpful because it tells
you where to find the requirements in the Dwelling Code for some

popular owner-builder roof coverings, such as wood shingles and shakes. You'll also note that the roof coverings mentioned in the exception are only to be used outside a fire district, which means they are only effective against light fire exposure. So be careful with that kind of covering if you have a wood or coal stove to heat your home.

The remaining kinds of roof coverings the Dwelling Code permits are: "Base Sheet Application" (§R-802); "Slate Shingles" (§R-804); "Asbestos Cement Shingles" (§R-805); "Metal" (the ole tin roof; §R-806); and "Tile, Clay, or Concrete Shingles" (§R-807).

All of these sections in Chapter 8 of the Dwelling Code bear an in-depth review by any owner-builder who is not sure of what materials to use for roof coverings. The provisions are very helpful, and cover the requirements of pitch of the roof for the different materials, the need for flashing, how some coverings require a heavier subbase, and more . . . All are important considerations for the owner-builder.

THE BBC This code places the subject of roof coverings in its chapter on "Fireresistive Construction Requirements" (Article 9). Section 903.3 establishes the roof-covering classifications—the same Classes A, B, and C that we saw in the Dwelling Code. There are further roof-covering requirements in §926. Wood shingles and shakes are specifically permitted in §854.8.2 (on the condition that your house is set back more than 12 feet from any other building).

THE NBC. This code covers the subject in §802. Class C coverings (the least restrictive) are allowed on dwellings according to §802.2a(1). There is a separate appendix (G) attached to the NBC that allows wood shingles and shakes, but if the local governmental body has adopted the NBC but not Appendix G, then you wouldn't be permitted to use wood shingles and shakes.

THE SBC. The topic of roof coverings in the SBC is found in §706, which contains the standard A, B, C Class rating we've seen in the other codes. Wood shingles and shakes are permitted on dwellings located outside a fire district (§706.6). You have to look all the way to §1707.9 to discover that "any roof covering permitted in this Code may be applied to dwellings."

THE UBC. This code devotes a whole separate chapter (32) to "Roof Construction and Covering," and the topic is extensively covered, and regulated, here. Sections 3203(c)7 and 8 require that all wood shingles and shakes bear the label of an approved inspection bureau or agency. In other words, only you owner-builders who aren't governed by the UBC may feel free to make your own shingles and shakes, since there is no similar requirement in the other model codes. I don't know why the UBC requires that wood roof coverings must have an inspection stamp; after all, the top of the roof does not support any other part of the house. To me, this is just another example of a regulatory organization not knowing when to stop.

SOME GENERAL COMMENTS. There is no actual list of the different roof coverings in the model codes, as there was in the Dwelling Code. Therefore, if you have a particular material in mind, you will have to check the standards in the back of these codes or inquire of your local building inspector to see if it's acceptable.

And speaking of planning, you should review very carefully the roof covering (and roof construction) provisions of whatever code you're governed by *before* designing your dwelling! How to support the roof and its cover, how to support anticipated snow loads, and how to protect against wind damage are all facts you need to know well before you start building . . . and the codes cover these subjects thoroughly.

CHIMNEYS AND FIREPLACES

Fireplace and chimney construction are proper subjects for a building regulation concerned with fire prevention. All of the codes go into extensive detail on how you can (and indeed, must!) build your fireplace and chimney.

The Dwelling Code devotes an entire separate chapter (9) to this subject. There are twenty-five sections—and detailed diagrams on fireplace foundations—within these pages. Important subjects such as chimney termination above a roof line (§R-904); wall thickness (§R-905); flue lining (§R-906 and §R-907); clearance from wood beams, joists, headers, and studs (§R-913); hearth extension (§R-919 and §920); and factory-built fireplaces (§R-924) . . . all are extensively covered.

The other model codes also devote separate chapters to this subject, and in general cover the same kind of regulations I listed for the Dwelling Code. You'll also note from the chapter titles in these other models that they include related topics—such as vent and duct systems—within their discussions of chimneys and fireplaces (BBC Article 10, "Chimneys, Flues and Vent Pipes"; NBC Article X, "Chimneys, Fireplaces, and Venting Systems"; SBC Chapter VIII, "Appurtenance Requirements"; and UBC Chapter 37, "Masonry or Concrete Chimneys, Fireplaces and Barbecues").

MECHANICAL SYSTEMS

This part of the Dwelling Code deals with the regulation of the different kinds of mechanical systems—such as heating and air-conditioning equipment—that you may place in your home.

The Dwelling Code places all the requirements for this subject in its manual because the authors want to place all the regulations that might be applicable to single-family dwellings in one book. The other model codes, however, don't include mechanical provisions within their own text. These codes have issued separate mechanical codes, just as they issued separate plumbing codes (see Chapter Six of this book).

The provisions in the *One- and Two-Family Dwelling Code* are similar to the mechanical codes of the other model groups—at least, that is, in the way they pertain to single-family residential construction.

The mechanical regulations are contained in Chapters 10, 11, 12, and 13 of the Dwelling Code.

If you are governed by the Dwelling Code, any mechanical system that you decide to heat and/or cool your house with must conform to the safety regulations found in these chapters. (If you design your home to use a *passive* solar-heating system with a wood stove backup, you can ignore a great majority of these mechanical regulations in the Dwelling Code because they just won't apply! If, however, you use an active solar-heating system, with fans and water pumps and other paraphernalia, you will be governed by the mechanical provisions of the Dwelling Code.)

If you are governed by one of the other model building codes (or a code developed locally), you then have to determine if your jurisdiction has also adopted a mechanical code. If it has not, you don't have to follow any mechanical regulations. (Though for safety's sake, you should be aware of these mechanical requirements so you don't burn your house down when you turn on your heat in the winter!)

There is nothing wrong, of course, with conforming to certain safety regulations when installing potentially dangerous heating equipment, and the Dwelling Code and mechanical codes perform a valid function when they insist that you install your heating equipment safely. But a building code oversteps its bounds when it requires you and me to install heating equipment that must produce a certain fixed level of heat.

Section 1411 of the Uniform Building Code does just that:

Every dwelling unit and guest room shall be provided with heating facilities capable of maintaining a room temperature of 70°F. at a point 3 feet above the floor in all habitable rooms.

That little provision has nothing to do with safe construction (the purpose of a building code) and *every*thing to do with making us all conform to a certain social sameness (*not* a valid purpose for a building code).

This provision means that you have to buy, or otherwise obtain, and install a heating system capable of producing a 70°F. creature comfort level. Even if you don't want that much heat. It effectively can preclude the installation of a passive solar/wood heating system— an alternative method of heating that (1) saves fossil fuel and money, (2) makes you less dependent on the big utility companies and large manufacturers, and (3) makes you more independent and self-reliant.

This provision also goes contrary to the new, enlightened energy-conservation attitude that our national leaders are now espousing. Furthermore, this provision goes contrary to the new energy-economy regulations for buildings, where the focus is on making the building more energy efficient. Why *require* a high-output heating system that uses fossil fuels?

In other words, this provision, in the final analysis, is just plain *bad*.

Thank goodness none of the other models make such a requirement! (You may find such a regulation in your local housing code, however.) In any case, check your local building and/or mechanical codes to determine if that provision has been adopted from the UBC. If it has, be prepared to show evidence to support your conclusion that your alternative solar/wood-burning heating system meets the intent of the requirement. Better yet, attempt to get that provision deleted from your local building code! (See how in Chapter Ten.)

9. Code Enforcement, Variances, Appeals

Now that we've covered all of the technical building and construction (and nonconstruction) requirements found in many, if not all, building codes, we're prepared to take a closer look at the administrative sections of the model building codes—and in particular, at the enforcement, variance, and appeals procedures found there.

This chapter is especially important to you as an owner-builder because it pulls together everything we've reviewed so far, and shows you how to use that knowledge to gain the right to build the kind of house *you* want to build. For instance, in this chapter you'll see how you can take advantage of the codes' alternative materials provisions—and the building inspector's right to approve certain methods of construction—to win a building variance. And, perhaps more important, I'll try to how you how to do all this with the building inspector's blessing—which is a much more desirable situation than being on the wrong end of a code-enforcement hearing in the courts.

Sure, you'll probably have to make some compromises. You won't get everything you want . . . but with a little study and effort on your part, I think you'll be surprised at how many of your original ideas can and will be incorporated into your self-built dwelling.

But wait, I'm getting ahead of myself. First, let's review the various methods by which a building code is enforced. Then I'll show you how to avoid many of the bad aspects of these enforcement provisions—and how to take advantage of the good ones—within the context of the variance and appeals procedures that the codes allow.

THE BUILDING PERMIT

In Chapter Two, we reviewed the procedures for obtaining a building permit. Now let's take a look at the role that governmental license plays in the overall code-enforcement process.

The process involved in applying for and obtaining a building permit is, in itself, the initial step in the code-enforcement process. If you live within a code-administered jurisdiction, you simply can't build without a permit (legally, that is), and to get that permit you have to give the building inspector an indication of what you plan to build, either by way of plans and specifications, simple drawings, or a statement. It is at this stage that what you plan to construct is checked out against what the building code you're governed by requires.

The end effect of this step, then, is cut-and-dried: if your plans don't conform to the code, you simply don't get a permit. Enforcement step number one.

Don't think, however, that once you've received your permit your code worries are over. That's not the case! At this point, the building inspector has reviewed only the barest of detail: your application, plans (or statement), and plot plan. And as we'll see (in Appendix B), these plans and specifications can be very sketchy, leaving many technicalities to be filled in during the actual construction of your home. And that's what the building inspector does when he reviews your plans—he makes an assumption that everything not shown on the plans *will* be built to conform to the building code.

Section 115.2 of the BBC reaffirms the tenuousness of the initial building permit: "The permit shall be a license to proceed with the work and shall not be construed as authority to violate, cancel or set aside any provision of this code. . . ."

The UBC, in §302(c), has a similar provision:

> Validity. The issuance or granting of a permit or approval of plans and specifications shall not be construed to be a permit for, or an approval of, any violation of any of the provisions of this Code. No permit presuming to give authority to violate or cancel the provisions of this Code shall be valid, except insofar as the work or use which it authorizes is lawful.
>
> The issuance of a permit based upon plans and specifications shall not prevent the Building Official from thereafter requiring the correction of errors in said plans and specifications or from preventing building operations being carried on thereunder when in violation of this Code or of any other ordinance of the city.

So the actual issuance of your building permit does not get you away from the building department's jurisdiction. The building inspector has to make sure that the house, *as built*, conforms to your approved plans and to the code. He accomplishes this by conducting a series of on-site inspections of your home during its construction.

BUILDING INSPECTIONS

This is step number two in the code-enforcement process.
Once you get your building permit and start to build—and in-

cidentally, you must do so within six months of the issuance of your permit under the BBC §114.2, NBC §102.16, and SBC §105.5, and four months under the UBC §302(d)—the building inspector will visit your building site to make a number of inspections of your work.

The Dwelling Code's §R-111 gives the full details as to what's involved in these inspections and when they occur:

> For on site construction from time to time the Building Official upon notification from the permit holder or his agent shall make or cause to be made any necessary inspections and shall either approve that portion of the construction as completed or shall notify the permit holder or his agent wherein the same fails to comply with this Code.
>
> (a) Foundation and Framing
> 1. Foundation Inspection: Commonly made after poles or piers are set or trenches or basement areas are excavated and forms erected and any required reinforcing steel is in place and prior to the placing of concrete.
> 2. Frame and Masonry Inspection: Commonly made after the roof, masonry, all framing, firestopping, and bracing are in place and all electrical pipes, chimneys, and vents are complete.
> 3. Lath and/or Wallboard Inspection: Commonly made after all lathing and/or wallboard interior is in place, but before any plastering is applied, or before wallboard joints and fasteners are taped and finished.
> (b) Plumbing, Mechanical and Electrical
> 1. Rough Inspection: Commonly made prior to covering or concealment and before fixtures are set.
> (c) Other Inspections
>   In addition to the called inspections above, the Building Department may make or require any other inspections to ascertain compliance with this Code and other laws enforced by the Building Department.
> (d) Final Inspection
> 1. Final Inspection: Commonly made after building is completed and ready for occupancy.
>
> Work shall not be done on any part of the building or structure beyond the point indicated in each successive inspection without first obtaining the written approval of the Building Official. Such written approval shall be given only after an inspection shall have been made of each successive step in the construction as indicated by each of the inspections required above.

The BBC's inspection provisions are found in §111, the NBC's in §103.7, the SBC's in §108, and the UBC's in §304. The BBC's and the NBC's requirements are rather slim in comparison to the Dwelling Code's §R-111. The SBC's and UBC's regulations are rather detailed and lengthy, with UBC §304(b) even requiring the permit holder to maintain a record card on the premises so "as to allow the Building Official conveniently to make the required entries thereon regarding the inspection of the work."

Inspections are the guts of the code-enforcement process. This is when your construction techniques and materials are examined in light of the code requirements to determine whether or not your dwelling complies with your local building regulation.

Of the four inspections the Dwelling Code (and most other codes) minimally require, the most important is the foundation inspection. Why? Because incorrectly designed footings or foundations placed on poor load-bearing soils can cause the rest of your planned structure to tilt, settle, or even come apart.

That's why the foundation inspection takes place after all the forms are set but *before* the concrete is poured. Obviously, any mistakes discovered before the finality of set concrete can be easily corrected, whereas only a sledgehammer will undo mistakes after the concrete has been poured. Remember: The building inspector has the legal power to force you to rip up an improperly laid foundation. As the last paragraph in §R-111 of the Dwelling Code states: "Work shall not be done on any part of the building or structure beyond the point indicated in each successive inspection without first obtaining the written approval of the Building Official."

You'll notice that most of the inspections required by the Dwelling Code take place before the work is covered up. Besides the foundations and footings, the plumbing, mechanical, and electrical inspections are all made prior to wallboards or lath being put into place. So keep that important fact in mind as you build your home! Don't get so carried away with getting your house built that you forget to call the building inspector to make an inspection at each key stop.

Keep in mind too that the inspector doesn't wait by the phone for your call and immediately run right out to your place to make an inspection. He or she will generally take anywhere from one or two days to a week before fitting you into his or her schedule—depending on how many inspections have to be made. So plan accordingly. In other words, don't call for an inspection after you've just completed the work in question. Anticipate when you'll get done and call a week before that time to make sure you get on the building inspector's schedule at a time that fits *your* schedule.

What happens if the building inspector finds a code violation during these inspections? The inspector has a whole arsenal of legal weapons at her or his disposal. As we saw in Chapter Three of this book, the building inspector has the right to stop the work and can force you to remove illegal or unsafe conditions. He or she can also revoke the permit if he or she thinks false or incorrect information was initially used to secure it.

Even more important to remember is the way the building inspector can use that power. I think you can now see, after reading all the technical building requirements that are found in any code, how difficult it is to match the words used in the requirement with the practical construction situations that those words are supposed to control. And the building inspector faces that same difficulty in interpreting the code. So if he or she is in a bad mood (or "doesn't like you"), the building inspector can find a lot of, admittedly minor, things that are wrong. These petty violations won't stop you completely, but they can certainly slow you down.

Remember that it pays to keep all these considerations in mind before and during the various building inspections required by your code.

THE CERTIFICATE OF OCCUPANCY

The Dwelling Code indicates in §R-111(d) that a final inspection must be made "after the building is completed and ready for occupancy." This final inspection is required simply to make sure everything in the house functions as intended by the code, and that the premises are safe. If that's the case, the building inspector then issues a certificate of occupancy. And *that* is your final contact with the building department!

But wait—what if you want to live in your house while it's being built?

The Dwelling Code doesn't cover this subject, but the other codes do. And at first glance these other codes seem to prevent an owner-builder from living in his or her partially completed structure during construction.

As an example, let's look at how §120.1 of the BBC prevents anyone from occupying a building prior to its completion:

> A building or structure hereafter erected shall not be used or occupied in whole or in part until the certificate of use and occupancy shall have been issued by the building official.

All the other codes have similar prohibitions: NBC §103.1, SBC §109.1, and UBC §306(a) (except that the UBC's certificate of occupancy regulations do not apply to Group I occupancies, meaning single-family dwellings).

Nevertheless, this is one time when the model-code groups do provide an alternative that owner-builders can take advantage of:

Each of the model codes provides for a "temporary certificate of occupancy" that permits an owner-builder to live in his or her dwelling while it is being built!

Section 120.5 of the BBC is a good example to quote:

> Temporary occupancy: Upon the request of the holder of a permit, the building official may issue a temporary certificate of occupancy for a building or structure, or part thereof, before the entire work covered by the permit shall have been completed, provided such portion or portions may be occupied safely prior to full completion of the building or structure without endangering life or public welfare.

Certainly, the condition that the partially completed premises be safe is a fair and reasonable one. And all the other models include similar conditions in their respective "temporary occupancy certificate" provisions—NBC §103.2, SBC §109.3, UBC §306(d).

Well, those code-enforcement provisions seemed simple and relatively harmless—if you're willing to bend and conform to the strict, but not always reasonable, letters of the law as embodied in your building code.

But suppose you don't want to change your dwelling—a building that you know is perfectly safe—just to conform to some technical requirement of the code. And suppose you can't convince your building inspector to change his or her mind and approve your unusual structure. What happens if you violate the code and the building inspector wants to throw the book at you?

Are there more serious consequences to code violations than the stop-work order (as serious as that would be)?

You bet there are.

VIOLATIONS AND PENALTIES

The consequences for violating the building regulations are found in the violations and penalties section of each of the codes. And because of the seriousness of the penalties for these code violations, I will discuss each code's sections on this topic in great detail. I cannot overly stress the importance of this discussion; the penalties that might fall upon you for violating the code hang over your head like an enormous sword, and must not be ignored.

THE DWELLING CODE. As an example, let's examine how serious it is to violate the Dwelling Code, the code that concentrates on the construction of a simple home. Section R-106 states:

It shall be unlawful for any person, firm or corporation whether as owner, lessee, sub-lessee or occupant to erect, construct, enlarge, alter, repair, improve, remove, convert, demolish, equip, use, occupy, or maintain any one and two family dwelling in the jurisdiction or cause or permit the same to be done, contrary to or in violation of any of the provisions of this Code.

It is hereby declared that any violation of this Code constitutes a public nuisance, and in addition to any other remedies provided by this Code for its enforcement, the City may bring civil suit to enjoin the violation of any provisions of this Code.

*   *   *

Any person, firm or corporation violating any of the provisions of this Code shall be guilty of a misdemeanor and each such person shall be deemed guilty of a separate offense for each and every day or portion thereof during which any violation of any of the provisions of this Code is committed, continued or permitted, and upon conviction of any such violation such person shall be punishable by a fine, or by imprisonment, or by both such fine and imprisonment as established by local applicable laws.

Yes, you could be subject to both civil *and* criminal penalties for building your own home if that construction does not conform to code standards—even if it's safe! Let me explain.

As the first paragraph of the above quote states, it is unlawful to do just about anything that is contrary to or in violation of any of the provisions of a building code. Just what happens to you if you do violate the code? Paragraphs 2 and 3 of the above quote tell you.

The second paragraph declares that a violation of the Dwelling Code "constitutes a public nuisance" which allows "the City" (meaning the jurisdiction—municipality or county—that adopted this code) to go into the courts of law in a civil suit to enjoin the violations. An injunction is a civil court procedure in which one party attempts to get the court to force another party to do or not to do something. There are generally no penalties involved—except if the enjoined party fails to follow the court's ruling.

To be specific, in the context of a building situation the building inspector or the governing body of the jurisdiction (this code does not say which) can start a lawsuit against you in which s/he or they ask the court to order you to change a nonconforming part of your building to meet code requirements. Of course, the court must find that you have in fact violated the building code before the court will order you to change your structure to conform to the Dwelling Code.

(You will have an opportunity to defend your construction in court, but unless you can prove that your building is code-approved according to the *technical requirements of the code* and not the alternative material provisions, you will not prevail. And since your testimony will be countered by the building inspector [to whom the judge might consciously or unconsciously give the edge], your chances of convincing the judge that you're right are low.)

So far, the situation is not too bad, because even if you're found to be in violation, the remedy is simply to force you to correct the matters in question. But unfortunately, there is more. As stated in the second paragraph of §R-106, the injunction is "in addition to any other remedies provided by this Code for its enforcement," and these other remedies—found in paragraph 3—are the tough ones.

Paragraph 3 states that "Any person, firm or corporation violating any of the provisions of this Code *shall be guilty of a misdemeanor*"— a criminal offense. (The emphasis is, of course, mine.) Yes, to violate a building code makes you a criminal, subject to a fine and/or imprisonment!

(The Dwelling Code does not indicate how long that prison sentence could be; it leaves that determination to each state's criminal statutes in which the length of time for misdemeanor convictions is set forth. Those prison terms are different in each state.)

Worse yet, the Dwelling Code also states that each and every day of a violation is a separate offense. *That* means that if you are in violation for thirty days, you can be charged with thirty *different* misdemeanors. In addition, if you're found guilty of each of those separate misdemeanors, you could get maximum jail terms for each offense—and those terms could be imposed consecutively, meaning that you would serve one before starting the next. In other words, you could end up spending a long time in jail!

You noticed, of course, that I said "could." That's because there is a great deal of flexibility and discretionary power built into the enforcement process, from (1) the building inspector's choice on how many "separate offenses" to charge you with, to (2) the jury's discretion to convict on one, most, or all counts, and (3) the judge's discretion as to whether to impose a prison sentence and whether to make multiple prison terms run concurrently or consecutively.

Now, I'll be the first to admit that building inspectors generally don't bring criminal charges against building-code violators, nor do convicted code violators often spend time in jail. But the language of the violation and penalty provisions of the Dwelling Code (and the other models, as we'll soon see) does permit such consecutive sentences to be handed out. Scary, isn't it?

As a matter of practice the building department will issue you a notice of violation and give you time to remedy the situation, and most code violations are cured at this point. The criminal process is usually the very last resort—and even if criminal charges were brought, you could negotiate to correct the code violation in return for the charges being dropped. (Of course, whether the charges are dropped is within the prosecution's discretion; he or she doesn't have to.)

So as you can see, the "bark" of the language of the penalties and violations section of your building code is worse than the "bite" of actual code-enforcement practice. But still . . . the criminal penalties *are* there and *can* be invoked. Be careful!

THE BBC. The BBC's violation section, §122, puts a little more emphasis on the practical notice and civil method of enforcement than some of the other codes (which solely emphasize the criminal-enforcement procedure). I'll quote the four subparts of this violation section in order that you may see how this model group handles its enforcement:

> 122.1 Notice of violation: The building official shall serve a notice of violation or order on the person responsible for the erection, construction, alteration, extension, repair, removal, demolition, use or occupancy of a building or structure in violation of the provisions of this code . . . and such order shall direct the discontinuance of the illegal action or condition and the abatement of the violation.
>
> 122.2 Prosecution of violation: If the notice of violation is not complied with promptly, the building official shall request the legal counsel of the jurisdiction to institute the appropriate proceeding at law or in equity to restrain, correct or abate such violation or to require the removal or termination of the unlawful use of the building . . .
>
> 122.3 Violation penalties: Any person who shall violate a provision of this code or shall fail to comply with any of the requirements thereof or who shall erect, construct, alter or repair a building or structure in violation of an approved plan or directive of the building official, or of a permit or certificate issued under the provisions of this code, shall be guilty of a [*specify offense*], punishable by a fine of not more than [*amount*], or by imprisonment not exceeding [*number of days*], or both such fine and imprisonment. Each day a violation continues shall be deemed a separate offense.
>
> 122.4 Abatement of violation: The imposition of the penalties herein prescribed shall not preclude the legal officer of the jurisdiction from instituting appropriate action to prevent unlawful construction or to restrain, correct or abate a violation, or to prevent illegal occupancy of a building . . . or to stop an illegal act, conduct, business or use of a building or structure in or about any premises.

(The bracketed material above appears in the original, to be filled in by the town, county, or state adopting the BBC as its own.)

There are several interesting aspects to this provision:

1. The BBC spells out very clearly that the intent of this code is to secure code compliance rather than impose criminal penalties, although, of course, fines and jail terms are a possibility under this code.

2. Criminal violations are not automatically considered misdemeanors. This model allows each jurisdiction to adopt its own maximum fines and jail terms, which are generally much less than the maximum penalties provided under misdemeanor statutes.

3. What §122.4 (quoted above) says in layman's language is that even if you are convicted of a code violation and pay a fine and/or go to jail, you can't retain the code violation in the building. You have to serve your sentence *and* get rid of the code nonconformity. It's not an either/or proposition.

4. Section 122.2 indicates that if the building department's notices go unheeded, the inspector then turns the court action over to the "legal counsel of the jurisdiction"—meaning the city attorney or county counsel—to institute the necessary legal proceedings. This takes the matter out of the hands of the building inspector (with whom you may have developed a serious personality conflict) and puts it into the care of someone who may be somewhat more objective.

THE NBC. This code has one section devoted to violations (§105) and another to penalties (§106):

> 105.1. Notices of Violations. Whenever the building official is satisfied that a building . . . is being erected, constructed, added to or altered, in violation of the provisions or requirements of this Code, or in violation of a detailed statement or plan submitted and approved thereunder, or of a permit or certificate issued thereunder, he shall serve a written notice or order upon the person responsible therefore directing discontinuance of such illegal action and the remedying of the condition that is in violation of the provisions or requirements of this Code.
>
> 105.2. Disregard of Violation Notices. In case a violation notice or order is not properly complied with, the building official shall notify the corporation counsel of such noncompliance, and the corporation counsel upon such notice shall institute an appropriate action or proceeding at law or in equity, to restrain, correct or remove such violation . . . or to require the removal of, or to prevent the occupancy or use of, the building . . . in violation of, or not in compliance with, the provisions of this Code . . .
>
> 105.3. Stopping Work. Whenever in the opinion of the building official, by reason of defective or illegal work in violation of a provision or requirement of this Code . . . he shall order, in writing, all further

work to be stopped and may require suspension of all work until the condition in violation has been corrected.

106.1. Noncompliance. A person who shall violate a provision of this Code or fail to comply therewith or with any of the requirements thereof . . . shall be guilty of a misdemeanor; also the owner of a building or structure, or portion thereof, or of the premises where anything in violation of this Code shall be placed or shall exist, and an architect, engineer, builder, contractor, agent, person or corporation employed in connection therewith and who assisted in the commission of such violations. Each such person shall be deemed guilty of a separate offense for each and every day or portion thereof during which any violation of any provision of this Code is committed or continued and upon conviction of such violation each such person shall be punished within the limits and as provided by State Laws.

106.2. Abatement. The imposition of the penalties herein prescribed shall not preclude the corporation counsel from instituting an appropriate action or proceeding to prevent an unlawful erection, construction . . . or use or to restrain, correct or abate a violation, or to prevent the occupancy of a building or structure or portion thereof, or of the premises, or to prevent an illegal act, conduct, business or use in or about any premises.

The criminal offense here is characterized as a misdemeanor, and leaves the maximum fine and/or penalty to the criminal statutes of each individual state. If you're convicted you'll have a criminal record.

This code also adds a twist to its penalties section that we haven't seen in the other codes. Section 106.1 states how far and to whom criminal responsibility reaches for infractions of the building code. Criminal responsibility applies to "a person who shall violate a provision of this Code . . . also the owner of a building . . . an architect, engineer, builder, contractor, agent, person or corporation." Of course, any or all of those persons must have "assisted in the commission of such violations." But in any case, this is a very good example of the "long arm of the law"!

(The words "corporation counsel" that appear in § 106.2 mean the city or county attorney.)

Please note, however, that the NBC includes a prior notice provision (as does the BBC) and attempts to get code-violation problems solved without resorting to the criminal-prosecution process.

THE SBC. The SBC seems to rely solely on criminal proceedings to enforce its code. Section 114 provides that

Any person, firm, corporation or agent who shall violate a provision of this code, or fail to comply therewith, or with any of the requirements thereof . . . shall be guilty of a misdemeanor. Each such person shall be deemed guilty of a separate offense for each day and every day or portion thereof during which any violation of any of the provisions of this code is committed or continued and upon conviction of any such violation such person shall be punished within the limits and as provided by State Laws.

I'm sure that most of the individual building inspectors who work under the SBC will give you notice of a violation, and attempt to resolve the matter out of court, but it's important to note that there is nothing in the language of this code that guarantees that approach.

THE UBC. This model group devotes a separate chapter (2) to "Organization and Enforcement." Only §205 of Chapter 2, however, deals with violations and penalties provisions:

It shall be unlawful for any person, firm, or corporation to erect, construct, enlarge, alter, repair, move, improve, remove, convert or demolish, equip, use, occupy, or maintain any building or structure in the city, or cause the same to be done, contrary to or in violation of any of the provisions of this Code.

Any person, firm, or corporation violating any of the provisions of this Code shall be deemed guilty of a misdemeanor, and each such person shall be deemed guilty of a separate offense for each and every day or portion thereof during which any violation of any of the provisions of this Code is committed, continued, or permitted, and upon conviction of any such violation such person shall be punishable by a fine of not more than $300 or by imprisonment for not more than 90 days, or by both such fine and imprisonment.

Here there is no civil action for abatement or injunction authorized—only a criminal suit. You would, if convicted, be guilty of a misdemeanor. But the code doesn't leave the length of sentence to your state's general criminal laws. The punishment is fixed in the UBC itself: not more than $300 fine and/or imprisonment for not more than ninety days. There's also the trusty "each day of the violation is a separate offense" provision that we've seen in all the other codes.

GENERAL COMMENTS. Our detailed review of the violations and penalty provisions within the model codes gives you an indication of how serious the penalties for code infractions can be.

Please don't ask me to tell you exactly when a building inspector is likely to invoke the relatively mild enforcement procedures outlined in the first part of this chapter, as opposed to when he or she will institute a criminal action for a code violation. I can't say . . . and neither can anyone else!

The codes themselves don't spell out this discretionary power. There is no one prescribed way for the building inspector to react to a code violation. Actual enforcement of the building code operates in a gray, undefined area between what the codes prescribe and what simple reason, under the circumstances, dictates. How the code is actually enforced between these two extremes depends upon (you guessed it) the personality and temperament of the building inspector. How that person envisions his or her job will dictate how and in what manner the building code by which you're governed will be enforced.

As a final note, if you think that the criminal process is not the correct way to enforce a building code, I want you to know that you're not alone; I couldn't agree with you more. I think it's absurd to use the criminal-justice system to regulate the home-construction field. There are enough civil remedies available that effectively deal with the situation without adding still more weight to the already overburdened criminal-court process.

OWNER-BUILDER REMEDIES: SUE THE BUILDING INSPECTOR?

Now that you know how building codes are enforced from the standpoint of municipal authority, let's take a look at the other side of the coin. Let's see what recourse *you* may have in your struggle to build your dwelling as you see fit.

Suppose, for instance, that your building inspector makes a mistake or illegally harasses you with needless and petty claims of code violations . . . What can *you* do?

Interestingly enough, one measure you *can't* take is to sue your building inspector for damages. Why? Because the writers of the building codes have taken as much care to insulate the building inspector from liability as they have to crack down on code violators.

The BBC's §107.8 is an example of the extent to which the code groups have gone to protect the building inspector:

> The building official, officer or employee charged with the enforcement of this code, while acting for the jurisdiction, shall not thereby render himself liable personally, and he is hereby relieved from all personal liability for any damage that may accrue to persons or property as a result of any act required or permitted in the discharge of his official duties. Any suit instituted against any officer or employee because of an act performed by him in the lawful discharge of his duties and under

the provisions of this code shall be defended by the legal representative of the jurisdiction until the final termination of the proceedings. The building official or any of his subordinates shall not be liable for costs in any action, suit or proceeding that may be instituted in pursuance of the provisions of this code; and any officer of the department of building inspection, acting in good faith and without malice, shall be free from liability for acts performed under any of its provisions or by reason of any act or omission in the performance of his official duties in connection therewith.

And don't think the BBC is alone. Each of the other model codes has similar protective provisions. NBC has §5 of Appendix Q; SBC, §103.7; UBC, §202(g). The Dwelling Code alone has no such provision!

Now let's take a closer look at the language of §107.8 of the BBC and analyze its legal implications so that you'll be able to look for similar subtleties in your own building code:

1. "The building official . . . while acting for the jurisdiction, shall not thereby render himself liable personally . . . for any damage that may accrue to persons or property as a result of any act required or permitted in the discharge of his official duties." That statement, or any similarly worded sentence, pretty much gets the building inspector off the legal hook. No matter what damage the building inspector has wrought upon you (by, for instance, causing unnecessary delays that forced you to pay rent elsewhere, or by forcing you to use more costly materials when less expensive items would have sufficed, etc.), you have no recourse against him or her. So the first thing you should be aware of is that you're not going to get anywhere by threatening a lawsuit against the building inspector.

You might say, "Well, if I can't sue the building inspector for personal liability, nothing prevents me from suing the local government that hired that inspector." Sorry, but there's a concept floating around American jurisprudence called "governmental immunity" that essentially prevents such a course of action. In effect, the widely accepted doctrine of governmental immunity means that you can't, in many cases, sue the government for damages for any of its mistakes, negligence, bureaucratic bungling, or whatever.

The concept of governmental immunity, however, is enforced differently from state to state. And I'm happy to report that it's slowly becoming a thing of the past as court decision after court decision opens more and more doors that allow a private citizen to sue the government.

The best advice I can give you on this subject is to suggest that you investigate the laws of your state very carefully before you spend money on a lawsuit against a building inspector or the government that hired him or her.

Now let's move on to the remaining significant statements in §107.8.

2. "Any suit instituted . . . shall be defended by the legal representative of the jurisdiction . . ." In other words, even if you decide to sue your building inspector (just as a matter of principle) you can expect that lawsuit to be defended by the municipal or county attorney, whose salary—not incidentally—is paid by you, the taxpayer.

3. "The building official . . . shall not be liable for costs . . ." Again, the building inspector is effectively insulated, in this case from even so much as paying court costs.

4. And "any officer of the department of building inspection, acting in good faith and without malice, shall be free from liability for acts performed . . ." This might be the only glimmer of hope in this otherwise oppressive code section—*if* (and this is a very big "if") you can prove the building inspector and/or his or her deputies were not acting in good faith (or acting with malice) in their dealings with you. If you can do so, this clause allows you to bring suit against them. But before you get your hopes up, I want you to know that it's extremely difficult to prove conclusively in a courtroom that someone has acted with malice and not in good faith toward you. Be prepared for a tough fight!

Okay. At least now you know where you stand. You know you can be subject to fines, imprisonment, stop-work orders, delays, and other sundry punishments for violating the code, and you know that the building inspector, personally, is practically immune from legal countermeasures. With that bit of realism in mind, let's now concentrate on the more positive aspects of the issue.

"BENDING" THE CODE

The fact is, in many cases you can avoid the code-enforcement process and/or criminal consequences by taking advantage of administrative provisions—and there are quite a few of them—that allow you to "bend" the seemingly straight line of the code in your favor. Some of the code sections you'll be seeing in the rest of this chapter I've mentioned before, others are new; but here—in one place—is everything you should know about the loopholes built right into nearly every building code.

PRELIMINARY STRATEGY. If you want to take advantage of the loopholes in your building code, you must realize right up front that sooner or later you're going to have to be straight with your building inspector; don't try to "sneak one by." It won't work! If the construction method you intend to use, for instance, doesn't follow the letter of the code—or if you intend to take advantage of a certain ambiguity in your code (as another for-instance)—you have no choice but to tell your building inspector, and go through the unavoidable red tape and delays necessary to get a decision or variance.

You *do* have somewhat of a choice, however, as to exactly *when* you inform the inspector of your intentions. And that option, in effect, is a basic strategic power you can often use to your advantage.

Generally speaking, there are two different times when your building inspector will know—whether you say so or not—that a new building technique or material is being used: either at plan-checking time or during one of the required physical inspections. Some items the building inspector will not discover until a physical inspection. For instance, he or she might not know (because you haven't labeled your plans as such) that you intend to use recycled and ungraded lumber. (Remember, I told you a while back that the building inspector *assumes* all matters not detailed on the plans will be performed according to code.) Other items, such as a new design or construction technique, might very well be revealed at plan-checking time.

There are two distinct advantages in waiting as long as possible in the construction process to tell the building inspector of your unusual construction method or material. One is that many inspectors will be naturally inclined to be a trifle more lenient with their decisions once a building is in progress, as opposed to when a site has just been cleared and nary a nail driven. Also, by nail-driving time you will have had plenty of opportunity to build a good working relationship with your inspector, and should have gained a useful insight into his or her personality and motivations.

Of course, before you decide to delay telling your building inspector of a potential code violation, you should consider the possible negative consequences as well. For instance: How far along will your building be when you *do* inform the officials? If the building inspector (or the board of appeals) fails to go along with your idea, might you have to tear down a great deal of work? If that's the case, forget about using delay tactics and tell your building inspector about the possible violation right away, so you can get a prompt decision. At least then you'll know exactly where you stand. Another negative factor is that a delay (to pursue these administrative remedies) during the construction process is much more upsetting to schedules and temperaments than a delay before the building was started.

If your building code is identical to or based on the NBC or BBC, you may also have the power to change your specific construction plans *during* the building process, and again, the advantage here is that your inspector may be more lenient in considering a departure from the norm when a structure has already been started. The NBC's provision concerning this subject, § 102.5, reads as follows:

> Nothing in this Code shall prohibit the filing of amendments to an application or to a plan or other record accompanying same at any time before the completion of the work for which the permit was issued. Such amendments shall be filed with and be deemed a part of the original application if approved before the certificate of occupancy has been issued, otherwise a new application for the alteration shall be made and a permit secured.

The BBC's § 113.8 is similar; the SBC and UBC have no such provisions.

Of course, the basic strategic powers I've discussed here relate only to the timing of the inevitable. Your choice as to when you inform your inspector of a possible departure to the code may give you an advantage, but it won't get you off the hook. Sooner or later, advantage or no advantage, you're going to have to gain official approval of that code departure, and you're going to have to do it within the guidelines (administrative loopholes) set forth in your particular code.

So now let's take a look at the different code-bending guidelines the model-code groups incorporated into their codes. Even though we'll review these loopholes from the standpoint of the particular code they're in, I would advise you to review *all* these provisions, even if you're not governed by one of these models. Why? Because the provisions and concepts detailed here may have been incorporated into your code no matter what model it's based on, and because these provisions are significant to all owner-builders, no matter what your particular code. (Especially if you intend to do some building-code reform, as suggested in Chapter Ten of this book, you'll want to know the best of the different alternatives available.)

We'll examine the BBC first, simply because it's somewhat unusual in this respect.

THE BBC: MATTERS NOT COVERED. The BBC has a provision that allows the building inspector to determine all matters not covered by the code. The language of this section, § 101.3, reads:

> Any requirement essential for structural, fire or sanitary safety of an existing or proposed building or structure, or essential for the safety of the occupants thereof, and which is not specifically covered by this code, shall be determined by the building official.

Now, the grounds upon which this clause can be invoked are rather limited. But you just might be able to convince the guardian of the code that what you intend to do *is* essential to structural, fire, or sanitary safety and that the matter is not really covered by the code. (Remember my oft-repeated view that it's difficult to match code language with a practical construction situation.)

The other model codes have no such provisions for "matters not covered."

THE BBC: RULE-MAKING AUTHORITY. The BBC has another provision which is helpful to owner-builders that isn't found in the other models. Section 109.1 gives the building inspector the

> power as may be necessary in the interest of public safety, health and general welfare, to adopt and promulgate rules and regulations to interpret and implement the provisions of this code to secure the intent thereof and to designate requirements applicable because of local climatic or other conditions; but such rules shall not have the effect of waiving working stresses or fireresistive requirements specifically provided in this code or violating accepted engineering practice involving public safety.

The ability to adopt rules is a very important power which the BBC has given to the building inspector. As you can see from the wording of §109.1, the building inspector can legally only adopt rules and regulations "to interpret and implement" the provisions of the BBC. He or she can also adopt rules "to designate requirements applicable because of local . . . conditions."

What you have to do is convince your building inspector that what you propose to do is safe but not within one of the many meanings of the language of a specific code section, or that it's unclear whether or not your proposed construction method is sanctioned under the code, or that local conditions are such that a new method (yours, of course!) can be used to achieve the same goals required in a code-approved method. Once you accomplish that (and that's a lot), then you have to persuade him or her to issue an official rule which contains an interpretation (favorable to your position) of the ambiguous code section, or a rule which modifies a code requirement because of local conditions.

The power of the building inspector to adopt rules is a discretionary one. That means there is nothing you can do to force him or her to adopt a rule at all, much less a rule favorable to you. And the procedures that the building inspector must follow to achieve a legally adopted rule are long and involved, as §109.3 points out:

A rule or regulation shall not become effective until four (4) weeks after the intention to adopt such rules shall have been published in accordance with local statutes in an official paper or public newspaper with general circulation in the jurisdiction, and only after a public hearing shall have been held on the rule.

Therefore, if you want to pursue this line of attack, you shouldn't wait until you are actually driving nails. Broach the subject with the building inspector as soon as your plans are sufficiently specific, because if the inspector agrees to adopt a favorable rule, he or she has to publish the proposed rule (and the notice of his or her intention to adopt it), hold a public hearing, and wait the required four weeks after publication of the above-described notice.

This method will be most successful with a sympathetic building inspector, but if a rule favorable to owner-builders is adopted you have achieved a significant reformation of the code, because, as §109.4 of the BBC points out:

All rules adopted by the procedure herein established shall have the same effect as provisions of this code; but such rules may be amended or repealed at any time by the same procedure herein prescribed for their adoption.

If you have a sympathetic building inspector but the building code in effect does not give her or him this rule-making authority, ask him or her to initiate, or join you, in asking the municipal council or county commissioners to amend the building code and incorporate such a provision. (See Chapter Ten of this book for some tips on how to change building codes.)

THE BBC: MODIFICATIONS. The BBC has another extremely important provision of which owner-builders can take advantage. Section 110 is entitled "Modifications," and its provisions come into play when you encounter *practical difficulties in carrying out actual code requirements*.

I'll quote all of §110 so that you can understand the full implications of this provision:

When there are practical difficulties involved in carrying out structural or mechanical provisions of this code or of an approved rule, the building official may vary or modify such provision upon application of the owner or his representative, provided that the spirit and intent of the law shall be observed and public welfare and safety be assured.

The application for modification and the final decision of the building official shall be in writing and shall be officially recorded with the application for the permit in the permanent records of the department of building inspection.

If you have the same or a similar provision in your local building code, consider yourself lucky. To be able to come within the purview of this section, you *don't* have to prove that the building code doesn't cover the topic in question (as in the "Matters Not Covered" section above) or that the code is ambiguous (as for interpretations in the "Rule-Making Authority" section). No, this provision anticipates that you—for one reason or another—may *have* to violate the code, and gives you a way to get around that violation.

The trick to taking advantage of this provision, of course, is in convincing your inspector that practical difficulties would arise if you followed the letter of the code. There are, however, no definitions or examples of what constitute "practical difficulties," so the full range of possibilities is open to you. You are free to suggest anything and everything that you consider a practical difficulty in order to induce the building inspector to modify the technical requirements of the code.

An important "plus" gained from this provision is that the decision whether to modify the technical requirement is left wholly to the building inspector's discretion. There's no committee or board of appeals to convince.

None of the other model codes puts quite as much discretionary power directly into the hands of the building inspector. As we shall see in the "Appeals" section, below, the other codes do provide procedures that allow you to avoid strict adherence to the code, but those procedures often involve either getting the opinion of an expert (which can be expensive), or going through a hearing before a board of appeals (and the appeals procedures involve convincing a lot more people than just the building inspector).

ALL MODEL CODES: ALTERNATE MATERIALS AND METHODS OF CONSTRUCTION. We've already discussed in Chapter Seven of this book each of the model-code sections that outlines the procedure for approval of alternate materials. I refer you to that chapter for a complete and in-depth review; it won't be repeated here.

I will, however, take another look at a typical alternate material provision to see what's involved in getting a different material or method of construction approved. Let's refresh our recollection of such a clause by reviewing §R-108 of the Dwelling Code:

The provisions of this Code are not intended to prevent the use of any material or method of construction not specifically prescribed by this Code, provided any such alternate has been fully approved.

The Building Official may approve any such alternate provided he finds that the proposed design is satisfactory and complies with accepted design criteria.

The Building Official may require that evidence or proof be submitted to substantiate any claims that may be made regarding its use.

Your building inspector may require you to substantiate your claims about a new method or material. In order to do that, you may have to pay an engineer or other expert to get the needed confirmation. So if you're considering applying for approval of an alternate material or method, you'd do well to weigh the time and expense it will take to get a decision, as opposed to the advantages you believe the material or method offers. For instance, if you want to use a noncode-approved material because it is less expensive, but find you'll have to pay an arm and a leg to substantiate your claim that the material is up to standards, you may be better off forgetting the whole issue. It's a matter of deciding what's most important to you.

Of course, if you do decide to go through with the application, and if your alternate is approved, you'll have the satisfaction of building your home more closely to the way you want it built, and you'll have the added pleasure of knowing that you've set a precedent for those who come after you. Because once an alternate material or method has been approved, it remains that way—no one in your code's jurisdiction will have to go through the process again in order to use it. (Building codes *can* be made more responsive to owner-builders' needs, *if* more people take advantage of such provisions!)

ALL MODEL CODES: APPROVED. The mention of the words "may approve" in §R-108 of the Dwelling Code, above, is not the first time we've encountered the concept. Do you remember way back in Chapter Six of this book, when we ran across a provision that required "plumbing fixtures and drainage piping to be connected to a public sewer or an approved private or individual sewage disposal system"?

We wondered then what "approved" meant, and found that the meaning was fixed in the codes, and important! In fact, we found a definition of the word in §R-114 of the Dwelling Code:

Approved refers to approval by the Building Official as the result of investigation and tests conducted by him, or by reason of accepted principles or tests by nationally recognized organizations.

All the other model codes place a similar meaning on the term in each of their respective definition chapters.

What all this means is that whenever the word "approved" appears in any section of a building code, it is not really referring to any one prescribed way of doing something. Rather, it is saying to you that this is a case where the building inspector has discretion to "approve" different solutions to the same problem.

Obviously, this provides a great deal of flexibility in terms of code compliance. It allows you an opportunity to convince the building inspector (again, however, you may need an expert's help) that your method of construction—or whatever you're fighting for—is just as good, or better, than any other "approved" approach.

This does not apply to just a few isolated instances, either. A great many sections in most codes base their "approved" requirements on the building inspector's say-so rather that on a fixed and single way of doing things. And owner-builders can use any section where the word "approved' appears as an opportunity to argue that their way of accomplishing the end result should be permitted. Look for the word "approved" as you read your code—it's a significant signal!

APPEALS

So far in this chapter we've focused on the wide range of matters on which the building inspector has discretion to decide, and the means at your disposal for gaining a favorable decision. The next question is obvious: What can you do when that decision goes against you? Do you have no choice but to conform to the code, or be found in violation—and be subject to penalties and fines?

The answer is an unequivocal no! There is yet another step—the appeals procedure—that all the codes have incorporated in order to give you the opportunity to challenge the decision of the building inspector before a higher tribunal. Sure, such an appeal is time-consuming and sometimes expensive, but at least the right to appeal exists and can be invoked if the need arises.

Before I review all the code-approved appeals procedures, however, let's look at an alternative appeals system that's not set forth in any books, but is nevertheless an accepted method.

I'm referring to situations where there are deputy inspectors in a multiperson building department. More than likely you'll be dealing with a deputy who has considerably less power and authority to make decisions than does his boss, the building inspector. (As we've noticed in all the codes we've reviewed, the right to make modifications, rule changes, or other variances is strictly the domain of the building inspector—not his deputies'.)

If the deputy inspector you're dealing with won't, or can't, bend the code a little in your favor, don't be afraid to take the matter directly to the chief building inspector. You'll often find that the matter can be favorably resolved at that point. If not . . . well, let's examine how to appeal a decision of the building inspector. We'll look at all of the codes' procedures carefully, for there are some subtle differences between them that make for interesting (and useful!) reading.

THE BBC. Section 127 of the BBC contains all the requirements for appeals, the makeup of the board of appeals, and the procedures under which decisions are rendered. I'll analyze this particular code section—and the others too—piece by piece so that you will be able to understand the appeals procedure set forth in *your* building code.

The most important stipulation you need to know about any appeals procedure is the *grounds* upon which that appeal can legitimately be brought. Section 127.1 outlines the grounds for appeal under the BBC:

> The owner of a building or structure or any other person may appeal from a decision of the building official refusing to grant a modification to the provisions of this code covering the manner of construction or materials to be used in the erection, alteration or repair of a building or structure to the board of appeals. Application for appeal may be made when it is claimed that: the true intent of this code or the rules legally adopted thereunder have been incorrectly interpreted, the provisions of this code do not fully apply, or an equally good or better form of construction can be used.

A quick glance at the first sentence gives you the impression that an appeal under the BBC is limited to the sole situation where you're appealing a refusal to grant a code modification. (A modification under the BBC, as you may remember from a few pages back, is the situation where you directly violate the code but where you can show practical difficulties in trying to follow the code and ask the building inspector to modify the technical code requirements.)

But the last sentence of §127.1 expands the grounds upon which you can appeal all the way from the situation when (1) the building inspector incorrectly interprets the code, to when (2) you claim that the code doesn't apply at all, to when (3) you contend *that an equally good or better form of construction can be used.* I can't emphasize that latter ground for appeal strongly enough. It's tailor-made for creative owner-builders who want to do things their way.

In any case, always structure any application you make under the BBC (or a code similar to it) to fit the grounds the code recognizes for a legitimate appeal.

Also, never be afraid to use your right to appeal. You won't get the building inspector mad at you, and even if you do, you have to place first things first—that house of yours should come before your inspector's feelings. As we learned in Chapter Three, a building inspector is generally somewhat conservative and reluctant to make waves. Many times, he welcomes the chance to be taken off the hook by having the board of appeals rather than himself grant you a code modification.

The next important item you need to consider is the kinds of people before whom you'll present your case. So let's see what the BBC requires concerning the backgrounds of the five members of a board of appeals. Section 127.2.2 states that

> Each member shall be a licensed professional engineer or architect, or a builder or superintendent of building construction, with at least ten (10) years experience, for five (5) years of which he shall have been in responsible charge of work; and there shall not be more than two (2) members of the board selected from the same profession or business; and at least one (1) of the professional engineers shall be a licensed structural or civil engineer of architectural engineering experience.

Chances are, the individuals who fit these requirements will make for a rather conservative, status quo group. So if you appear before such a board, you'd better be prepared with hard facts and figures and be ready to substantiate any and all of your contentions.

Here is a list of essential items to look for in the appeals portion of your building code: (1) the time limit within which you must appeal from the building inspector's decision (the BBC sets no such limit); (2) the quorum required to hear an appeal (five, under §127.4.3 of the BBC); and (3) the number of members who must agree on a decision (three, in §127.5.1).

Now, exactly *how* to initiate a hearing and the ground rules for that hearing are generally covered by the rules and regulations adopted by each local board of appeals. So your first step will be to obtain those rules and regulations and study them carefully. The following is a general guideline to the hearing procedure; you will, of course, have to stay within the dictates of your own particular rules if they're different.

There usually are appeal forms which you have to fill out, serve a copy or two on the building inspector, and file with the board of appeals. The board will set a hearing date and give all parties notice of that date.

The board's rules and regulations might also tell you how the hearing will be conducted—in other words, who presents evidence first, the order of witnesses, etc. These hearings are generally not conducted as a court of law; strict rules of evidence are not followed and the hearings are informal. In most cases you don't need a lawyer to argue for you (some even say an attorney jeopardizes your chances of success), but you should make up your own mind on that issue.

Be prepared to present the best kind of evidence possible, including expert testimony from engineers and architects, if possible. Don't mount an attack against the building inspector personally. The only issue is whether you should be granted a code modification (or whatever ground you appealed on) and all the evidence you present should refer directly to that issue.

Another hint: Make sure a court reporter is taking down all the testimony at the hearing. Sometimes the rules and regulations provide that the board shall supply a court reporter; in other cases you might have to bear the expense yourself. But it's worth it because it lets the board of appeals know that you are serious about your claim and that you might appeal a negative decision to a higher court.

For, the BBC, in §127.6, tells you that if you don't like the decision of the board of appeals, you can always go to a court of law. (I'd like to see a code try to say that you can't appeal to a court of law!) The catch is that this section limits your appeal to a court strictly to correct any errors of law. This means that you can't get another hearing on the facts, nor will you have an opportunity to present new evidence; you can only claim that the local board of appeals applied the law incorrectly to the facts presented to it. (That's why you have a court stenographer present. You want the testimony transcribed accurately and fully.) Let me quote from §127.6 in an effort to show you more clearly how limited the right of appeal is under the BBC:

> Any person aggrieved by a decision of the board of appeals, whether or not a private party to the decision, or any officer or official board of the jurisdiction, may apply to the appropriate court for a writ of certiorari to correct errors of laws in such decisions. Application for review shall be made to the proper court of jurisdiction within fifteen (15) days after the filing of the board's decision in the office of the building official.

Though the codes can't constitutionally prohibit you from seeking a review of a decision of the board of appeals in a court, they certainly do try to limit that right as much as they can. (Maybe someone will successfully challenge the right of a building code to limit the jurisdiction of a court of law.)

152   BUILDING REGULATIONS

THE NBC. Let's see what the NBC requires on the points we've just discussed. The grounds for appeal are put in short, simple, and very broad terms. Section 107.6a states that

> Any person aggrieved or the head of any agency of the municipality may take an appeal to the Board of Appeal from any decision of the building inspector.

Now, that's about as liberal as any of the codes get. Under the NBC, you can appeal any decision of the building inspector. But §107.6.b requires you to make that appeal within thirty days of the date of the decision. (If you file an appeal beyond the time limit stipulated in the code, the board could well throw out your claim on the procedural grounds that you applied too late. So take those time periods seriously.)

The NBC is not so concerned about stacking the board with conservative members of the building establishment as is the BBC. The only condition the NBC requires—in §107.1—is that the five members be "qualified by experience and training to pass upon matters pertaining to building construction"—which might allow people with a broader outlook to sit on the board.

A quorum, according to NBC §107.3, is four members, with three concurring votes needed to reach a decision.

The board of appeal's power to modify this code under §107.7 is broad:

> The Board of Appeal, when so appealed to and after a public hearing, may vary the application of any provision of this Code to any particular case when, in its opinion, the enforcement thereof would do manifest injustice, and would be contrary to the spirit and progress of this Code or public interest, or when in its opinion, the interpretation of the building official should be modified or reversed.

And last but not least, this code also states—in §107.9—that a person aggrieved by a decision of the board (notice that this is not as broad as the BBC, which gives just about anyone—even people not personally involved in a case—the right to appeal) has fifteen days to appeal to a court of law "to correct errors in law in such decisions."

THE SBC. This code calls the body to whom you appeal the "Board of Adjustments and Appeals." The members of this board (five members to "be composed of one Architect, one General Contractor or Engineer and three Members at large from the building industry"), their term in office, quorum requirements (three), records, and procedure are all set forth in §111.

The grounds for an appeal are set forth in §112.1(a):

> Whenever the Building Official shall reject or refuse to approve the mode or manner of construction proposed to be followed or materials to be used in the erection or alteration of a building or structure, or when it is claimed that the provisions of this code do not apply, or that an equally good or more desirable form of construction can be employed in any specific case, or when it is claimed that the true intent and meaning of this code or any of the regulations thereunder have been misconstrued or wrongly interpreted, the owner of such building or structure, or his duly authorized agent, may appeal from the decision of the Building Official to the Board of Adjustments and Appeals. Notice of appeal shall be in writing and filed within ninety (90) days after the decision is rendered by the Building Official. A fee of $10.00 shall accompany such notice of appeal.

These grounds are fairly broad and include the one most favorable to owner-builders: that an equally good or more desirable form of construction can be employed. The stipulated time limit within which to appeal a decision—ninety days—is certainly long enough. But do note that a fee of $10 must accompany the notice of appeal.

Under the SBC, the grounds upon which the Board of Adjustments and Appeals can base its decision are found in §113.1(a):

> The Board of Adjustments and Appeals, when so appealed to and after a hearing, may vary the application of any provision of this code to any particular case when, in its opinion, the enforcement thereof would do manifest injustice, and would be contrary to the spirit and purpose of this code or public interest, or when, in its opinion, the interpretation of the Building Official should be modified or reversed.

This code is refreshingly silent on the right to appeal to a court of law from the decision of the Board of Adjustments and Appeals. This doesn't mean that you don't have the right to go to a court of law— you certainly do. What is refreshing is that there is no attempt to limit that appeal to questions of law.

THE UBC. And then there's the UBC!

This code tends to be the most technical and restrictive of all the models, and it certainly exhibits that quality on the subject of appeals. Why do I say this? Because this code does not provide the mechanism for you to appeal a decision of the building inspector!

Sure, §204 is entitled "Board of Appeals," but that's the last of the similarities, because the board's jurisdiction is only "to determine the suitability of alternate materials and methods of construction and to provide for reasonable interpretations of the provisions of this code. . . ."

That's it. No right to appeal a decision of the building inspector—except directly to the civil courts! That's expensive, time-consuming, and probably not worth the effort unless you have a very vital matter to be resolved. The power of the building inspector in such an appeal-free situation can be truly stifling to creative owner-builders unfortunate enough to live in a UBC-dominated jurisdiction.

I think you can see now why major attacks against building regulations originated in California—the state that virtually makes the UBC mandatory for all its citizens. (It's also the state where some significant changes for owner-builders are taking place, as we shall see in the next chapter.)

SOME CONCLUDING COMMENTS

I still can't give you *the* definitive answer to the question we asked partway through this chapter: When is the criminal process used against code violators and when are the civil remedies involved? But I think you now have enough insight into the enforcement proceedings as a whole to understand that there are much time and many things you can do between the detection of a code violation and the bringing of a lawsuit—either criminal or civil.

You can either tell the building inspector about your new material or method of construction at plan-checking time or at some stage in actual construction; you can ask him or her to grant you a code modification; and—if he or she doesn't decide in your favor—you can take the matter to the board of appeals.

Even if an undisclosed departure from the code is detected during a construction inspection, you still have time to ask the inspector for a modification, receive his decision, and—if it's adverse—appeal to the board of appeals *and not be in violation of the criminal provisions of the code and subject to suit.*

It is *only* after the board of appeals has rendered a decision against you and you've exhausted all other appeals procedures and still refuse to conform that you'll be in violation.

And one more comment. Remember the time limitations within which you must appeal from a decision of the building inspector? Well, if you fail to appeal within that time, you could then be subject to code-violation charges too.

My best advice? Plan ahead. Anticipate code violations. Time your disclosure of that potential violation to your advantage, if you wish. But in any case, be prepared to stop work at the time the violation comes to light, and be ready to expeditiously pursue any and all administrative remedies. That will keep the building inspector from charging you with a code violation!

10. How to Change Your Building Code

You've plowed through a lot of material to get to this point! I know it hasn't been easy, for the very nature of building codes—even when put into everyday language as I've attempted to do here—often makes for dry and tedious reading. I do hope, though, that you've found at least some of the information new and interesting and—most important—useful.

You see, I've tried to do more here than just show you how building codes are organized and list what's in them. I've tried to give you a working knowledge of the subject, by reviewing single-family dwelling construction requirements from the point of view of the owner-builder, and by criticizing those regulations and provisions that I and many others feel don't allow owner-builders the freedom to choose low-cost, ecological, and/or nonconventional materials and designs for their shelters.

This chapter builds on that criticism, and concentrates on how to change (not abolish) the codes to give owner-builders more freedom of choice. But some of you may be thinking even now: "Okay. I've read to this point and you still haven't convinced me. I don't want to change the building codes because—despite their drawbacks—they really do ensure safely constructed homes . . . And that's of paramount importance."

Well, let's take another look. Before we find out *how* to change the building codes, let's find out *why!*

WHY CHANGE THE BUILDING CODES?

Yes, the basic purpose of any building code—safety—is completely valid. The code groups themselves rightfully emphasize this point in the "purpose" sections of their respective manuals. Section 102 of the UBC is a good example:

> The purpose of the Code is to provide minimum standards to safeguard life or limb, health, property, and public welfare by regulating

and controlling the design, construction, quality of materials, use and occupancy, location and maintenance of all buildings and structures within the city and certain equipment specifically regulated herein.

The NBC's §100.2 and the SBC's preface state similarly lofty objectives. These objectives are particularly valid in a society that has become so specialized and departmentalized that few of us truly provide for our own food, clothing, or shelter anymore. Instead, we depend upon a relative handful of others to produce the things we need—and concentrate on making money so that we can buy those necessities. In this kind of consumer-oriented—rather than provide-for-yourself—society, building codes play an important role.

Building codes protect the housing consumer from unscrupulous, slipshod, or just plain lousy builders. Obviously, if you're buying an already constructed, mass-produced subdivision home—and putting out hard-earned dollars for it—you want to be sure that the plumbing, for instance, really is hooked up behind those shiny chrome faucets, that there are substantial supporting studs behind the paper-thin paneling, that the furnace will produce heat, that the stairs leading up to the bedrooms won't collapse, that the toilets are hooked up to a functioning sanitary disposal system, and so on and so forth. Building regulations and the inspection system we examined in the previous chapter help to ensure that the homes we buy are safe, livable, and conducive to good health.

Building codes protect us in another important way too. They regulate the construction of our supermarkets, libraries, movie theaters, stores, business offices—all the structures that we use (and therefore entrust our lives to) daily. And I, for one, wouldn't want it any other way. Building codes really are necessary and vital to our well-being.

But, on the other hand, what of the individuals, friends, or families who want to be more involved with their own lives, who are weary of this buy-and-sell society and want to build their own self-designed shelters? What of the homesteaders, the suburbanites, the city dwellers who want to use their own resources and the materials they have at hand to live self-reliant rather than dollar-reliant lives? These people are not asking anything unreasonable; they simply want to be able to live in houses they designed and built themselves. And they want the freedom to use their own ideas to accomplish that end.

And that's where the rub comes in. As we have seen, existing building codes don't allow the full range of alternatives; they don't take into account the fact that different ways exist of accomplishing similar ends without sacrificing safety. The code groups have solidi-

fied construction regulations into a rigid mold and, as we discussed in
Chapter Nine, they have perpetuated that rigidity by making it time-
consuming, expensive, and otherwise downright difficult to make
changes, modifications, or appeals to the codes.

Building regulations have also gone way beyond their original
purpose of safety and are now used to accomplish ends that were not
initially contemplated. (See Chapter One of this book.) Furthermore,
they have helped to increase the cost of a single-family dwelling to
the point where it is today impossible for many low- and even mod-
erate-income families to purchase a home.

The book *The Owner-Builder and the Code* documents this
costly aspect of building codes:

> Why would a house which is built to code cost hundreds and even
> thousand of dollars more? In the 1920s, Secretary of Commerce Her-
> bert Hoover, advised Congress that 10% of all building costs—from
> foundation to roof—would be saved by eliminating conflicting, out-
> dated elements of building codes. In more recent years, the National
> Commission on Urban Problems raised this estimate to be a saving of
> 15% on all building costs for home builders. The Commission lists
> many "excessive code requirements" which, in 1969, added $1,838 to
> the cost of a $12,000 house of 1,000 square feet. Some of these impor-
> tant items are listed below:

FREQUENT CODE REQUIREMENTS AND THEIR COSTS

1. Foundations dug to clay when piers and grade beam would do as well.	$150
2. Extra number and sizing of joists.	63
3. 2x4 studs supporting outside walls 16″ o.c. when 24″ o.c. entirely adequate.	125
4. Extra sheathing.	125
5. Separate siding and sheathing instead of single ⅜″ panel.	330
6. Double framed 2x4s for window and door openings although single 2x4s considered sufficient.	40
7. Each door and window must have own header when continuous double 2x6 atop outside wall is better.	45
8. Extra door and window headers.	20
9. Extra fire wall requirements in frame construction.	50
10. Interior walls 4″ thick even though 2″ walls safe when non-load bearing.	310
11. Subfloor must be ¾″ instead of ½″ plywood.	500

12. Double 2x4 plate on all wall partitions where single member sufficient.   30

13. Trusses on 16" centers where 24" sufficient.   100

14. Masonry chimney when Class B flue would do a better job.   150

15. Extra electric over National Electric Code when rigid conduit required.   300

16. Metal conduit required for wiring when Romex (non-metallic sheathed cable) just as good.   200

17. All electrical wiring to be accomplished by a licensed electrician.   100

18. All plumbing, drainage, waste and vent size must be 2" minimum.   30

19. Install lead pan under all shower bases regardless of type instead of other means of water protection.   50

20. Central cold air return cannot be used in heating. Each room must have its own air return to furnace.   85

Not included in the Commission report were alternative building methods and materials which, if permitted, would provide even greater savings. Builders may save $300, for example, on the cost of a $30,000 construction if they are not required to form the foundation footing with wood. A simple trench footing performs satisfactorily and provides equivalent strength. A survey by the National Association of Home Builders of 1,200 communities indicates that the code prohibits half of them from using a concrete post and grade beam foundation. Using a 2-inch, non-bearing partition wall saves $400 in an average-size house, but code requires *all* walls to be 4-inches thick.

Rex Roberts in *Your Engineered House* lists what he considers is wrong with building codes:

> The basic purpose of a building code for single-family residential areas is to prevent the erection of structures which give offense to the eye. This is a difficult proposition to write into law. Most residential building codes begin with such innocent injunctions as staying back seventy-five feet from the street, and using some kind of exterior covering other than tar paper, both aimed at avoidance of visual nuisance.
>
> It is when building codes start trying to tell you how to build your house that they themselves become nuisances. Their intentions are excellent: sanitary safety, fire safety, structural safety, all aimed at keeping you from pinching the wrong penny, getting into trouble, and becoming a nuisance to the community. The trouble with these stipulations is, many of them don't work.

They don't work because it is almost as difficult to codify safety as it is to codify aesthetics. For example, if the sanitary rule specifies fifty feet between well and septic tank, and is measured in horizontal feet, what became of the vertical distance? How can you define water purification in terms of feet without specifying the type of leach? How can you know what is going on down there, anyway? The only possible way to be sure your citizens are drinking pure water is to specify that each well be tested twice a year. I have never yet read any such code.

Fire-safety codes don't agree with each other. Some mention fire-retarding walls but say nothing about the roof. Some specify that outside doors be of solid wood, but allow hollow core doors on the inside. If the fire code were seriously concerned with personal safety, it would prohibit sleeping upstairs.

Structural safety rules attempt to control the thickness of earth-retaining walls, without mention of reinforcing and without examining the horizontal load. They specify wall stud spacing without reference to the weight being held. They insist on fir but prohibit spruce, or vice versa.

And I'm sure you can add your own particular criticism of building codes, now that you've made the thorough review of your own building code which this book more or less forced you through.

Builders who construct homes that they themselves intend to live in should be treated differently from contractors who mass-produce homes for others to live in. Even the founder (Rudolf Miller) of the Building Officials and Code Administrators of America (the authors of the BBC), stated the very same concern way back in 1915:

> The building laws should provide only for such requirements with respect to building construction and closely related matters as are absolutely necessary for the protection of persons who have no voice in the manner of construction or the arrangement of buildings with which they involuntarily come in contact. Thus, when buildings are comparatively small, are far apart, and their use is limited to the owners and builders of them, so that, in case of failure of any kind that are not a source of danger to others, no necessity for building restriction would exist.

It is with this spirit and in this context that I call for a change in—not abolition of—building codes in favor of owner-builders.

THE KIND OF CHANGE

I'm not, however, advocating any one particular kind of change. You personally might be interested in amending the sanitation provisions of your code, while another group might concentrate on a different section.

I will, on the other hand, give you a few examples of building-code reform that have developed in California. There, a group of owner-builders, under the name United Stand, were confronted with a state-mandated building code based almost entirely on the UBC—in many respects the most restrictive model code of all. (The UBC is the code that requires a building permit for all construction, even repairs; requires high permit fees; fails to provide civil remedies for code violations; has no board to which to appeal decisions of the building inspector; and contains many other restrictive provisions.)

The confrontation between the California building hierarchy and United Stand is producing some very beneficial results for owner-builders in that state, and is important to owner-builders everywhere. I want to pass some of this information on to you so that you can analyze your own situation and observe some of the various ways and means open to you for establishing and accomplishing your own objectives.

River, in her book *Dwelling*, records an interesting and productive department-owner/builder meeting. It contains some extremely helpful information and deserves close scrutiny:

A few weeks ago, after a picnic at the beach, our family went to a meeting called by the red tag committee. The purpose of the meeting was to further communication between the officials charged with this task and the community whose homes are in question. We found ourselves in a crowded school auditorium, surrounded by friends and neighbors, and facing the committee. One of our county supervisors chaired the meeting; he began by stating that it was the desire of the committee to hear the needs and wishes of the people. Mr. Adams, representing the District Attorney's Office, stated that the committee (called BLUR: Buildings Land Use Review) was trying to determine just how far they could go in making broad changes in a law mandated by the State (in California, each county is required to adopt the building code, but the county can also make changes that have to do with local conditions). The Attorney General's Office is currently working to discover what changes can be made, and what can be called "a local factor." Here, the big question is, can a change be based on such a factor as economics? In an area plagued by a continuing severe housing shortage and a very high unemployment rate, consideration of such a factor seems at least logical.

Following this brief introduction and statement of good faith from the Attorney General's office, the floor was opened to the community. We were asked to address ourselves to the following questions: should the Building Code be changed, and why? What followed was as heartening an exchange of ideas, proposals, reactions and considerations as ever I've heard at a public gathering. I came away somewhat stunned and extremely pleased to be part of a community that is learning to be respectful and considerate enough to create a climate of clear communication.

The following is a small sampling of some of the statements made that evening.

Jim: The issue is really bigger. It's not merely whether a code book which we've got our heads buried into should be obeyed or not, it's whether the world situation of scarcity of materials should be looked into in this case.

Carol: I'm working for a governmental agency, the only one in the county currently working with problems of housing. . . . The vacancy rate in this county is 1%, which is just impossible. The state vacancy rate is 4.2%. The rate that is considered acceptable is 10%. We need houses and there's no housing. I was talking to a man, a representative of a Mexican-American organization, and he wanted to know what we were going to do about housing for *his* people, who don't speak English, and don't get to the Board of Supervisors, who are working on crops, and I asked him, "if you could build a house that would be legal for $1–2,000, would you do it?" He got so excited, and said, "That *would* be the answer!" And that *is* the answer.

John: Would it be possible, for those who want to build according to the code, to have some way to, say, register the house at the county seat, if they follow the code. And if they don't follow the code they'd not be able to register the house, and therefore if the time came that they wanted to sell it, the person buying it would know that there's no registry and therefore they're taking a chance, and, "buyer beware." Has this been considered?

Philip: I would like to see a change in materials. I like to make my own beams, and I think they're just as good as the ones you can buy at the store. Also I would like to make earth blocks, which would be a very cheap method of construction for the people around here.

One person who spoke, a lawyer from a tiny inland town, having listened to most of the proposals, summarized for us the basic changes he thought should be implemented. These included approval of the following:

a. Alternative human waste disposal systems such as compost privies ("in fact, after this meeting, I'd like to ban flush toilets and septic tanks").

b. Use of recycled materials (used wood, etc.) and use of home-made wood products—posts, beams, slabs, shakes, etc.

c. Relaxation of foundation requirements.

d. Plastic pipe for plumbing.

In addition, he suggested that:

a. In developing building classifications, the following factors be considered: economics, geography, density, access to water, soil conditions, proximity to neighbors, etc.

b. There be no legal impediment to registering of noncode dwellings with title to protect a second buyer who would then know if house was built to code or not.

    c. Whatever changes were made, there still be room for variances for local or individual circumstances and

    d. Review procedures by inspectors should be liberalized and red tape eliminated, as well as insuring that adequate notice be given homeowners of building inspection visits.

On a more general level, he suggested that the committee recognize that the building code is subsidiary to the Constitution, which provides in effect that each person should be free to utilize and develop his property consistent with public health and safety, and that the purpose of the codes is to protect the health and safety of the community to the extent that alternate means of building do not interfere with the health or safety of neighbors.

The impetus for change did not stop at a meeting or two, either. With the backing of Governor Jerry Brown, the fight for code reform in California reached the state administrative level. Here the debate, the give-and-take of the political process, has resulted in a proposed (and significant) amendment to the state building code.

I quote this proposal in full for your review:

Special Guidelines for Dwellings in Rural Areas

152. Purpose. Health and Safety Code Section 17958.5 permits a city or county to determine that changes or modifications in the State's building requirements are appropriate because of local conditions. Health and Safety Code Section 17925 confers similar authority on local appeals boards. The Commission of Housing and Community Development hereby finds and declares that in deciding whether to make such determinations regarding dwellings in rural areas, such local bodies may consider the following local conditions, among others: the general development of the area (including low housing density which minimizes dangers to the health and safety of occupants of neighboring dwellings), the availability of electricity and water in the area, the need for low-cost housing in the area, and the need to maximize freedom of choice by owner-builders in order to encourage the development of new techniques in energy conservation and aesthetic design. It is the intent of the Commission to reserve to such local bodies the authority and discretion to make such determinations or choose not to do so.

In the event that such a determination is made by the local body, it may designate the area or areas in its jurisdiction which it deems to be rural. It is the intent of the Commission to reserve to such local bodies that authority to designate as rural such portion or portions of their jurisdictions as they, in their discretion, deem appropriate, and that such designation shall not affect other local zoning categories and requirements unless the local body so specifies.

In the event that such a determination is made by the local body, it shall then adopt regulations which protect the public health and safety in such rural areas. In order to further uniformity of such regulations throughout the state, the Commission hereby recommends that the following proposed regulations be adopted, by such local bodies, to apply in rural areas. Modification of some of these proposed regulations may be appropriate in some cities and counties, such as where enforcement of a certain regulation would normally be performed by an official other than the one specified in the regulation.

It is also the intent of the Commission that these recommended regulations serve as guidelines for local building officials in exercising their discretion under Health and Safety Code Section 17951, Subsection (b), Uniform Building Code Section 106, Uniform Mechanical Code Section 105, Uniform Plumbing Code Section 201, and National Electrical Code Section 90-4, in approving alternate building methods and materials in areas of low population density.

It is the intent of the Commission to review the impact and operation of this Article six months after its enactment.

*   *   *

154. Recommended Regulations. (a) Purpose. The purpose of these regulations is to provide minimum requirements for the construction of owner-built dwellings and appurtenant structures in rural areas, to protect the public health and safety, while allowing for maximum flexibility as to design and materials employed.

(b) Structures and Activities Affected. These regulations shall apply only to construction, enlargement, conversion and alteration of owner-built dwellings and appurtenant structures. "Owner built" shall mean not more than two stories in height and constructed by the property owner(s) or their agent(s) and not intended for sale, lease, or rent. For purposes of this section, sale, lease, or renting within one year of the date of occupancy is presumptive evidence that a structure was erected for the purpose of such sale, lease, or renting.

Except as otherwise indicated in these regulations, dwellings and appurtenant structures constructed under these regulations need not comply with construction requirements contained in the latest applicable editions of the Uniform Building, Plumbing, or Mechanical Codes or Article Four of Chapter One, Subchapter One, of Title 25 of the California Administrative Code.

All structures affected by these regulations which constitute a hazard to health or safety may be declared to be a public nuisance and shall be abated by repair, rehabilitation, or removal in accordance with Health and Safety Code Sections 17980–17990 and Sections 124 through 148 of Chapter One, Subchapter One, of Title 25 of the California Administrative Code.

(c) Sanitation Requirements.

(1) Sanitation facilities approved by a local health official shall be provided to the dwelling site, but need not be provided within the dwelling unit.

(2) A water closet need not be provided when an alternate system for disposal of sewage wastes is provided and has been approved by a local health official.

(3) A bathtub or shower and a lavatory (or other bathing and washing facilities approved by a local health official) shall be provided to the dwelling site.

(4) Potable water shall be available to the dwelling site, although such water need not be pressurized nor treated. Where water is not piped from a well, spring, cistern or other source, there shall be a minimum of fifty (50) gallons of potable water available.

(5) A system for the disposal of greywater which has been approved by a local health official shall be provided for the dwellsite. "Greywater" means the waste water from the dwelling site (exclusive of toilet wastes), such as water from a laundry, bath, shower, or sink.

(d) Structural Requirements.

(1) Each structure shall be constructed in a safe and sound condition, to protect the health and safety of the occupants, including protection from fire and from vertical and lateral forces to which the structure may be subjected.

(2) Footings and Foundations. Pier foundations, pressure treated lumber, or equivalent materials may be used, provided that the bearing is sufficient for the purpose intended. If steel poles are used, they shall be protected as required by the building official. Footings and foundations may be of field stone, provided the stone is clean, not decomposed or spalling, and set in standard mortar. Where the foundation is not reinforced, the minimum footing width shall not be less than twelve inches and the overall unsupported height of footing and foundation shall not exceed 24 inches, and load on such foundation and footing shall not exceed 600 pounds per lineal foot of exterior wall for single story dwellings. When foundations support structures over one story in height, they shall be sufficient to support the entire structure.

(3) Lumber. Salvaged lumber or owner-produced new lumber may be used, unless found by the building official to contain dry rot, excessive splitting or other defects obviously rendering the material unfit as lumber or not of sufficient strength or durability to perform the function intended.

(4) Shingles and Shakes. Owner-produced wood shingles and shakes may be used unless found by the building official not to be of sufficient quality or durability to perform the function intended.

(e) Mechanical Requirements. Fireplaces and heating and cooking appliances shall be installed and vented in accordance with the requirements of the latest edition of the Uniform Mechanical Code and Chapter 37 of the Uniform Building Code, except that an alternate method of venting shall be allowed if substantially equivalent in safety, and compliance with this section shall be verified only at an inspection allowable by Subsection (h) of this section.

(f) Electrical Requirements. Electrification and wiring therefore shall not be required, and where electrical usage is confined to one room of a structure, the remainder of the structure need not be wired. However, where electrical wiring or appliances are installed, they shall be installed in accordance with the National Electrical Code, except that compliance with this section shall be verified only at an inspection allowable under Subsection (h) of this section.

(g) Room Dimension Requirements. No habitable room shall be less than seven feet in any dimension nor less than 70 square feet in area.

(h) Permits, Inspections, and Fees.

(1) Permits. The building official shall grant a permit for the construction of a dwelling or appurtenant structure where the permit application shows construction methods that do not violate the requirements of these regulations. No permit shall be required for small or unimportant work or alteration or repair which does not endanger health or safety. Permit applications shall contain the following information: (1) name and mailing address of the applicant, (2) address and location of the proposed structure(s), (3) a basic description of the structure(s), including type of heater and/or stove installation, with all clearances and venting procedures described, (4) a plot plan indicating the location of the dwelling in relation to property lines, other structures, sanitation and bathing facilities, water resources, and water ways, (5) a permit for installation of sanitary facilities from the local health official.

(2) Inspections. To determine compliance with these regulations, only a final inspection of the structure(s) shall be conducted after the structure(s) is completed and ready for occupancy, except in unusual circumstances which require additional inspections. A foundation inspection shall be conducted only where the permit application and review indicate that footings are subject to serious lateral movement. A frame inspection shall be conducted only where the permit application and review indicate that wallboards, plaster, or other covering will conceal under-lying construction. This subsection shall not be construed to limit inspections made after completion of construction and commencement of occupancy to ensure compliance with code requirements concerning proper maintenance of dwellings and sanitary facilities.

(3) Fees. Permit and inspection fee for schedules covered by these regulations shall be adjusted to reflect savings resulting from the application of this section.

I think you'll agree with me that this proposal touches upon many, if not most, of the problems we've reviewed in this book. If you're really into launching a major assault toward changing your code, you certainly have enough ammunition from all these sources to map out a hard-hitting campaign.

There are, of course, more limited solutions to building-code reform. You might advocate the change of just a specific section rather than the whole code (as was done in California). Your own local politics will dictate how broad a change you should, and can, realistically seek. The California experience is set out here only as an example of what you can accomplish!

CHANGING A LOCAL BUILDING CODE

There are many levels on which true building-code reform can take place. Accomplishments at the local—municipal or county—level sometimes go unnoticed or unrecognized as the significant changes they represent. In fact, we just mentioned a very significant kind of code reform in the last half of Chapter Nine, whereby every time an owner-builder achieves a modification in the building code, or succeeds in getting a favorable rule adopted, or gets an alternate material or method of construction approved, the local building code has been reformed!

Unfortunately there will be times when you can't get the building inspector's or the board of appeal's approval for a significant owner-builder code change. You then have to go to the next step, and that is to ask the municipal or county governing body (the same group which adopted the building code in the first place) to *amend* the code.

The process you must engage in to achieve code reformation is a political one. Don't ever forget that fact. That means you have to exert the same kind of pressure that any special-interest group would have to exert in order to achieve the desired result.

Here's a brief—yes, even simplistic—general outline of some necessary steps. The exact procedure, of course, will vary from municipality to municipality.

First, you'll have to seek out a "friendly" councilperson or county commissioner to present the amendment before the whole governing body. (United Stand, for instance, might never have gotten as far in the reform of the California building code if Governor Brown hadn't taken a personal interest in the problem.)

The proposed amendment will then have to be sent to the building committee for debate and review. I'm sure the local building inspector's opinion will be sought, so if you've cultivated him or her properly, you might get a favorable recommendation. The amendment will then be presented to the full voting members of the local or county governing body, and will be voted upon.

All during this process, however, it's important that you and your fellow owner-builders try to educate *everyone* as to the issues involved, including, but not limited to, the issue of individual freedom versus government control. You will also have to be completely prepared to back up all of your proposals and claims with facts, figures, logic, and examples.

How well you have (1) analyzed your local political situation, (2) organized your group, (3) cultivated the "right" political person *and* the building inspector, (4) educated the governing body in particular and the public in general, and (5) backed up your position with substantiating facts . . . all these will determine the outcome of code reform in your community.

It's not easy, but it's well worth the struggle!

CHANGING A STATE BUILDING CODE

Before you attempt to change a state building code, you will have to analyze the kind of state code that's now on the books. And believe me, there is a bewildering array of various kinds of state-adopted codes:

1. A state building code may be mandatory throughout the state and prohibit the local government from making any amendments to that code.

2. A state building code may be mandatory throughout the state but allow local governments to make amendments that are as or more restrictive than state requirements.

3. A state building code may be mandatory throughout the state but allow local governments to make any amendments to the state code—even amendments that are less restrictive.

4. A state building code may be permissive and give the local governments the option to adopt the state code, adopt another building code, or not adopt any code at all. (I have compiled, in Appendix C, a list of the building regulations in effect in each state of the union, including—among other things—whether a state which has a statewide building code makes that code mandatory [with or without local amendments] or permissive.)

In those states that have state building codes like those described in numbers (3) and (4) above, you can proceed to amend at the local level, as described in the section on "Changing a Local Building Code," above.

Or you can proceed (as the United Stand group did in California) to get the state administrative agency that is entrusted with code writing to adopt a statement of "Special Guidelines" to help local governments focus their attentions on the unique needs of owner-builders.

Now, you may have noticed that I mentioned getting a "state administrative agency"—rather than the legislature—to adopt a statewide building code. That's right. If you want to change a mandatory state code that allows no local amendments (or only local amendments that are as restrictive as the state code), you don't bring your fight to the state legislature. A statewide building code is not adopted by the state legislature. What generally happens is that the state legislature will pass a bill which declares that a state building code *should* be adopted, and will then appoint a committee or one of the administrative agencies of state government to make a study, conduct hearings, and finally adopt a building code.

So, if you want to achieve code reform at the state level, you must take your case to the state administrative agency entrusted with adopting the building codes. (Appendix C also lists the names and addresses of the state agencies responsible for building-code review in a statewide building-code jurisdiction.)

The process of code reform at this level is different from the politics involved at the local level. A state administrative agency is more impersonal and its members are not subject to the vote of the people. Yet politics—of a different sort—*is* involved. Find out about the makeup of your state agency and how to go about getting matters considered before it. Maybe a call to a friendly yet influential state senator or representative will get the ball rolling. Or maybe a petition directly to the agency is best. You'll simply have to investigate the method that will give you the best results.

A code-amendment hearing before a state administrative agency will be a formal hearing. You'll really have to support your contentions for code reform in favor of owner-builders substantially, because state agencies generally have a whole host of engineers, architects, and other experts who will review your proposals. The agency will, of course, look upon your proposed amendment with more favor if an important state government figure (such as Governor Brown, in California's case) comes out in favor of building-code reform for owner-builders.

The process is difficult and your group may not achieve satisfactory results on the first try, but if you keep the pressure on, favorable amendments may come to pass—so stick with it!

CHANGING A MODEL BUILDING CODE

Let me reemphasize a few comments I made about the model codes in Chapter One. These codes are only models; they carry no legal effect unless and until a municipality, county, or state adopts them. But quite a few of those governmental entities have adopted a model building code as their own, almost word for word, without significant amendment. Thus, if a model building code is amended in favor of owner-builders at the national level, these changes will automatically be incorporated into many state and local codes. If more alternatives and more special guidelines for owner-builders appear in a model code, then more owner-builders would be benefited countrywide.

But just as reforming a model code would bring the greatest benefit to owner-builders, achieving that reform is probably the most difficult.

Sure, each of the model-code groups sets forth an elaborate process by which amendments may be suggested, studied, reviewed, debated, and acted upon in yearly meetings, but it is the makeup of the voting members of these model-code groups that presents the problems. *Building inspectors themselves are the voting members!*

Just look (again) at the titles of the model groups and I think you'll see what I mean. Building Officials and Code Administrators (for BBC), International Conference of Building Officials (for UBC), Southern Building Code Congress International (for SBC), and the voting membership of these groups live up to their names. The NBC is developed by the American Insurance Association and is the only model-code group not directly made up of building inspectors.

The BBC has eleven different classes of membership, from Active Membership (restricted to governmental units that administer and enforce building codes) and Individual Active Membership (a qualified employee of a governmental unit that is not as a body a member), to Industry Members, Commercial, Professional, and Technical membership (all four associated in some way with the building business). It is, however, only the Active and Individual Active members who have a vote—which means that it's only building inspectors who vote on code reform. The other models have similar membership breakdowns.

But even though the reform of a model code in favor of the do-it-yourselfer might be difficult, let me tell you how the Southern Building Code Congress International conducts its code-amending program, as an example of how the process works.

Suggestions for code changes are submitted in writing to the Southern Building Code Congress. Article VIII of the Constitution of the Southern Building Congress does not state whether the proposed changes must come from members. I do know from my review of the actual changes suggested that both voting and nonvoting building associations, industry, commercial, and professional members do submit proposals. If you can't directly submit a proposed amendment to a model-code group, ask a sympathetic member to submit the proposal for you.

Each proposal is published in the June/July issue of *Southern Building,* the official magazine of the congress. The section to be amended, the proponent of the proposal, the wording of the proposal, and the reason for the suggestions are all set forth.

Here's an example of a proposed change to §105 of the SBC as contained in the June/July 1975 *Southern Building:*

ITEM NO. 3—SECTION 105—APPLICATION FOR PERMITS

PROPONENT: B. Glenn Hatfield, Chief, Inspections and Code Enforcement Division, Columbus, Georgia

Delete Section 105.1, paragraph (b) in its entirety and add the following in lieu thereof:

A general permit shall be accompanied by specifications and drawings and indicate the total scope of the work to be done. A separate permit shall be required for any installations, alterations, repairs, replacements, maintenance or relocation performed within the scope and under the regulations of the plumbing code, the gas code, the electrical code, the mechanical code, and the elevator code.

A separate permit shall also be required to demolish or move a building, and to construct or erect a sign of any description.

REASON: Most of the Building Inspection Departments today require separate permits for the sub-contractors who are responsible for that scope covered by regulations separate from the building code. Each of the standard codes requires that the responsible contractor secure a permit and pay a permit fee to perform the work covered in the scope of the particular standard code (plumbing, gas, mechanical, etc.).

Section 105.1, paragraph (b) is now in conflict with the Standard Gas and Standard Mechanical Codes which require a separate permit for work done within the scope and under the requirements of these codes.

Then the Building Code Revision Committee (there's a separate revision committee for the Gas, Mechanical, Plumbing, and Fire Preventive Codes) of the congress "shall schedule an open meeting of such length as is required to receive comments from interested persons." The Building Code Revision Committee then recommends to the membership one of the following actions on each proposed code change: Approval, Approval As Revised, Disapproval, or Further Study.

This report is then published in the October/November issue of the congress's magazine. To follow through on the amendment known as item No. 3 quoted above, here is the recommendation of the Building Code Revision Committee on the proposed change:

ITEM NO. 3—SECTION 105—APPLICATION FOR PERMITS

PROPONENT: B. Glenn Hatfield, Chief, Inspections and Code Enforcement Division, Columbus, Georgia

As proposed: See June/July Magazine.

COMMITTEE RECOMMENDATION: DISAPPROVAL

REASON: Adequately covered by present code text and such specific requirements should be left to the local authority having jurisdiction.

Then the congress has an annual research conference at which each of the revision committees holds open public (meaning you and I could attend) hearings on the proposed code changes, "at which time every member of the Congress, active and associate, shall have full right of the floor" (meaning you and I, as lay persons, can't be heard!).

This annual research conference then votes on the revision committee's recommendations. The recommendations that are approved are then mailed to all active members for a ballot vote. So active membership has the final say.

To continue the history of the proposal change to Section 105 (Item No. 3), Application for Permits, the proposal was not accepted; the code revision committee's recommendation was upheld.

In fact, from my review of the score sheet, each and every proposed change that the code revision committee recommended was adopted and each change the committee disapproved was not passed. And the margin of victory was significant also. Out of a total of 354 ballots cast, the closest vote of approval for a proposed change was 326 for, 21 against, and 7 abstentions.

I think it is evident that in the Southern Building Code Congress, the code revision committee has enormous influence. That is where the fight will have to be waged for significant owner-builder amendments. But what also is evident is that only 354 members vote on code amendments. Not a very wide cross section when you consider the enormity of the consequences. What this suggests is that a mail campaign to the voting members (you can get their names from the director of each model-code group) would not be too expensive to accomplish!

All of the model codes have annual reviews and revisions of their respective building codes, similar in most respects to the method used for the Southern Building Code Congress. If your group plans to wage a campaign in any of the model-code groups for owner-builder reform, you'll have to get the constitution, by-laws, rules, and regulations for the model-code group and follow the procedures outlined there.

I've left many gaps concerning the process of changing a building code on the local, state, or national level. That's because I can't possibly cover every individual procedure you might face; they vary greatly on all levels. Instead, I've tried to give you an idea of how the process works in general, and suggested at least one way you might start your own code-reform program.

A FEDERAL CODE?

There is, at present, no federal building code applicable throughout the United States. But that doesn't mean that such a code won't be a reality sometime in the future, for talk about a federal building code has been an on-again, off-again proposition. We should be aware, therefore, of the implications that such a code presents and be ready to have the voice of owner-builders heard on the issues involved.

The main thrust of the proponents for a federal code is that one code throughout the country would allow the manufacturers of buildings and building products to conform to one code and not to the multitudinous building regulations that now exist on every level of government throughout this country. A single federal code, the argument continues, will allow for more streamlined production of building products and result in lower cost to the housing consumer.

But from the point of view of the owner-builder, a federal building code would be a disaster.

First, it would create another bureaucratic maze through which you would have to find your way in order to build your own house.

Second, I would hate to imagine the process owner-builders would have to go through to amend that all-pervasive code, or achieve local exceptions to its countrywide application. If there's anything we've learned from our review of the procedure to amend the local, state, and national building codes, it's that the farther you get from the local level, the more difficult it is to achieve true code reform.

Could you see an owner-builder trekking to Washington to propose an amendment to a federal building code, which amendment seeks major concessions for owner-builders? I can't

So fight a national building code tooth and nail. Make sure that owner-builders' opinions and concerns are properly voiced. Because even if the weight of owner-builder opinion is not enough to stop the adoption of a federal building code, it may be enough to achieve a significant owner-builder exemption built right into the code in the first place. Am I dreaming pie-in-the-sky? Maybe.

Whether or not a federal building code will ever come to be, at all, remains to be seen. And if it does come to be, the exact wording of that code, and how it handles the needs of owner-builders, also remains to be seen. The outcome, to a large extent, rests upon the shoulders of each individual citizen—you and me and millions of others like us.

In fact, that's one of the reasons why I've enjoyed writing this book so much. I've never had to worry about writing an ending. I've done everything I can to give you all the ammunition you need to build your own home exactly as you see fit . . . or to change your local or state codes in your favor . . . or even to pave the way for a national code that looks kindly upon owner-builders.

I've given you the beginning and middle of a story, complete with characters both good and bad—and suggested a plot line or two. But now it's up to you to write that final chapter for yourself. Use this book, and I think the final scene will find you and your family living in a safe, comfortable home of your own design and construction— happily ever after.

A Sample Application for a Building Permit

Following is a typical application for a building permit. You will, in all likelihood, not encounter exactly the same application form where *you* intend to build.

I've filled in the form as if the house shown in Appendix B were being built. (This application is not, however, the one used in the town of Watche Fall, New York.) Even though applications for building permits are different—and sometimes longer—in different localities, there are a few points you can pick up from a study of how this application has been filled in.

Note how you can make reference to attached plans and specifications and save yourself redrawing the same information on the application form itself. You can also reference the attached plans when you are asked to describe the length and width of an irregularly shaped house in two small spaces.

Also don't be afraid to use "N/A," the initials used when a question is not applicable to your project. And since one application form is used for many construction permits, many questions just don't apply to you. Note, near the top of the form, the listing of the different kinds of permits you can apply for on this one application.

With regard to cost of the work and the amount of the building permit fee, please see my comments on pages 27 to 29 of this book. The cost figures used on the application are purely conjecture. I didn't go out and attempt to price the cost of materials to build this particular home.

APPLICATION FOR PERMITS

June 10   , 19 78

Type of Permit: New, Addition, Repairs, Reroof, Moving, Sign, Demolition, Other. (Specify)

1. **LOCATION:**
   Street_____3040 Mill Rush Rd., Watche Fall, N.Y. 12440_____ First Fire District___N/A___ Zone___N/A___

2. **TYPE AND COST:** Single-family residential
   Use of Property_____ Occupancy Class_____ Residence

   Estimated Cost:

		Cost	Permit Fee
Building (Contr. Name)	Mr. & Mrs. Michael Sadowy	$ 10,000	$ (Based on
Electrical (Contr. Name) " " " "		$ 1,500	$ ordinance)
Plumbing (Contr. Name) " " " "		$ 2,000	$
Heating (Contr. Name) " " " "		$ 2,000	$
Other (Contr. Name)		$	$
TOTAL COST		$	$

3. **CHARACTERISTICS OF BUILDING:** Irregular; see attached
   Size of Building: Width___40'___ Depth___20'___ plans Area Appr. 1700 Sq. Ft.
   Height___2___Story; Type of Construction___Post and beam___ Type Heat___Oil fires___ No. of Rooms___6___
   No. of Living Units___1___ No. of Parking Spaces___N/A___ No. of Baths___1½___ No. of Bedrooms___2___

4. **IDENTIFICATION:**   Address
   Owner___Mr. & Mrs. Michael Sadowy, 3040 Mill Rush Rd., Watche Fall,N.Y. 976-5432___Tel. No.
   Contractor___Same as owner___
   City License No.___N/A___ State License No.___N/A___
   Architect___Walter B. Melvin___

5. **PLOT PLAN**
   Draw plot plan accurately. Show dimensions of lot and locate buildings by dimensions from property lines.
   Show dimensions of all buildings, or attached; Plans___Attached___ Const. Details___Attached___

   SEE ATTACHED PLOT PLAN

Area of Lot___94,675 Sq. Ft.___ Corner Lot: Yes_____ No___X___
REMARKS_____

IF PERMIT IS GRANTED___we___AGREE TO CONFORM TO ALL CITY ORDINANCES AND THE LAWS OF THE STATE OF (your
state) REGULATING SUCH WORK AND THE SPECIFICATIONS OR PLANS SUBMITTED ___I___HEREBY SWEAR THAT
THE FOREGOING STATEMENTS ARE ACCURATE AND CORRECT TO THE BEST OF MY UNDERSTANDING AND KNOWLEDGE.
Signature of Applicant_S/ Michael Sadowy___ Address 25 Maple St.___ Tel. No.976-5432

FOR OFFICE USE ONLY

Refused By_____ Date_____ Reason_____
Approved By_____ Date_____ Permit No._____
APPLICANT'S COPY

A Sample Set of Building Plans

The plans that follow have been drawn by Walter B. Melvin, an architect in New York City (who also does work in the more rural areas of the state). I specifically told him to prepare a set of plans that are as detailed as possible for a building permit application and which show a rather complicated house. (Two-story construction is not easy for an owner-builder.) If your local building inspector does not require all these details, you don't have to worry. If he or she does, you then at least have a guide here.

Though you may not want to tackle a two-story house, if you do, these plans will give you an insight into the construction problems you might face. The plans depict a two-story single-family dwelling using post-and-beam construction.

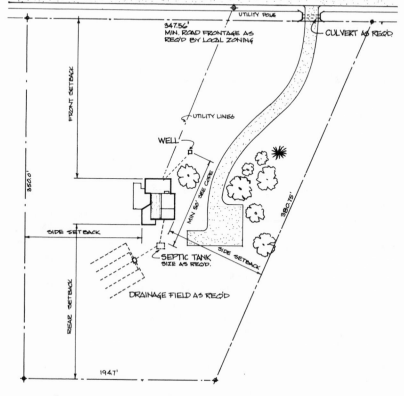

← PAVED ROADWAY →

UTILITY POLE

347.56'
MIN. ROAD FRONTAGE AS REQ'D BY LOCAL ZONING

CULVERT AS REQ'D

FRONT SETBACK

UTILITY LINES

WELL

350.0'

MIN. 50' SEE CODE

380.75'

SIDE SETBACK

SIDE SETBACK

SEPTIC TANK
SIZE AS REQ'D.

REAR SETBACK

DRAINAGE FIELD AS REQ'D

194.7'

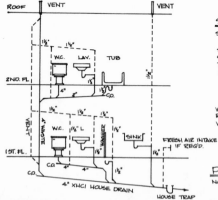

ROOF   VENT   VENT

1½"   1½"
W.C.   LAV.   TUB

2ND. FL.
4"   2"   C.O.   1½"

VENT

1½"   1½"   1½"
W.C.   1½" L   WASHER   SINK   FRESH AIR INTAKE IF REQ'D.

1ST. FL.
C.O.
4"   4"   1½"   1½"

C.O.

4" XHCI HOUSE DRAIN   HOUSE TRAP

SITE PLAN

SCALE : 1" = 20'-0"

SEPTIC TANK & DRAINAGE FIELD DETAILS ARE OFTEN REQUIRED. DETAILS OF APPROVED TYPES ARE AVAILABLE FROM LOCAL OR STATE AGENCIES OR LOCAL SUPPLIERS.

WATER SUPPLY DIAGRAM IS NOT USUALLY REQUIRED.
VENTING REQUIREMENTS VARY

PLUMBING DIAGRAM

NOT TO SCALE

REGISTERED ARCHITECT
WALTER BASIL MELVIN JR.
10297
UNIVERSITY OF THE STATE OF NEW YORK

drawing title

N

RESIDENCE for MR. & MRS. MICHAEL SADOWY
3040 MILL RUSH ROAD
WATCHE FALL, NEW YORK 12440

1

site plan
plumbing

date

walter b. melvin, architect
94 mac dougal street new york, n.y.

scale
1" = 80'-0"

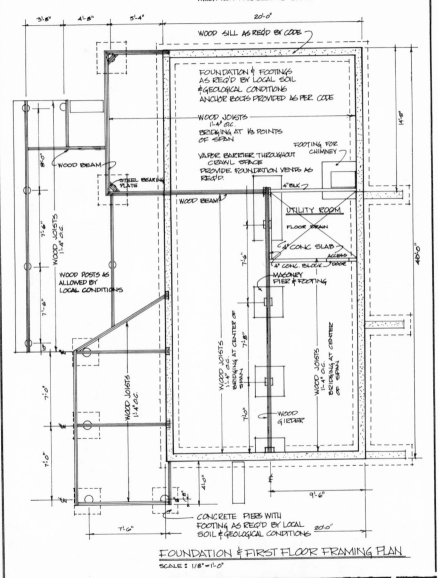

PROVIDE TERMITE PROTECTION AS REQUIRED BY CODE

WOOD POSTS, BEAMS & JOISTS TO BE SIZED ACCORDING TO
LOCAL CODE, LOADING & SPECIES GRADE REQUIREMENTS

PROVIDE DOUBLE JOISTS UNDER ALL PARTITIONS
WHICH RUN PARALLEL TO JOISTS.

WOOD SILL AS REQ'D BY CODE

FOUNDATION & FOOTINGS
AS REQ'D BY LOCAL SOIL
& GEOLOGICAL CONDITIONS
ANCHOR BOLTS PROVIDED AS PER CODE

WOOD JOISTS
1'-4" O.C.
BRIDGING AT 1/3 POINTS
OF SPAN

VAPOR BARRIER THROUGHOUT
CRAWL SPACE
PROVIDE FOUNDATION VENTS AS
REQ'D.

FOOTING FOR
CHIMNEY

WOOD BEAM

STEEL BEARING
PLATE

WOOD BEAM

4" BLK

UTILITY ROOM

FLOOR DRAIN

4" CONC SLAB

ACCESS

4" CONC. BLOCK   DOOR

MASONRY
PIER & FOOTING

WOOD JOISTS
1'-4" O.C.

WOOD POSTS AS
ALLOWED BY
LOCAL CONDITIONS

WOOD JOISTS
1'-4" O.C.

WOOD JOISTS
1'-4" O.C.
BRIDGING AT CENTER OF
SPAN

WOOD JOISTS
1'-4" O.C.
BRIDGING AT CENTER
OF SPAN

WOOD
GIRDER

CONCRETE PIERS WITH
FOOTING AS REQ'D BY LOCAL
SOIL & GEOLOGICAL CONDITIONS

3'-8"   4'-8"   5'-4"   20'-0"   14'-8"

8'-0"   7'-6"   7'-6"   7'-0"   7'-0"   7'-6"

40'-0"

7'-6"   4'-0"   9'-6"   20'-0"

7'-8"   7'-0"

FOUNDATION & FIRST FLOOR FRAMING PLAN
SCALE: 1/8" = 1'-0"

drawing title

foundation

date

N

RESIDENCE for MR. & MRS. MICHAEL SADOMY
3040 MILL RUSH ROAD
WATCHE FALL, NEW YORK 12440

walter b. melvin, architect
94 mac dougal street new york, n.y.

2

scale
1" = 8'-0"

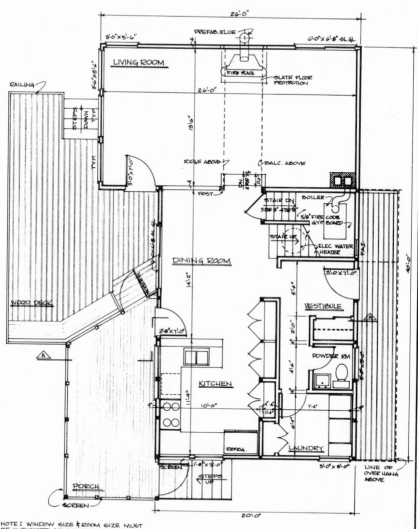

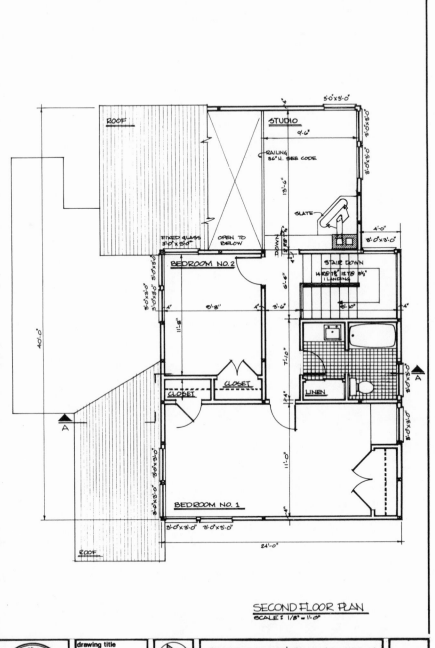

NOTE : BEAM SIZES ARE DEPENDENT UPON
LOCAL WIND & SNOW LOADING CONDITIONS AS
WELL AS LOCAL CODE REQUIREMENTS FOR
LIVE LOADS, AND SPECIES/GRADE OF LUMBER
USED. CONSULT WITH A QUALIFIED PROFESSIONAL
FOR SPECIFIC STRUCTURAL DESIGN.

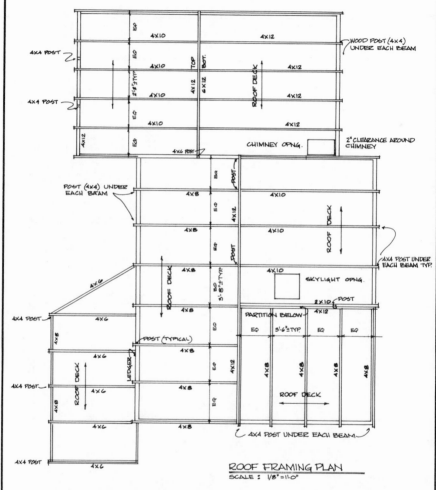

ROOF FRAMING PLAN
SCALE : 1/8" = 1'-0"

NOTE : IF FRAMING PLANS ARE REQUIRED BY
LOCAL INSPECTOR, ALL FLOORS AS WELL AS
ROOF MUST BE INDICATED. IF THE BUILDING
IS A SIMPLE SHAPE, A BUILDING SECTION
WILL OFTEN MEET THE REQUIREMENT.

ROOF DECK TO BE EXPOSED
AT UNDERSIDE - INSULATION TO
BE APPLIED ABOVE DECK.

drawing title		RESIDENCE for MR. & MRS. MICHAEL SADOWY	5
		3040 MILL RUSH ROAD	
		WATCHE FALL, NEW YORK 12440	
date		walter b. melvin, architect	scale
roof framing		94 mac dougal street new york, n.y.	1" = 8'-0"

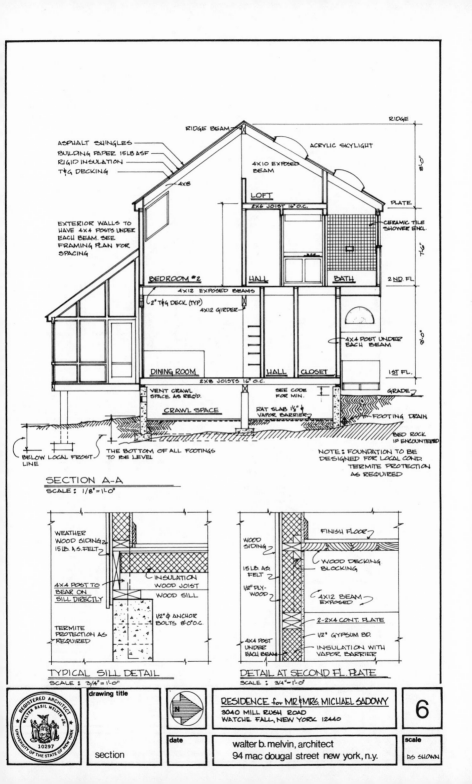

RIDGE BEAM

RIDGE

ACRYLIC SKYLIGHT

8'-0"

ASPHALT SHINGLES
BUILDING PAPER 15 LB ASF
RIGID INSULATION
T&G DECKING

4x10 EXPOSED BEAM

4x8

PLATE

LOFT
2x6 JOIST 16" O.C.

CERAMIC TILE
SHOWER ENCL.

7'-6"

EXTERIOR WALLS TO
HAVE 4x4 POSTS UNDER
EACH BEAM. SEE
FRAMING PLAN FOR
SPACING

BEDROOM #2   HALL   BATH

2 ND. FL.

4x12 EXPOSED BEAMS
2" T&G DECK (TYP)
4x12 GIRDER

4x4 POST UNDER
EACH BEAM

8'-0"

DINING ROOM   HALL   CLOSET

1ST. FL.

2x8 JOISTS 16" O.C.

VENT CRAWL
SPACE AS REQ'D.

SEE CODE
FOR MIN.

GRADE

CRAWL SPACE

RAT SLAB 1½" &
VAPOR BARRIER

FOOTING DRAIN

BED ROCK
IF ENCOUNTERED

BELOW LOCAL FROST
LINE

THE BOTTOM OF ALL FOOTINGS
TO BE LEVEL

NOTE: FOUNDATION TO BE
DESIGNED FOR LOCAL COND.
TERMITE PROTECTION
AS REQUIRED

SECTION A-A
SCALE : 1/8"=1'-0"

WEATHER
WOOD SIDING
15 LB. A.S. FELT

INSULATION
WOOD JOIST
WOOD SILL

4x4 POST TO
BEAR ON
SILL DIRECTLY

½"∅ ANCHOR
BOLTS 8'-0"O.C.

TERMITE
PROTECTION AS
REQUIRED

TYPICAL SILL DETAIL
SCALE : 3/4"=1'-0"

WOOD
SIDING

15 LB AS
FELT

½" PLY-
WOOD

4x4 POST
UNDER
EACH BEAM

FINISH FLOOR

WOOD DECKING
BLOCKING

4X12 BEAM
EXPOSED

2-2X4 CONT. PLATE

½" GYPSUM BD.

INSULATION WITH
VAPOR BARRIER

DETAIL AT SECOND FL. PLATE
SCALE : 3/4"=1'-0"

drawing title

RESIDENCE for MR. & MRS. MICHAEL SADOWY
3040 MILL RUSH ROAD
WATCHE FALL, NEW YORK 12440

6

section

date

walter b. melvin, architect
94 mac dougal street new york, n.y.

scale
AS SHOWN

REGISTERED ARCHITECT
WALTER BASIL MELVIN JR.
10297
UNIVERSITY OF THE STATE OF NEW YORK

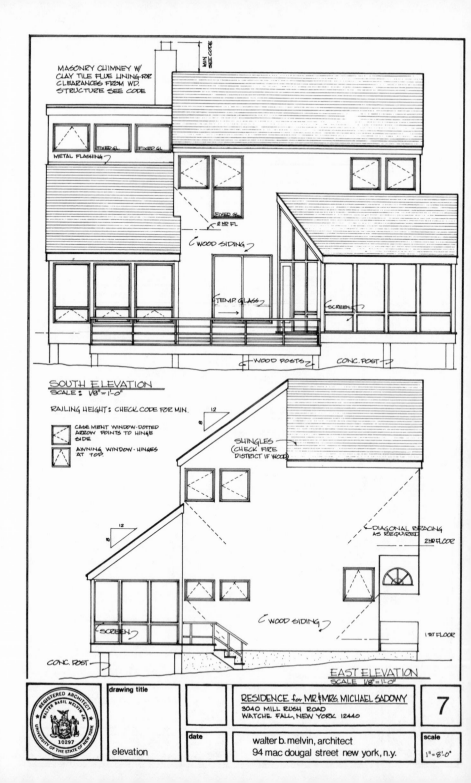

MASONRY CHIMNEY W/
CLAY TILE FLUE LINING-FOR
CLEARANCES FROM WD.
STRUCTURE SEE CODE

MIN
SEE CODE

METAL FLASHING

FIXED GL.   FIXED GL.

2 ND FL

WOOD SIDING

TEMP. GLASS

SCREEN

WOOD POSTS   CONC. POST

SOUTH ELEVATION
SCALE: 1/8"=1'-0"

RAILING HEIGHT: CHECK CODE FOR MIN.

CASEMENT WINDOW-DOTTED
ARROW POINTS TO HINGE
SIDE

AWNING WINDOW-HINGES
AT TOP.

12
8

SHINGLES
(CHECK FIRE
DISTRICT IF WOOD

12
8

DIAGONAL BRACING
AS REQUIRED
2ND FLOOR

WOOD SIDING

SCREEN

1 ST FLOOR

CONC. POST

EAST ELEVATION
SCALE 1/8"=1'-0"

drawing title		RESIDENCE for MR. & MRS. MICHAEL SADOWY	7
		3040 MILL RUSH ROAD	
		WATCHE FALL, NEW YORK 12440	
date		walter b. melvin, architect	scale
elevation		94 mac dougal street new york, n.y.	1"=8'-0"

REGISTERED ARCHITECT
WALTER BASIL MELVIN JR.
UNIVERSITY OF THE STATE OF NEW YORK
10297

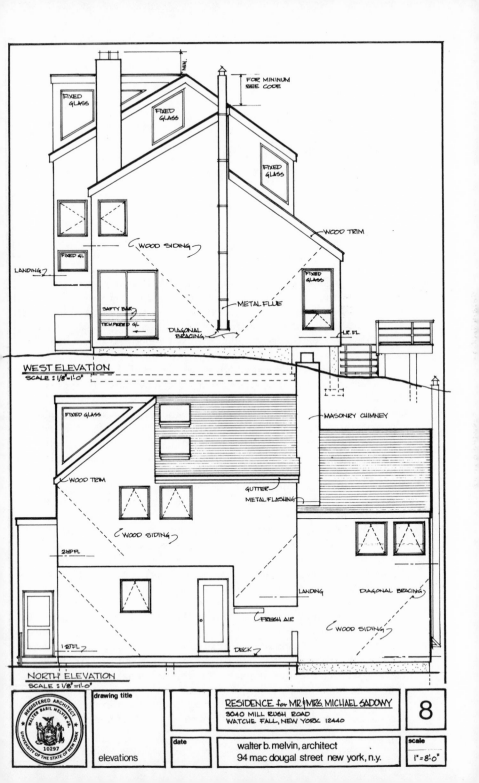

FOR MINIMUM
BEE CODE

FIXED GLASS

FIXED GLASS

FIXED GLASS

WOOD TRIM

WOOD SIDING

FIXED GL

LANDING

METAL FLUE

SAFTY BAR

FIXED GLASS

TEMPERED GL

DIAGONAL BRACING

LR. FL.

WEST ELEVATION
SCALE : 1/8"=1'-0"

FIXED GLASS

MASONRY CHIMNEY

WOOD TRIM

GUTTER

METAL FLASHING

WOOD SIDING

2ND FL

LANDING

DIAGONAL BRACING

FRESH AIR

WOOD SIDING

1 ST FL

DECK

NORTH ELEVATION
SCALE : 1/8"=1'-0"

drawing title

RESIDENCE for MR.&MRS. MICHAEL SADOWY
3040 MILL RUSH ROAD
WATCHE FALL, NEW YORK 12440

8

date

elevations

walter b. melvin, architect
94 mac dougal street new york, n.y.

scale

1" = 8'-0"

REGISTERED ARCHITECT · WALTER BASIL MELVIN JR. · UNIVERSITY OF THE STATE OF NEW YORK
10297

Building Regulations— A State-by-State Survey

I said earlier in this book that, generally speaking, it is the local jurisdiction that adopts the building regulations you would be governed by. But as my research continued, I was surprised to find out how many states have mandatory building regulations—construction codes that the legislature mandates must be followed throughout the state.

This appendix tells you which states have such far-reaching codes and which don't. In those places that have statewide building codes, I've attempted to tell you (1) upon which model the state code is based, (2) whether it is mandatory or voluntary, (3) whether it allows alternate materials and methods of construction, (4) the code-amendment process, and (5) the name and address of the state official or office where you can get further information. I also tell you whether the state has a mandatory mechanical, plumbing, fire-prevention, and electrical code and whether the licensing laws for electricians permit owner-builders without licenses to perform their own electrical work on their homes.

Now, some of this information is not precise. States that don't have a statewide building code when this guide is being written might have one when this is read. Also, those states that do have building codes might significantly amend and change those regulations in the interim. And finally, each of these statewide codes are interpreted and enforced at a local level and there can be a wide divergence *within* the state as to how the code is applied to an individual construction problem.

You have to check your local situation. That's especially true for those of you in states that don't have mandatory codes. You have to consult with community officials to determine what building regulations have been locally adopted.

Most of the information for this appendix came from Cooke and Eisenhand's study for the U.S. Department of Commerce, National

Bureau of Standards, entitled *A Preliminary Examination of Building Regulations Adopted by the States and Major Cities.* The analysis of the electrical codes came from a publication by the National Electrical Contractors Association, Inc., 7315 Wisconsin Ave., Washington, D.C. 20014.

Like everything else in this book, my remarks here are limited to single-family dwellings. A state may have all kinds of mandatory building regulations, but if they are not applicable to single-family residential construction, I don't dwell on the code.

ALABAMA

There are no statewide building, plumbing, or mechanical codes—either voluntary or mandatory—in this state.

Alabama does not have a statewide electrical code but electricians are licensed at the state level. Fortunately for owner-builders, the licensing requirements specifically exempt firms or persons constructing private dwellings or making any building improvements to properties they own.

The Alabama legislature has incorporated the Standard Building Code into its fire prevention code, but the SBC is not enforced as a building code, nor is it applicable to single-family dwellings.

The state health laws—in §73 of title 22 of the Alabama statutes—allow privies (outhouses) under controlled conditions. Sections 117 to 140 of the same title contain the state's water regulations.

ALASKA

This jurisdiction has no statewide building, plumbing, or health regulations.

There are, however, state mechanical, electrical, and fire prevention codes, but they don't apply to single-family dwellings. Alaska requires electrical contractors to be licensed, but I could find no exception to that requirement for owner-builders.

ARIZONA

Arizona has no statewide constriction, of any sort. The 1971 Arizona Electrical Code, which purports to be of statewide application, is advisory only. So you have to check your local jurisdiction to determine what building regulations have been adopted. If you find local building regulations, they will in all likelihood be based on the Uniform Building Code.

ARKANSAS

This state has no building, mechanical, or electrical codes. So check your municipal ordinances to see if these building regulations have been locally adopted. There is an applicable statewide plumbing code, enforced through the state Board of Health, Division of Public Safety, 4815 W. Markham St., Little Rock, Ark. 72201.

Arkansas' electrical licensing requirements specifically exempt from their provisions persons constructing private dwelllings.

Arkansas' statewide fire prevention code is based on the National Building Code (which we've reviewed extensively in this book) and does apply to single-family residential construction. This code is enforced by the State Fire Marshall's office, which is part of the state police. For more information, write the Fire Marshall's Section, Arkansas State Police, 1818 W. Capital St., Little Rock, Ark. 72209.

CALIFORNIA

The California legislature has adopted the Uniform Building, Mechanical, and Plumbing Codes. The statewide fire prevention code is based on the National Fire Prevention Association's model and the electrical code is generally based on the National Electrical Code. All of these codes are applicable to single-family dwellings.

A few comments about California's building code:

The Commission of Housing and Community Development is primarily responsible for the adoption and amendments to the code. But, as we saw in Chapter Ten, each county can adopt amendments to the building code because of local conditions peculiar to it.

Even though this is a state-mandated building code, it is—like most codes of statewide application—enforced by the local county and city building inspectors. Most, if not all, of the comments I made about the UBC in this book are applicable to the California version. Especially the alternate materials provision (UBC §106), which has been incorporated right into the state enabling statute.

For further information about the California building code, write the Division of Codes and Standards, Department of Housing and Community Development, 921 10th St., Sacramento, Calif. 95814.

Owner-builders can do their own electrical work on their own homes which are not intended for sale. This is an exception to the state's electrical contractors' licensing requirements. However, if the owner-builder sells his or her house within a year of its construction, that constitutes presumptive evidence of construction or improvement for the purpose of sale—which *is* a violation of the electrical contractors' licensing law.

COLORADO

There are no statewide building, mechanical, or fire prevention codes that govern single-family construction in Colorado. There is, however, a statewide plumbing regulation (patterned after the National Plumbing Code) and a statewide electrical code (based on the National Electrical Code). It seems that owner-builders can't do their own electrical work on their homes without getting a license.

CONNECTICUT

This state has a mandatory statewide building code (based on the Basic Building Code), a mechanical code (patterned after the Basic Mechanical Code), a plumbing regulation (based on the National Plumbing Code), an electrical code (following the National Electrical Code), and a fire prevention code (using the National Fire Prevention Association's model).

With regard to Connecticut's building code, the Department of Public Works (165 Capital Ave., Hartford, Conn. 06115) is responsible for its adoption and enforcement. A separate statewide interpretation committee takes interpretations out of the hands of the local governments. A state board of appeals exists, which centralizes that function also.

The Connecticut building code is patterned after the Basic Building Code, but there have been some significant changes made from that model code. The right to (1) make rules, (2) grant modifications, and (3) approve new materials and methods of construction are not given to the local building inspector but are all exercised at the state level. This centralization of power makes it more difficult for owner-builders to take advantage of some of the procedures I outlined in this book—at least not without expending a lot of time and money. It is also difficult, under the Connecticut building regulations scheme, to get a local exception to the statewide building regulation.

The electrical licensing laws of Connecticut do not permit nonlicensed owner-builders to do their own electrical work.

DELAWARE

Delaware has no statewide building, mechanical, or plumbing codes. All electrical installations in the state are required to conform to the National Electrical Code. There is no exception to the electrical licensing requirements for owner-builders.

The state's mandatory fire prevention code does *not* apply to single-family dwellings.

FLORIDA

Florida has an interim state building code, which is becoming more and more permanent since funds for the study of a final code have not been forthcoming. The interim code requires local governments to adopt either the state building code, the BBC, the UBC, the South Florida Building Code, or the *One- and Two-Family Dwelling Code*. So, as you can see, you'll have to check your local town hall to determine which of those codes is in effect. The Department of Community Affairs, 2571 Executive Center, Circle E, Tallahassee, Fla. 32301, has more detailed information on the status of the interim state building code.

No statewide mechanical code has been adopted. The statewide plumbing code and Fire Marshall's Rules and Regulations are mandatory.

The National Electrical Code has been adopted by Florida as its electrical code. Owner-builders can do their own electrical work without state license.

GEORGIA

Georgia has a voluntary state building code (based on the Standard Building Code), which means that local governments have the option to adopt or not adopt the state model.

This state also has a voluntary Heating and Air Conditioning Code (another name for a mechanical code), and a mandatory fire prevention code that does not apply to single-family residences. The state's electrical code also does not apply to single-family residential construction. For more specific information, write: State Building Administrative Board, 166 Pryor St. S.W., Atlanta, Ga. 30303.

HAWAII

This state has no building, mechanical, plumbing, or electrical codes. The mandatory fire prevention code does not apply to single-family dwellings. The electrical licensing statute excludes work on single-family dwellings. So consult your local ordinances to determine what building regulations, if any, you're governed by.

IDAHO

Idaho has a building code based primarily on the UBC (Idaho Statute §39-4101). The statute says that the code is mandatory, but state officials say the building regulation is not enforced in all places throughout the state. In fact, recent legislation has been introduced to make the code voluntary. Code officials also told me that local amendments are allowed as long as they are as strict or stricter than the state-adopted code, but the statute itself does not seem to give the local jurisdictions that power.

The Idaho Code Advisory Board, a state rather than local organization, passes on the suitability of alternate materials and methods of construction. The board also functions as a board of appeals and gives code interpretations. Write the Department of Labor and Industrial Services, 317 Main St., Room 400, Boise, Idaho 83720, for the current status of the building regulations in this state.

Idaho has also adopted the Uniform Mechanical and Plumbing Codes, and has a fire prevention code that's applicable to single-family dwellings.

The National Electrical Code is enforced in Idaho. All electrical contractors must be licensed, but persons performing electrical work on their own property are exempt from the licensing provisions.

ILLINOIS

This highly populated state has very few statewide building regulations. There are no state building, mechanical, or plumbing codes—but I'm sure many of the local governments have them.

There is a fire prevention code that is not applicable to single-family dwellings. There is no statewide electrical code as such, but I understand that all electrical installations are required to conform to the National Electrical Code according to the fire prevention code. There is no statewide licensing requirement for electricians.

INDIANA

This state has adopted the *One- and Two-Family Dwelling Code.* There have been, however, many amendments to the model Dwelling Code that we reviewed in this book. The alternate materials provision is unusual: the new material or method of construction must have the approval of the sponsoring model-code groups themselves.

The Indiana legislature gave the Administrative Building Council the right to adopt and amend the building code. Its address is 215 N. Senate Ave., Indianapolis, Ind. 46202.

This state has also adopted the Uniform Mechanical and Plumbing Codes. It also uses the Uniform Building Code as its fire prevention code.

The National Electrical Code is followed on a statewide basis but there are no state electrical licensing requirements. So check your local laws to determine if you can do the electrical work on your own home.

IOWA

Iowa has a voluntary building code (based on the UBC). Not many local jurisdictions have adopted it, however, because of the lack of personnel to enforce the code and the fact that the state code does not allow local amendments. You can contact the Division of Municipal Affairs, 523 E. 12th St., Des Moines, Iowa 50319, for more information.

This state's mechanical code is voluntary. The Health Department for the state has a plumbing code that is mandatory if the voluntary state building code has not been locally adopted. The state's fire prevention code is not applicable to single-family residential dwellings.

Iowa's electrical code is also voluntary and there are no state licensing regulations. Check the locality in which you intend to build to determine whether owner-builders may do their own electrical work.

KANSAS

Kansas has adopted the Uniform Building Code as a statewide code but has made it applicable only to assembly occupancies. So you'll have to check with your town and county officials to determine if there's a local building code that governs single-family construction.

Similarly, the state's mechanical and plumbing codes (both based on the Uniform models) also apply only to assembly occupancies. The fire prevention code applies to all occupancies *except* single-family dwellings. There is no statewide electrical code nor statewide licensing of electrical contractors.

KENTUCKY

Kentucky has not adopted a statewide building code. The mandatory mechanical code (based on the National Fire Protection Association's model) does apply to single-family dwellings.

This state's plumbing code is a mandatory regulation that sets forth the minimum requirements to be followed throughout the state. (It is a code of the state's own creation and is not based on any of the national models that we've examined in this book.)

Kentucky's fire prevention and electrical codes (the latter based on the National Electrical Code) are mandatory throughout the state and both are applicable to single-family dwellings. There are, however, no statewide electrical licensing requirements. Check locally.

LOUISIANA

There are no statewide building, mechanical, or plumbing codes in this state. The Fire Marshall's Code (based on the National Fire Protection Association's model) is applicable throughout the state.

The state's electrical code exempts single-family dwellings from its regulations. And since you don't have to follow the state code to wire your house (you might check local codes, however), I would assume you don't have to be state licensed to perform that work.

MAINE

This state has no building or mechanical codes of statewide application. There is a statewide mandatory plumbing code. But don't forget, this is the first state (at the time of this writing) that allows composting privies instead of the water-flush toilets.

Maine's fire prevention code does not apply to single-family residences, whereas the electrical code (patterned after the National Electrical Code) does. Electrical contractors must be licensed—with *no* exceptions for owner-builders.

MARYLAND

The state building code (based on the BBC) is voluntary and only one county had adopted it by 1976. Many towns and county governments have adopted their own codes, so check locally. The mechanical code is also voluntary.

Maryland's plumbing code controls if local jurisdictions have not adopted a similarly strict plumbing code of their own. The state's fire prevention code is not applicable to single-family dwellings.

The National Electrical Code is not state mandated; it's only required for the more populous counties. There are no statewide electrical licensing requirements.

MASSACHUSETTS

Massachusetts has adopted the BBC and the *One- and Two-Family Dwelling Code* as the models for its state-mandated building code, but both models have been significantly amended in this state.

Some differences are that Massachusetts has its own new materials and methods of construction provision (§108.13), the rule-making authority is in the hands of the state building commission and not with the local building inspector (§109), and the appeal process does not stop at the local level but can go to a State Appeals Board (§126).

One important similarity in the Massachesetts Building Code and the BBC is that the numbering systems are the same. This will, with the help of this book, make your analysis of the state code easier to accomplish. Another "plus" is that the state code has a good index.

The Massachusetts State Building Code Commission has the authority to amend the code (local amendments must have state approval). The address of the commission is McCormick St. Office Building, 13th Floor, Boston, Mass. 02108.

The mandatory statewide mechanical and plumbing regulations (based on the BBC) have been incorporated into the state's building code. There's no fire prevention code that is mandatory throughout the state.

Massachusetts has adopted—with a few exceptions and additions—the National Electrical Code. There are no owner-builder exemptions to the state's electrical licensing requirements. In other words, you can't do your own wiring.

MICHIGAN

This is a statewide-building-code jurisdiction. The State Construction Code Commission adopted the BBC with little modification, so that the review of the BBC in this book will help you to review this state's construction requirements. The state commission also has the power to amend the state code. A town, village, or township can exempt itself from the state code by adopting one of the nationally recognized model codes without amendment. The small number of communities that have adopted other models have chosen the UBC or the unmodified BBC. For a complete, updated list of the building codes adopted in each and every municipality in the state, together with the names, addresses, and telephone numbers of each building inspector, write: Michigan Department of Labor, Construction Code Commission, State Secondary Complex, 7150 Harris Dr., Lansing, Mich. 48926.

As part of the State Construction Code, the Commission has also adopted mechanical and plumbing codes which are mandatory—unless the local communities have adopted other nationally recognized models without amendment. Michigan's fire prevention and electrical codes do not apply to single-family dwellings. Local communities may, however, adopt their own electrical codes. Owner-builders are exempt from state electrical licensing requirements.

MINNESOTA

This state's building code (based on the UBC) is mandatory for those communities that had a building code before July 1, 1972. Also, if any local jurisdiction adopts a building regulation after that date, it must use the state code. So there may be parts of Minnesota that are not governed by any code.

The state code has a useful index to help you track down those provisions that relate to single-family dwellings. Alternate materials and methods of construction are allowed by the "Building Official," but I could not determine from reading this code whether the reference was to the state or local building official. The code is locally enforced.

Amendments to the state code may be proposed by any interested person to the commission of Administration, Building Code Division, 7th and Roberts Sts., St. Paul, Minn. 55101.

There are also state mechanical, plumbing, and fire prevention codes that are enforced locally and do apply to single-family dwellings.

The National Electrical Code is the model for the state's own electrical code. All electrical contractors must be licensed and there are no exceptions for owner-builders.

MISSISSIPPI

There are no building, mechanical, plumbing, fire prevention, or electrical codes of statewide application in Mississippi. Electrical licensing is done locally.

MISSOURI

There are no statewide building, mechanical, plumbing, fire prevention, or electrical codes or statewide electrical licensing requirements.

MONTANA

This state has adopted the Uniform Building Code as part of its statewide mandatory building regulations. The code is supposed to be locally enforced, and if there is no local enforcement state officials are supposed to do it. But there are not always local or state officials to do the job, so the code doesn't always get enforced in all the nooks and crannies in this big state.

Local amendments to the state code are not allowed (but this may be changed). The Department of Administration, Building Code Administrative Bureau, Capital Station, Helena, Mont. 59601, is responsible for amending the code. Write to them for further building regulation information.

Montana has also adopted the Uniform Mechanical and Plumbing Codes, applicable to single-family dwellings. The state's fire prevention code is based on the National Fire Protection Association's model. The National Electrical Code is the basis for Montana's electrical code. Owner-builders are exempt from electrical contractor licensing requirements.

NEBRASKA

Nebraska has no statewide building, mechanical, or electrical codes. The National Plumbing Code has been adopted for statewide application. The state's fire prevention code is based on the National Fire Prevention Association's code and is applicable to single-family dwellings. The National Electrical Code is used in Nebraska. The mandatory state licensing requirements have no exemptions for people doing their own electrical work on their own dwellings.

NEVADA

Nevada has no state building or mechanical codes. The more populous counties and cities do have building regulations, generally patterned after the Uniform Building Code. The National Plumbing Code, the National Electrical Code, and the National Fire Prevention Association Code are the models for similarly named regulations in this state. Though electrical contractors are licensed, journeymen are not.

NEW HAMPSHIRE

There are no statewide building, mechanical, plumbing, fire prevention, or electrical codes in New Hampshire. All electrical contractors, however, must be licensed—with no exceptions for owner-builders.

NEW JERSEY

This state has recently adopted the Basic Building Code as its mandatory, statewide building regulation. The first article of the BBC (the sections on administration) has been completely changed in the New Jersey version. There aren't many changes to the rest of the

BBC, however. No local amendments are allowed, so the code is truly uniform throughout the state; but the code is enforced locally—which can make for some divergence in interpretation.

The Commissioner of the Department of Community Affairs has the power to amend the code. Write the New Jersey Department of Community Affairs, P.O. Box 2768, Trenton, N.J. 08625, for more information.

New Jersey has no statewide mechanical code yet. There are, however, statewide plumbing and fire prevention codes, both of which are applicable to single-family dwellings.

The National Electrical Code must be followed for code-approved electrical installations. There are no exemptions for owner-builders to the state's electrical licensing requirements.

NEW MEXICO

The Uniform Building Code is the basis for this state's building regulation. It's administered by the Construction Industries Commission. The rules are promulgated by the General Construction Board. This board also certifies local inspectors and approves alternate materials and methods of construction. There's also a State Board of Appeals. As you can see, this is a centrally administered building code.

For more information, write the General Construction Board of the C.I.C., P.O. Box 5155, Santa Fe, N.M. 87503.

The Uniform Mechanical and Plumbing Codes, as well as a fire prevention code, are in effect in this state. The National Electrical Code is enforced and all electrical contractors are licensed.

NEW YORK

New York has developed its own State Building Construction Code. It's not based on any of the national model codes that we've discussed in this book. It is also not mandatory throughout the state. Many towns and villages in New York have adopted this code because of the many services the State Building Code Council provides. You can write the council at Two World Trade Center, New York, N.Y., 10047.

The code New York has put together is a good one. One book outlines the performance requirements that must be achieved (found in the small yellow-covered books), while a larger book contains a manual of performance practices that have already been approved. These performance practices are not mandatory. This allows you to choose from many different techniques (or invent your own) to achieve and comply with a single performance objective.

Mechnical, plumbing, electrical, and fire prevention regulations are part of New York's voluntary State Building Construction Code. There is no statewide licensing of electrical contractors; that function is done locally, if at all.

NORTH CAROLINA

The first statewide building code in this country was adopted in North Carolina in 1903. Up until recently, single-family dwellings were exempt from the mandatory State Building Code. Today the Uniform Residential Building Code is also mandatory, though local governments can amend its provisions if the state approves the change.

But the actual construction situation is not as regulated as it sounds. That's because enforcement of the code is local (the state does not have a team of building inspectors to cover the state). If a city or county does not appoint and pay for a building inspector (they don't have to under state law), the building codes just don't get enforced. An interesting situation.

The State Building and Uniform Residential Building Codes do permit alternate materials and methods of construction, but the new process first has to be accepted by the building inspector and then forwarded to the Building Code Council for final approval.

Write to the Department of Insurance, P.O. Box 26387, Raleigh, N.C. 27611.

There are also statewide mechanical and plumbing codes, but no fire prevention code. The National Electrical Code is the model for North Carolina's electrical code. (Enforcement is a local responsibility, which means this code, also, may not get enforced.) There are no owner-builder exceptions to the state's electrical licensing requirements.

NORTH DAKOTA

There are no building, mechanical, or fire prevention codes applicable throughout the state of North Dakota. There are, however, plumbing and electrical codes (the latter based on the National Electrical Code) whose requirements must be observed in constructing single-family residences in the state. Owner-builders are not exempted from the state's electrical licensing requirements.

OHIO

This state has developed its very own code without relying on any of the national models. The document entitled the Ohio Building

Code is mandatory but does not apply to single-family dwellings, whereas the separate Ohio 1, 2, and 3 Family Dwelling House Code is applicable—but it's voluntary. If a local community has not adopted the Ohio Dwelling House Code, you are free to build without having to meet the requirements of a building code. Once a town or county adopts Ohio's Dwelling House Code, local amendments are permitted without state approval.

Ohio's mechanical, plumbing, fire prevention, and electrical codes are incorporated into the building code—but remember, they're not applicable to single-family dwellings. There is no state licensing of electrical contractors. For more information on Ohio's Building Code or Dwelling House Code, contact the Board of Building Standards, P. O. Box 825, Columbus, Ohio 43216.

OKLAHOMA

Oklahoma has no statewide building, mechanical, plumbing, or electrical codes. The state does have a fire prevention law, which is based on the National Fire Prevention Association's model. There's no statewide licensing of electrical contractors.

OREGON

Oregon has a statewide code called the Structural Speciality and Fire and Life Safety Code. There are also the Mechanical and Plumbing Speciality Codes. They are all based on the Uniform codes published by the International Conference of Building Officials in California. Amendments to all those codes require a public hearing before the Department of Commerce, Building Code Division. The division's address is: Labor and Industrial Bldg., Room 401, Salem, Ore. 97310.

This state has also adopted the National Electrical Code and has a fire prevention regulation. Owner-builders are exempt from electrical licensing requirements.

PENNSYLVANIA

This state has no building, mechanical, plumbing, electrical, or fire prevention codes of statewide application. There is also no state licensing of electrical contractors.

RHODE ISLAND

Rhode Island has adopted the Basic Building Code model, together with the *One- and Two-Family Dwelling Code.* So if you're an owner-builder in that state, you can use—to good advantage—the review of that code found throughout this book.

The State Building Code Standards Committee has the power to amend these codes. It also acts as a Board of Standards and Appeals, and passes upon new construction and materials. Local officials are responsible for the enforcement of these codes. Local amendments are allowed only if approved by the Code Standards Committee. The address of that committee is 150 Washington St., Providence, R.I. 02903.

There are also mechanical and plumbing codes—both patterned after the BOCA models—that are applicable throughout the state. Rhode Island has adopted a fire prevention code. The state's electrical code is based on the National Electrical Code. Owner-builders are specifically exempted from the electrical contractors' licensing requirements.

SOUTH CAROLINA

This state does not have a building code, but there is legislation that promotes "conformity in local building laws" and the adoption of the Standard Building Code by local municipalities. There are no plumbing, mechanical, or electrical codes. The statewide fire prevention code is based on the Standard Building Code, but I think just the fire safety aspects of that model are followed and not all of the construction requirements. Only electrical contractors who work on projects totaling more than $10,000 in value need to be licensed.

SOUTH DAKOTA

South Dakota has no statewide building, mechanical, plumbing, or electrical codes. However, there is a statute that requires all electrical installations to conform to approved methods (conformance to the National Electrical Code would be okay). There is a state fire prevention code but it does not apply to single-family dwellings. There's no owner-builder exception to the state's electrical licensing requirements.

TENNESSEE

There are no state building, mechanical, or plumbing codes in Tennessee. The State Fire Marshall enforces the National Fire Prevention Association's model and the National Electrical Code. Owner-builders are exempted from the state's electrical licensing requirements.

TEXAS

There are no statewide building, mechanical, plumbing, electrical, or fire prevention codes in Texas. There is also no state licensing of electrical contractors.

UTAH

Utah has no statewide building or mechanical codes. The state's plumbing code is applicable to single-family dwellings while the state's fire prevention code is not. All electrical installations are required to conform to the National Electrical Code. There are no exceptions to the state's electrical licensing requirements for owner-builders.

VERMONT

There's no statewide building code here, but the Vermont legislature has mandated that if a municipality adopts a building code, it must use the National Building Code—a model we've reviewed extensively in this book.

Vermont does not have a mechanical or plumbing or fire prevention code, and all electrical installations must conform to the National Electrical Code. All electrical contractors must be licensed—no exceptions.

VIRGINIA

Virginia's Uniform State Building Code—which is based on the BBC—also incorporates the Basic Mechanical and Plumbing Codes. The state has also adopted the *One- and Two-Family Dwelling Code*, which makes the owner-builder's code-reading task a bit easier.

The State Board of Housing is entrusted with adopting amendments to this code. It gets technical assistance from the Board of State Building Code Review, which also interprets the code and hears appeals from local boards of appeal. Write the Office of Housing, 6 N. 6th St., Richmond, Va. 23219.

There is no statewide fire prevention code. The National Electrical Code is followed for all electrical installations. There are no owner-builder exemptions to the state's electrical licensing requirements.

WASHINGTON

A Washington State statute (Chapter 96 of the laws of 1974) proclaims that after January 1, 1975, there shall be in effect in all cities, towns, and counties of the state, a state building code which shall consist of the following codes which are hereby adopted by reference:

1 The Uniform Building Code
2 The Uniform Mechanical Code
3 The Uniform Fire Code
4 The Uniform Plumbing Code

What this means is that the legislature, and not a commission or board, has adopted these model codes. It also means that these codes were adopted without changes to conform to state conditions. Any amendments on the state level must be approved by the state legislature, yet I understand that local amendments are allowed without state approval.

A State Building Code Advisory Council has been appointed. Its function seems to be to coordinate the efforts of the local governments. The address of the council is 106 Insurance Bldg., Olympia, Wash. 98504.

All electrical installations must conform, by statute, to approved methods for safety of life and property. There's no owner-builder exemption to the state's electrical licensing requirements.

WEST VIRGINIA

No state building, mechanical, or plumbing codes exist in West Virginia. There is a state fire prevention code applicable to single-family residences, however. The National Electrical Code is the model that's been adopted for electrical installations. Owner-builders are not exempt from the state's electrical licensing requirements.

WISCONSIN

This state's building code includes heating, ventilating, and air-conditioning provisions but it doesn't apply to single-family residences. Recent legislation has been passed authorizing the adoption of a single-family dwelling code; the Single-Family Residential Code is not yet in effect at the time of this writing. Contact the Department of Industry, Labor, and Human Relations, P.O. Box 7946, Madison, Wis. 53707, for more current information.

There's also a statewide plumbing code that *is* applicable to single-family dwellings, whereas the fire prevention code is not. The state enforces the National Electrical Code. There are no state electrical licensing requirements.

WYOMING

There are no statewide building, mechanical, or plumbing codes in Wyoming. The National Electrical Code must be followed. The state's fire prevention code is not applicable to single-family dwellings. Owner-builders are exempt from Wyoming's electrical licensing requirements.

INDEX

before buying property, *see* property-
   buying considerations
BOCA code, *see* Basic Building Code
building codes, 6, 12-14
  administration, 20
  adoption, 13-14
  background, 7
  complexity, 5-6
  criticism, 2, 156-60
   codify aesthetics, 159-60
   cost, 158-59
   flush toilets, 60, 67-68, 71, 80
   heating provisions, 125-26
   no alternatives, 49, 67-68, 80-81
   openable windows, 54
   overregulation, 24-25
   smoke detectors, 55-56
   subjects covered, 13
   when permit required, 22-25
   wood grading, 111-12
  enforcement, 33-34, 127-39
  good aspects, 156-57
  how to read, 20, 21
  local, 12-14, 167-68
  model, 12-14, 21, 169-73
  numbering systems, 21
  origin, 12
  purpose, 156-58
  reform, 2-3, 156-74
   background, 7
   basis, 160
   how, 167-73; local code, 167-68;
    model code, 169-73; state code,
    168-69
   kind of change, 160-66
   suggested proposals, 163-66
   why, 156-60
  requirements, 12
  state, 12-14, 168-69
building inspector, 20-21, 33-38
  alternatives, power to approve, 92,
   94-103
  don't underestimate, 92-93
  duties, 33-34
  helpful hints, 26, 35-36
  him- or herself *as* the code, 25, 34, 139
  how to approach, 35-36
  job insecurity, 35
  the person, 36

plans and specs, 32
protected, 139-41
standards, 84, 103-4
**Building Officials and Code Adminis-
  trators International** (BBC), 13,
  170
  address, 13
  founder's remarks, 160
building permit, 6, 20-32
  alternatives, proposed, 166
  amendments, 142-43
  application, 25-27
  code enforcement, 127-28
  expiration, 129
  fees, 27-29
  as license, 21, 25
  plans and specs, 29-32
  repairs, 22-25
  revocation, 33
  site plan, 29-30
  when required, 22

ceiling heights, 58
certificate of occupancy, 131
  temporary, 132
chimneys and fireplaces, 124
code enforcement, 127-55
Code-Reading Techniques
  ambiguous words, 61
  definitions, 23, 28
   habitable space, 57
   where to look for, 23
  discretionary rules, 34-35
  fuzzy language, 43
  habitable rooms, 51
  how to find a topic, 115
  how to use conflicting sections, 93
  how to use introductory remarks, 95
  introduction, 2
  regulations spread out, 65
  residential uses, 45
  time periods, 25
code reform, *see* building codes, reform
composting toilets, 68, 76-77, 80-81
construction, types of, *see* types of construction
Council of American Building Officials
  (Dwelling Code), 13